IXL MATH WORKBOOK

THE ULTIMATE

SIXTH GRADE MATH WORKBOOK

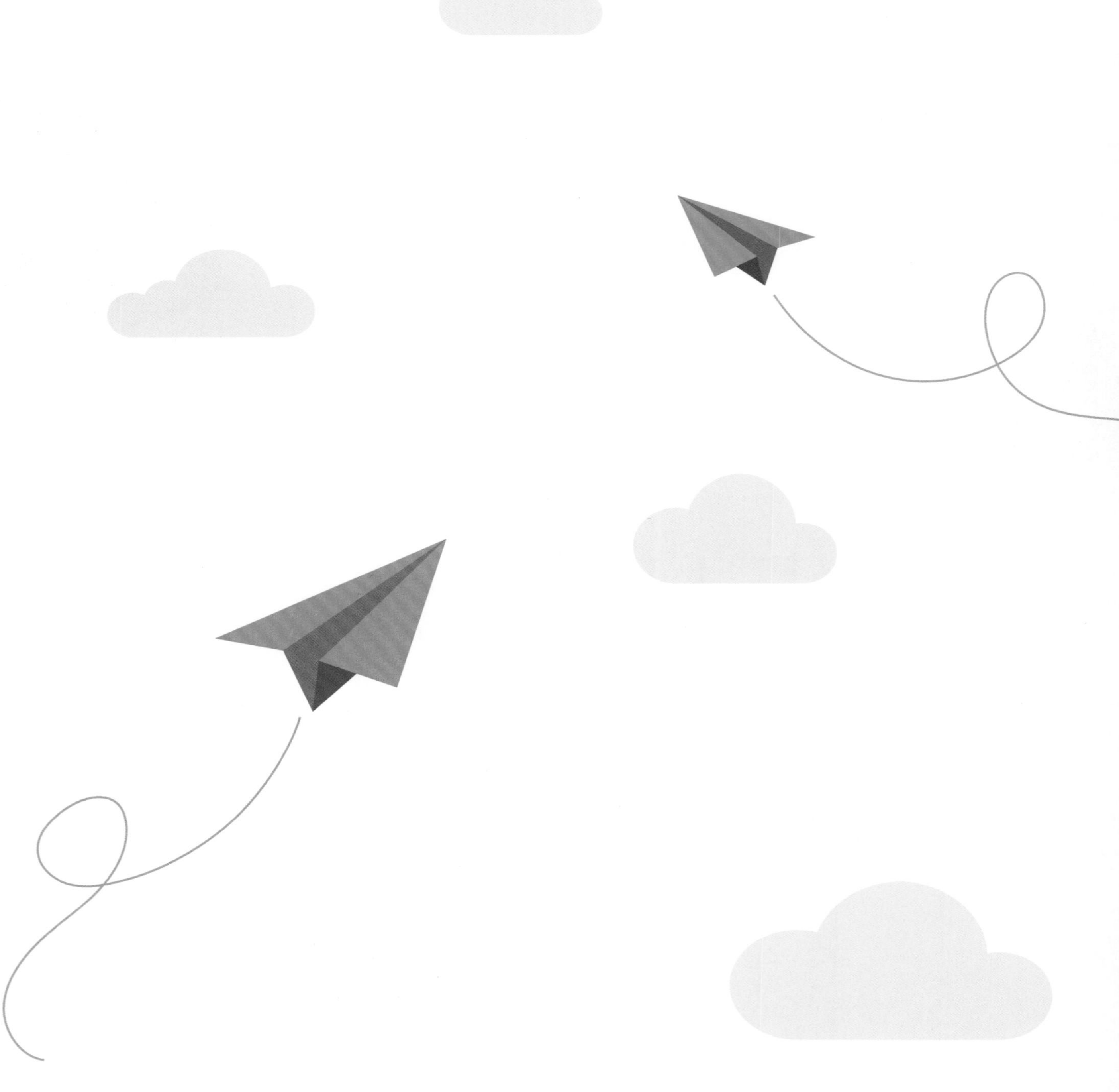

ISBN: 9781947569614
27 26 25 24 23 2 3 4 5 6
Printed in China

Table of Contents

4 Exponents

Learn!

You can use an **exponent** to write repeated multiplication. Take a closer look.

$$3^4 = 3 \times 3 \times 3 \times 3$$

Base: the factor that is repeatedly multiplied

Exponent: tells how many times the base is used as a factor

Expanded form: shows the repeated multiplication written out

Write the expression in expanded form.

4^2 = ______________________

2^5 = ______________________

9^3 = ______________________

12^4 = ______________________

$(0.6)^3$ = ______________________

$\left(\frac{1}{8}\right)^4$ = ______________________

Write the expression using an exponent.

6×6 = ______________________

$5 \times 5 \times 5 \times 5$ = ______________________

$3 \times 3 \times 3 \times 3 \times 3$ = ______________________

$8 \times 8 \times 8$ = ______________________

$0.2 \times 0.2 \times 0.2 \times 0.2$ = ______________________

$\frac{1}{4} \times \frac{1}{4} \times \frac{1}{4}$ = ______________________

IXL.com skill ID **TY5**

For more practice, visit IXL.com or the IXL mobile app and enter this code in the search bar.

Exponents

Evaluate each exponent.

8^2 = 8 × 8 = 64

4^3 = ____________

2^4 = ____________

12^1 = ____________

10^4 = ____________

1^5 = ____________

9^1 = ____________

7^3 = ____________

6^3 = ____________

11^2 = ____________

3^5 = ____________

5^3 = ____________

2^5 = ____________

8^3 = ____________

12^2 = ____________

6 Prime factorization

Learn!

Factors are numbers that you multiply together to get another number. You can write the **prime factorization** of a number by writing the number as a product of its prime factors. If a number is already prime, its prime factorization is the number itself. Try it with 36.

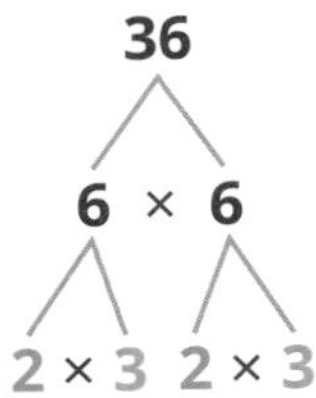

Start by writing 36 as the product of any two of its factors.

If the factors are not prime, continue breaking them down until you have all prime factors.

36 = 2 × 2 × 3 × 3

Then you can write the prime factorization. Make sure to write the prime factors in order from least to greatest.

Write the prime factorization of each number.

24 = ______________________

30 = ______________________

53 = ______________________

48 = ______________________

Write the prime factorization of each number.

27 = ______________________

41 = ______________________

77 = ______________________

100 = ______________________

84 = ______________________

32 = ______________________

DIG DEEPER! | Go back and rewrite the prime factorizations on this page using exponents wherever possible.

8 Greatest common factor

Learn!

The **greatest common factor** (**GCF**) of two or more numbers is the largest factor that the numbers share. Try it with 18 and 45.

18: 1, 2, 3, 6, 9, 18 First, find all of the factors of each number.
45: 1, 3, 5, 9, 15, 45

18: 1, 2, 3, 6, 9, 18 Next, look for the common factors. Find the largest one.
45: 1, 3, 5, 9, 15, 45 So, the greatest common factor of 18 and 45 is 9!

Find the greatest common factor of each pair of numbers.

8 and 12

GCF: ________

16 and 24

GCF: ________

25 and 40

GCF: ________

60 and 100

GCF: ________

27 and 36

GCF: ________

32 and 48

GCF: ________

Greatest common factor

Learn!

You can also use prime factorization to find the GCF. Try it with 12, 24, and 60.

12 = 2 × 2 × 3
24 = 2 × 2 × 2 × 3
60 = 2 × 2 × 3 × 5

First, list the prime factorization of each number.

12 = 2 × 2 × 3
24 = 2 × 2 × 2 × 3
60 = 2 × 2 × 3 × 5

Next, look for the common prime factors shared by all of the numbers. If there are no common prime factors, the greatest common factor is 1.

2 × 2 × 3 = 12

Then, multiply the common factors.
So, the greatest common factor of 12, 24, and 60 is 12.

Find the greatest common factor of each group of numbers.

4, 6, and 18

GCF: ________

8, 16, and 20

GCF: ________

15, 27, and 33

GCF: ________

14, 30, and 45

GCF: ________

10 Factoring expressions

Learn!

If the terms in an expression share a common factor, you can **factor** the expression by rewriting it as a product. Try it with the expression 42 + 12.

First, find the greatest common factor of 42 and 12. The GCF is 6. Then, rewrite the expression as a product using the distributive property.

42 + 12 GCF: 6

42 + 12 = (6 × 7) + (6 × 2)

= 6(7 + 2)

Write the GCF. Then factor the expression using the GCF.

16 + 20 GCF: 4

16 + 20 = (4 × 4) + (4 × 5)

= 4(4 + 5)

15 + 9 GCF: ______

15 + 9 = ______

= ______

40 + 30 GCF: ______

40 + 30 = ______

= ______

28 + 42 GCF: ______

28 + 42 = ______

= ______

85 + 20 GCF: ______

85 + 20 = ______

= ______

24 + 36 GCF: ______

24 + 36 = ______

= ______

TAKE ANOTHER LOOK! Check your answers by applying the distributive property. You should get the original expression!

Least common multiple

Learn!

The **least common multiple** (**LCM**) of two or more numbers is the smallest multiple that the numbers have in common. Try it with 4 and 6.

4: 4, 8, 12, 16, 20, 24 . . .
6: 6, 12, 18, 24, 30, 36 . . .

Start by listing the multiples of each number.

4: 4, 8, (12), 16, 20, 24 . . .
6: 6, (12), 18, 24, 30, 36 . . .

Next, look for the common multiples. Find the smallest one.

So, the least common multiple of 4 and 6 is 12.

Find the least common multiple of each pair of numbers.

3 and 12

LCM: ________

5 and 9

LCM: ________

6 and 15

LCM: ________

8 and 10

LCM: ________

3 and 20

LCM: ________

5 and 11

LCM: ________

8 and 9

LCM: ________

12 Least common multiple

Learn!

You can also use prime factorization to find the LCM. Try it with 10, 15, and 20.

First, write the prime factorization of each number.

10 = 2 × 5
15 = 3 × 5
20 = 2 × 2 × 5

Find the greatest number of times each prime factor appears in a single prime factorization.

The most the factor **2** appears is twice.
The most the factor **3** appears is once.
The most the factor **5** appears is once.

Then, multiply each of those prime factors that many times. 2 × 2 × 3 × 5 = **60**

So, the least common multiple of 10, 15, and 20 is 60.

Find the least common multiple of each group of numbers.

5, 6, and 10

LCM: ________

6, 7, and 12

LCM: ________

3, 11, and 18

LCM: ________

7, 10, and 50

LCM: ________

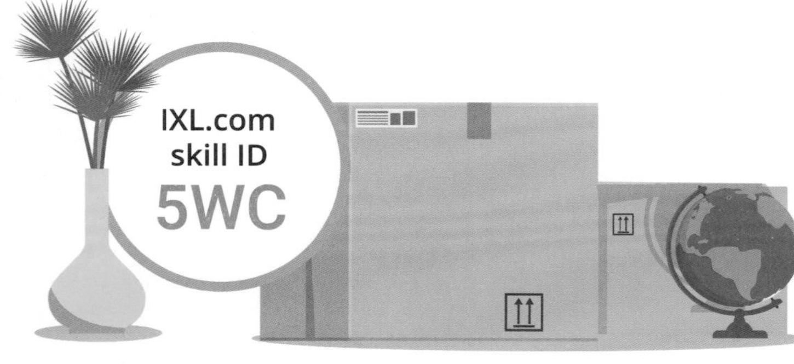

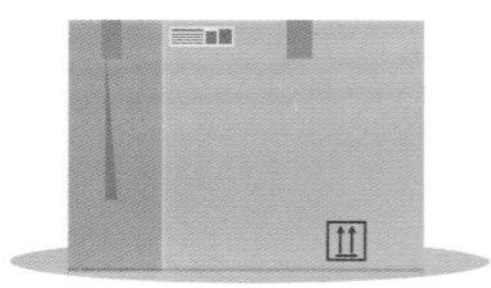

Answer each question.

Ling and Wes saw each other at the market today. Ling goes to the market every 6 days, and Wes goes every 8 days. How many days will it be until they go to the market on the same day again? ______________

Shivani is making balloon centerpieces to decorate for the spring dance. She has 24 yellow balloons and 32 green balloons. She wants to have the same number of each color balloon in every centerpiece. If she uses all of the balloons, what is the greatest number of centerpieces she can make? ______________

Antonio is making sandwiches for his soccer team's year-end party. He has 18 slices of cheese and 27 slices of turkey to use for the sandwiches. He wants to make identical sandwiches that use up all of the slices. What is the greatest number of sandwiches Antonio can make? ______________

Kiera is making goody bags at the party store. She has 36 pencils and 54 stickers that must be split evenly among the bags. If Kiera uses all of the items, what is the greatest number of bags she can make? ______________

Natalie is moving to a new house and is packing up her room. The small moving boxes are 12 inches tall and the medium boxes are 16 inches tall. Natalie wants to put the boxes into stacks of small boxes and stacks of medium boxes so that the stacks are the same height. What is the shortest height, in inches, that each stack of boxes could be? ______________

IXL.com skill ID **ZB8**

Multi-digit division

Divide.

$$\begin{array}{r} 18 \text{ R33} \\ 40\overline{)753} \\ -40 \\ \hline 353 \\ -320 \\ \hline 33 \end{array}$$

$25\overline{)850}$

$12\overline{)245}$

$16\overline{)192}$

$55\overline{)360}$

$62\overline{)992}$

$34\overline{)272}$

$68\overline{)7{,}080}$

$46\overline{)5{,}713}$

$17\overline{)1{,}972}$

$76\overline{)4{,}943}$

$94\overline{)9{,}024}$

Divide.

$82 \overline{)8{,}692}$

$43 \overline{)1{,}204}$

$52 \overline{)3{,}008}$

$79 \overline{)5{,}302}$

$35 \overline{)43{,}820}$

$80 \overline{)86{,}004}$

$64 \overline{)79{,}335}$

$92 \overline{)99{,}267}$

$71 \overline{)14{,}768}$

Multi-digit division

Divide.

$410\overline{)9{,}020}$ $205\overline{)3{,}485}$ $815\overline{)8{,}204}$

$141\overline{)2{,}032}$ $313\overline{)8{,}205}$ $473\overline{)3{,}311}$

$737\overline{)9{,}581}$ $525\overline{)73{,}008}$ $811\overline{)89{,}210}$

Divide.

$280 \overline{)456,120}$	$924 \overline{)680,145}$	$372 \overline{)683,904}$
$457 \overline{)770,965}$	$566 \overline{)194,138}$	$214 \overline{)300,670}$

18 Multi-digit division

Divide to complete the crossword puzzle.

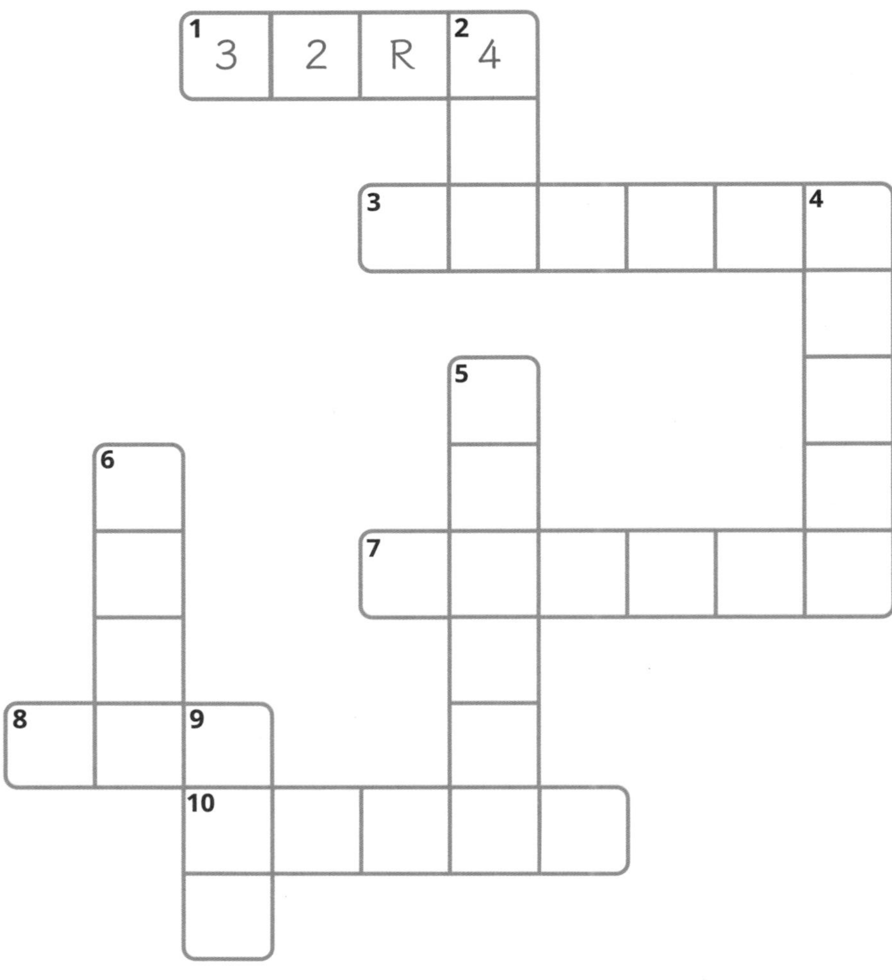

Across

1. 932 ÷ 29 = 32 R4

3. 4,898 ÷ 25

7. 17,818 ÷ 140

8. 6,336 ÷ 11

10. 754 ÷ 21

Down

2. 7,824 ÷ 16

4. 20,158 ÷ 65

5. 44,373 ÷ 126

6. 43,554 ÷ 42

9. 72,450 ÷ 115

Word problems

Answer each question.

Ms. Baxter needs 35-inch pieces of string for an art project in her classroom. How many pieces can she cut from a ball of string that is 945 inches long? ____________

Jamar has $160 to spend on video games. The cost of each game is $39. How many games can Jamar buy? ____________

The Bobcats baseball team placed an order for 18,000 baseballs. The baseballs are packaged in cases with 72 balls in each case. How many cases of baseballs did the team order? ____________

The 273 sixth-grade students at Regus Middle School are going on a field trip to the zoo. Each of the buses they will use can fit 48 students. How many buses will they need? ____________

Rita earned 2,867 points playing an online trivia game. She can buy new levels in her game for 350 points each. How many new levels can Rita buy? ____________

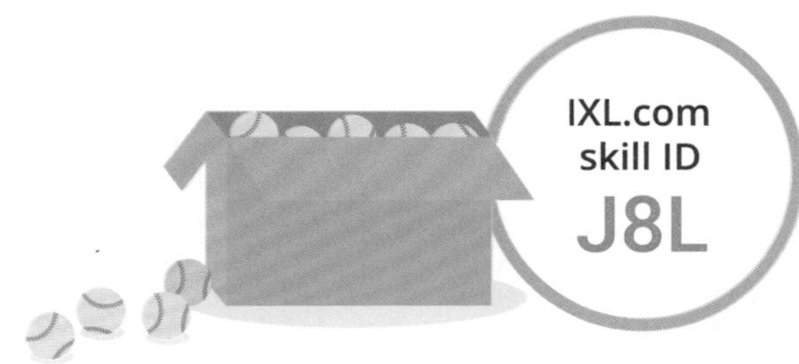

20 Adding and subtracting decimals

Add or subtract.

58.7 + 63.25 = 121.95

$$\begin{array}{r} \overset{1}{5}8.70 \\ +\ 63.25 \\ \hline 121.95 \end{array}$$

94.83 − 13.22 = ________________

388.67 − 212.09 = ________________

245.95 + 36.25 = ________________

78.6 + 94.53 = ________________

987.4 − 65.31 = ________________

67.936 − 8.25 = ________________

406.81 − 93.005 = ________________

641.71 + 225.6 = ________________

6.747 + 18.59 = ________________

890.5 − 46.307 = ________________

Fill in the missing number to make each statement true.

__________ − 12.17 = 70.12

26.09 − __________ = 7.55

__________ − 126.7 = 14.82

7.61 + __________ = 104.524

__________ + 73.67 = 210.4

__________ − 6.89 = 184.3

714.26 − __________ = 353.6

614.73 + __________ = 683.8

__________ + 90.7 = 92.004

__________ − 81.923 = 52.67

__________ + 317.6 = 411.239

22 Word problems

Answer each question.

For lunch, Kelsey ordered spaghetti and meatballs for $10.99 and an iced tea for $3.99. How much did she pay for those two items? __________

Rafael's dog, Duke, weighed 9.8 kilograms at his checkup last year. This year, Duke weighs 11.3 kilograms. How much more does Duke weigh now than last year? __________

One stormy weekend in Auburn City, it rained 1.6 inches on Saturday and 3.88 inches on Sunday. What was the total amount of rainfall that weekend? __________

Tammy's favorite cereal, Cocoa Flakes, comes in two sizes. The small box is 20.35 ounces and the large box is 39.4 ounces. How much heavier is the large box? __________

Aria had 5.4 milliliters of a solution at the beginning of her science experiment. By the end, 1.6 milliliters of solution remained. How much solution did Aria use during the experiment? __________

Kamal swam the 100-meter freestyle in a 50-meter pool. He swam the first lap in 42.277 seconds and the second lap in 44.85 seconds. What was Kamal's total time? __________

IXL.com skill ID **97T**

Multiply.

$$\begin{array}{r} \overset{1}{1}4.1 \\ \times \quad 1.3 \\ \hline 423 \\ +\,1410 \\ \hline 18.33 \end{array}$$

$$\begin{array}{r} 21.8 \\ \times \quad 3.4 \\ \hline \end{array}$$

$$\begin{array}{r} 7.24 \\ \times \quad 8.1 \\ \hline \end{array}$$

$$\begin{array}{r} 96.4 \\ \times \ 0.26 \\ \hline \end{array}$$

$$\begin{array}{r} 62.8 \\ \times \ 0.15 \\ \hline \end{array}$$

$$\begin{array}{r} 35.2 \\ \times \quad 6.4 \\ \hline \end{array}$$

$$\begin{array}{r} 2.46 \\ \times \ 0.25 \\ \hline \end{array}$$

$$\begin{array}{r} 76.93 \\ \times \quad 7.8 \\ \hline \end{array}$$

$$\begin{array}{r} 5.19 \\ \times \quad 1.3 \\ \hline \end{array}$$

$$\begin{array}{r} 75.42 \\ \times \ 0.89 \\ \hline \end{array}$$

$$\begin{array}{r} 16.23 \\ \times \quad 4.7 \\ \hline \end{array}$$

$$\begin{array}{r} 80.96 \\ \times \ 0.72 \\ \hline \end{array}$$

Multiplying decimals

Multiply.

$$\begin{array}{r} 78.3 \\ \times \quad 6.7 \\ \hline \end{array}$$

$$\begin{array}{r} 30.85 \\ \times \quad 9.2 \\ \hline \end{array}$$

$$\begin{array}{r} 19.45 \\ \times \quad 4.1 \\ \hline \end{array}$$

$$\begin{array}{r} 4.118 \\ \times \quad 0.35 \\ \hline \end{array}$$

$$\begin{array}{r} 29.08 \\ \times \quad 3.4 \\ \hline \end{array}$$

$$\begin{array}{r} 6.352 \\ \times \quad 5.6 \\ \hline \end{array}$$

$$\begin{array}{r} 2.67 \\ \times \quad 0.18 \\ \hline \end{array}$$

$$\begin{array}{r} 3.849 \\ \times \quad 0.85 \\ \hline \end{array}$$

Divide.

6.7 ÷ 2 = 3.35

$$\begin{array}{r} 3.35 \\ 2\overline{)6.70} \\ -6 \\ \hline 07 \\ -6 \\ \hline 10 \\ -10 \\ \hline 0 \end{array}$$

96.5 ÷ 5 = ______

64.96 ÷ 8 = ______

1.854 ÷ 9 = ______

0.946 ÷ 11 = ______

70.8 ÷ 15 = ______

296.1 ÷ 42 = ______

6.804 ÷ 72 = ______

26 Dividing decimals

Learn!

You can use long division to divide a decimal by a decimal. Try it with 8.64 ÷ 2.4.

$2.4\overline{)8.64}$

First, change the divisor to a whole number. You can do that by multiplying by 10. Then, multiply the dividend by 10, since 8.64 ÷ 2.4 is the same as 86.4 ÷ 24. Notice that for both numbers, you've moved the decimal point one place to the right.

$$\begin{array}{r} 3.6 \\ 24\overline{)86.4} \\ -72 \\ \hline 14\,4 \\ -14\,4 \\ \hline 0 \end{array}$$

Next, use long division to divide until there is no remainder.

Remember to include a decimal point in your quotient. The decimal point will go above the decimal point in the dividend.

So, 8.64 ÷ 2.4 = 3.6.

Divide.

460 ÷ 0.8 = 575

$$\begin{array}{r} 575 \\ 0.8\overline{)460.0} \\ -40 \\ \hline 060 \\ -56 \\ \hline 40 \\ -40 \\ \hline 0 \end{array}$$

1.74 ÷ 0.3 = ______

42.7 ÷ 0.7 = ______

72 ÷ 0.04 = ______

Keep going! Divide.

96.6 ÷ 0.6 = ______

86.38 ÷ 0.7 = ______

0.215 ÷ 0.02 = ______

120.18 ÷ 1.5 = ______

1,080 ÷ 0.24 = ______

319.95 ÷ 47.4 = ______

28 Dividing decimals

Divide. Compare each pair of quotients using <, >, or =.

54.9 ÷ 0.9 (<) 36.9 ÷ 0.6

$$\begin{array}{r} 61 \\ 0.9\overline{)54.9} \\ -54 \\ \hline 09 \\ -9 \\ \hline 0 \end{array} \qquad \begin{array}{r} 61.5 \\ 0.6\overline{)36.90} \\ -36 \\ \hline 09 \\ -6 \\ \hline 30 \\ -30 \\ \hline 0 \end{array}$$

38.5 ÷ 0.7 ◯ 1.05 ÷ 0.02

49.2 ÷ 1.5 ◯ 20.35 ÷ 0.55

65.52 ÷ 4.2 ◯ 117 ÷ 7.5

Exploration Zone

You can use your knowledge of place value to help you divide decimals. Look at the examples below. What pattern do you notice?

48 ÷ 6 = 48 ones ÷ 6 ones = 8

4.8 ÷ 0.6 = 48 tenths ÷ 6 tenths = 8

0.48 ÷ 0.06 = 48 hundredths ÷ 6 hundredths = 8

0.048 ÷ 0.006 = 48 thousandths ÷ 6 thousandths = 8

TRY IT YOURSELF!

Try the examples below using what you noticed above.

0.036 ÷ 0.006 = _______ thousandths ÷ _______ thousandths = _______

0.1 ÷ 0.05 = _______ hundredths ÷ _______ hundredths = _______

0.056 ÷ 0.007 = 56 ______________________________ ÷ 7 ______________________________ = ______

1.8 ÷ 0.3 = 18 ______________________________ ÷ 3 ______________________________ = ______

Divide.

0.32 ÷ 0.08 = __________

2.1 ÷ __________ = 3

0.03 ÷ 0.006 = __________

0.1 ÷ 0.005 = __________

0.108 ÷ __________ = 9

__________ ÷ 0.11 = 11

Word problems

Answer each question.

Becca has 13.5 gigabytes available on her tablet. She wants to download some movies before she goes on a trip. If each movie uses 1.5 gigabytes of storage, how many movies can Becca download? ____________

Sanjay earns $22.50 per hour working as a lifeguard at Silver City Pool. Yesterday, Sanjay worked 3.5 hours. How much money did he earn? ____________

U-Pick Berry Farm charges $3.40 for every pound of strawberries that is picked. If Kinsley paid $7.65 for her strawberries, how many pounds of strawberries did she pick? ____________

A boat holds 12.5 gallons of gas. If gas costs $4.40 per gallon, how much would it cost Janet to fill the gas tank from empty? ____________

Time for review! Add, subtract, multiply, or divide.

45.72 − 6.04 = ____________

56.48 ÷ 0.8 = ____________

19.68 + 5.24 = ____________

4.5 × 7.9 = ____________

131.4 ÷ 2.5 = ____________

32.71 − 11.8 = ____________

7.81 × 0.53 = ____________

7.269 + 15.8 = ____________

1.56 ÷ 0.16 = ____________

87.6 − 3.125 = ____________

Decimal operations

Keep going! Add, subtract, multiply, or divide.

65.4 × 1.8 = ________________

343.21 − 51.8 = ________________

16.15 ÷ 1.9 = ________________

12.5 + 8.972 = ________________

19.5 − 7.63 = ________________

7.32 × 0.95 = ________________

82.6 ÷ 2.8 = 

64.3 + 0.781 = ________________

47.1 − 8.462 = ________________

342.7 × 0.61 = ________________

For more practice, visit IXL.com or the IXL mobile app and enter this code in the search bar.

Follow the path from start to finish.

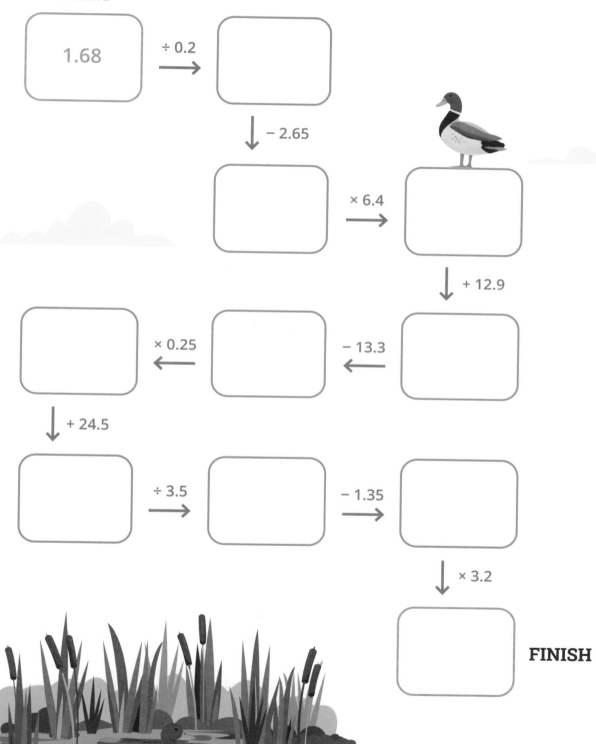

1.68 → ÷ 0.2 → ☐

↓ − 2.65

☐ → × 6.4 → ☐

↓ + 12.9

☐ ← × 0.25 ← ☐ ← − 13.3 ← ☐

↓ + 24.5

☐ → ÷ 3.5 → ☐ → − 1.35 → ☐

↓ × 3.2

☐ FINISH

Word problems

A group of friends went to the Deer Creek Fair for an afternoon of rides, food, games, and fun! This sign shows the prices of a few snacks and tickets they could have purchased while at the fair.

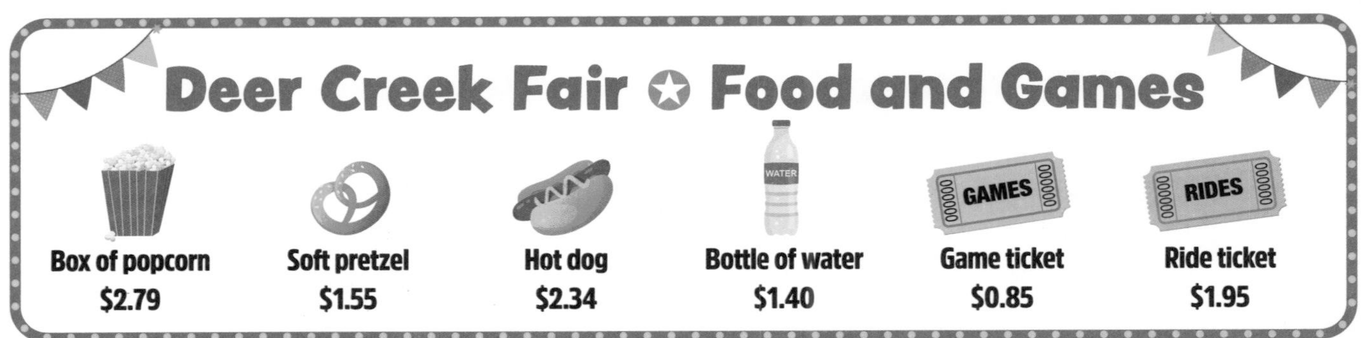

Deer Creek Fair ✪ Food and Games
WATER
GAMES
RIDES
Box of popcorn
$2.79
Soft pretzel
$1.55
Hot dog
$2.34
Bottle of water
$1.40
Game ticket
$0.85
Ride ticket
$1.95

Use the sign to answer the questions.

Carmen spent $5.10 playing games. How many game tickets did she purchase? ____________

Latrell needed to buy 3 ride tickets in order to ride the Ferris wheel. He also bought a soft pretzel to eat while on the ride. How much money did he spend? ____________

While playing a game, Jada won a coupon for $0.75 off any food purchase. She used it when she bought a bottle of water and a box of popcorn. How much money did she spend? ____________

Travis bought 3 hot dogs to split with his friend Jo. If they split the cost evenly, how much did they each spend? ____________

Daphne bought 6 ride tickets and a box of popcorn. She paid with a $20 bill. How much change did she get back? ____________

IXL.com skill ID **8HT**

Multiply.

$3\frac{1}{2} \times \frac{2}{3} =$ $2\frac{1}{3}$

$\frac{7}{2} \times \frac{2}{3} = \frac{14}{6} = 2\frac{1}{3}$

$\frac{1}{5} \times 9 =$ ______

$\frac{10}{11} \times \frac{3}{8} =$ ______

$\frac{3}{5} \times 2\frac{3}{4} =$ ______

$\frac{5}{12} \times \frac{3}{5} =$ ______

$\frac{5}{6} \times \frac{2}{3} =$ ______

$5\frac{1}{3} \times \frac{1}{8} =$ ______

$\frac{7}{9} \times 1\frac{3}{5} =$ ______

$3\frac{3}{4} \times \frac{2}{5} =$ ______

$\frac{5}{12} \times \frac{4}{15} =$ ______

$\frac{3}{10} \times 2\frac{1}{6} =$ ______

36 Multiplying mixed numbers

Multiply.

$2\frac{1}{3} \times 5\frac{1}{2} =$ ________________

$1\frac{4}{5} \times 3\frac{2}{3} =$ ________________

$1\frac{3}{5} \times 3\frac{3}{4} =$ ________________

$1\frac{1}{4} \times 2\frac{2}{3} =$ ________________

$2\frac{1}{4} \times 4\frac{1}{5} =$ ________________

$1\frac{2}{5} \times 6\frac{2}{3} =$ ________________

$3\frac{1}{8} \times 2\frac{1}{2} =$ ________________

$2\frac{5}{6} \times 7\frac{1}{2} =$ ________________

IXL.com
skill ID
Z9M

Keep going! Multiply.

$3\frac{1}{3} \times 2 \times \frac{1}{2} =$ ______________

$\frac{2}{3} \times 3 \times 1\frac{1}{4} =$ ______________

$\frac{1}{2} \times 2\frac{2}{3} \times \frac{1}{6} =$ ______________

$4\frac{1}{3} \times \frac{3}{5} \times \frac{2}{3} =$ ______________

$\frac{3}{4} \times \frac{2}{5} \times 3\frac{1}{2} =$ ______________

$1\frac{2}{3} \times 2\frac{1}{2} \times \frac{4}{5} =$ ______________

IXL.com
skill ID
W5G

38 Fractions and exponents

Evaluate.

$\left(\frac{2}{3}\right)^4 = \frac{16}{81}$

$\frac{2}{3} \times \frac{2}{3} \times \frac{2}{3} \times \frac{2}{3} = \frac{16}{81}$

$\left(\frac{9}{10}\right)^2 =$ ______

$\left(\frac{1}{2}\right)^5 =$ ______

$\left(\frac{3}{5}\right)^3 =$ ______

$\left(\frac{7}{8}\right)^1 =$ ______

$\left(\frac{5}{6}\right)^2 =$ ______

$\left(\frac{2}{5}\right)^2 =$ ______

$\left(\frac{1}{3}\right)^5 =$ ______

$\left(\frac{3}{7}\right)^3 =$ ______

$\left(\frac{3}{4}\right)^4 =$ ______

Answer each question.

Darius is making blueberry pancakes for breakfast. The recipe calls for $\frac{3}{4}$ of a cup of milk for one batch of pancakes. Darius plans to make $\frac{1}{2}$ of a batch. How much milk should he use? ____________

Meg bought $4\frac{1}{2}$ yards of fabric to make purses to sell at a craft fair. Each purse will use $\frac{1}{3}$ of the fabric Meg bought. How much fabric will be used for each purse? ____________

Noah and Jasmine are learning how to knit scarves. Noah's scarf is $1\frac{1}{2}$ feet long. Jasmine's scarf is $2\frac{1}{2}$ times that length. How long is Jasmine's scarf? ____________

Valerie walks her dog, Dodger, 2 times every day. They walk $\frac{4}{5}$ of a mile each time. How many miles will Valerie and Dodger walk in 5 days? ____________

Bryan's soccer team has played 12 games this year. They won $\frac{3}{4}$ of their games. Of the games they won, they celebrated with pizza after $\frac{2}{3}$ of them. How many games did Bryan's team celebrate with pizza? ____________

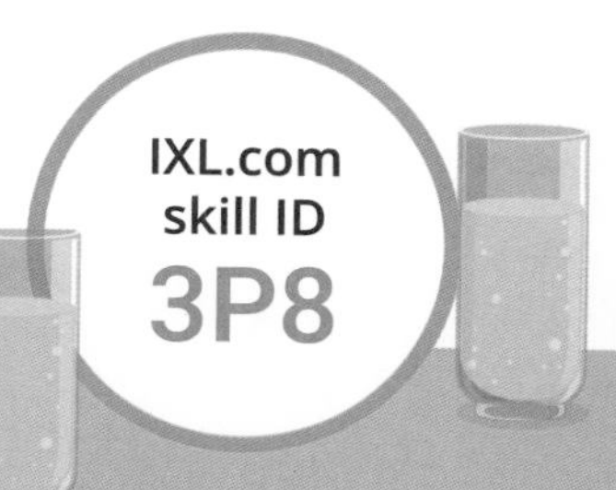

IXL.com
skill ID
3P8

40 Dividing fractions with models

Learn!

You can divide a whole number by a fraction using a model. Try it with $3 \div \frac{2}{5}$. Start by breaking 3 wholes into $\frac{1}{5}$ pieces.

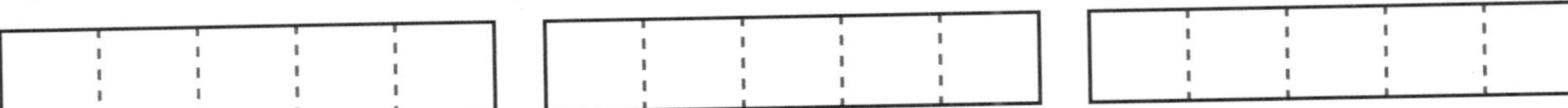

Then, count the number of groups of size $\frac{2}{5}$.

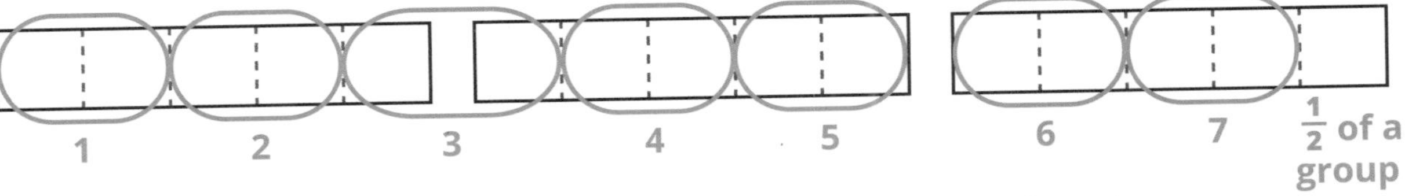

There are 7 groups of size $\frac{2}{5}$ and $\frac{1}{2}$ of a group of size $\frac{2}{5}$. So, $3 \div \frac{2}{5} = 7\frac{1}{2}$.

Divide. Use the models to help.

$5 \div \frac{1}{2} =$ ______

$3 \div \frac{3}{4} =$ ______

$1 \div \frac{3}{5} =$ ______

$3 \div \frac{2}{3} =$ ______

IXL.com skill ID DXW

Learn!

You can divide a fraction by a whole number using a model, too. Try it with $\frac{3}{4} \div 6$. Start with a model of $\frac{3}{4}$. Divide $\frac{3}{4}$ into 6 equal groups. What fraction of the whole is each group?

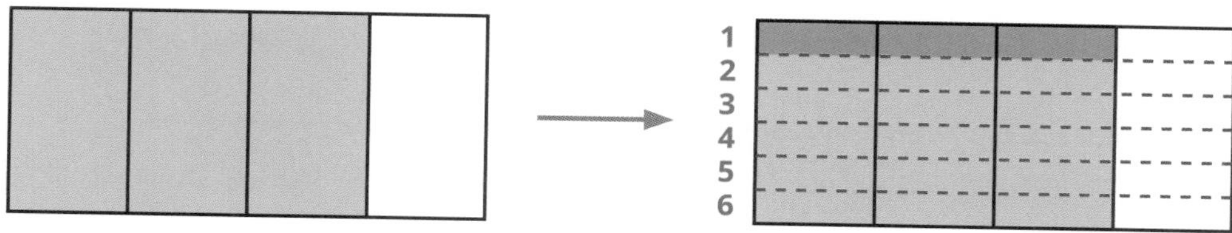

Each group is $\frac{3}{24}$ or $\frac{1}{8}$ of the whole. So, $\frac{3}{4} \div 6 = \frac{1}{8}$.

Divide. Use the models to help.

$\frac{1}{4} \div 3 =$ ________

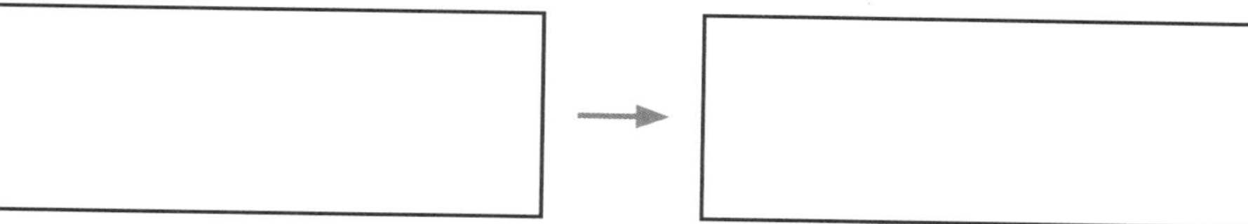

$\frac{4}{5} \div 2 =$ ________

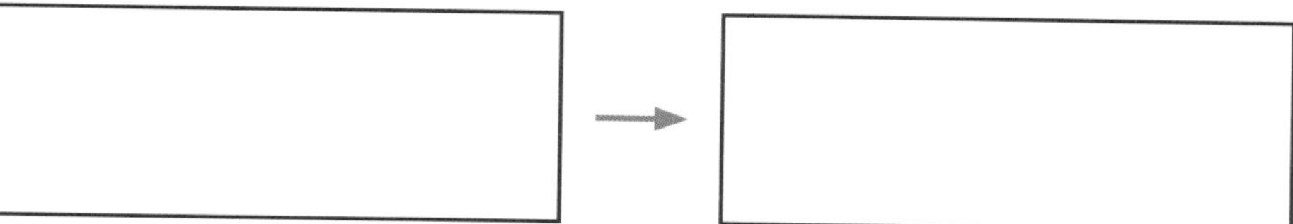

$\frac{2}{3} \div 4 =$ ________

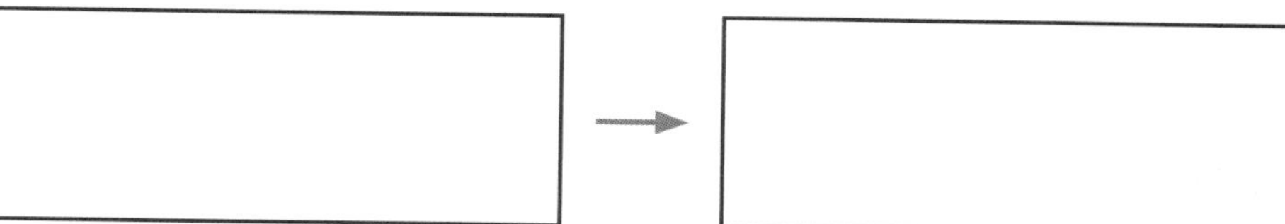

$\frac{2}{5} \div 6 =$ ________

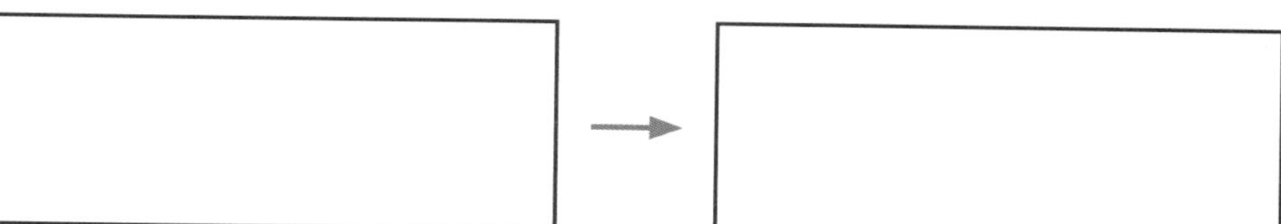

IXL.com skill ID **MF8**

Dividing fractions with models

Learn!

You can also divide a fraction by a fraction using a model. Try it with $\frac{5}{6} \div \frac{1}{3}$. Start with a model of $\frac{5}{6}$ and a model of $\frac{1}{3}$. How many groups of $\frac{1}{3}$ are there in $\frac{5}{6}$?

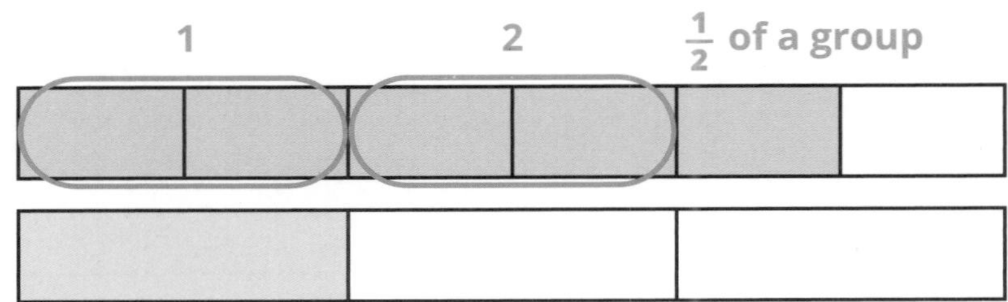

There are $2\frac{1}{2}$ groups of $\frac{1}{3}$ in $\frac{5}{6}$. So, $\frac{5}{6} \div \frac{1}{3} = 2\frac{1}{2}$.

Divide. Use the models to help.

$\frac{1}{2} \div \frac{1}{6} =$ ________

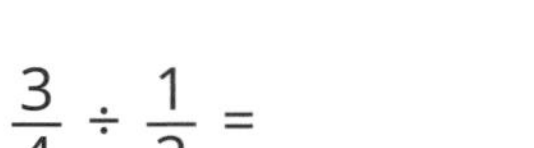

$\frac{3}{4} \div \frac{1}{2} =$ ________

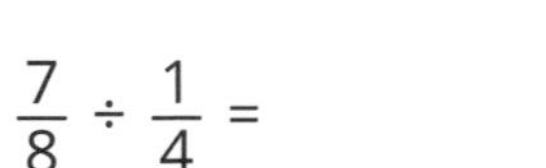

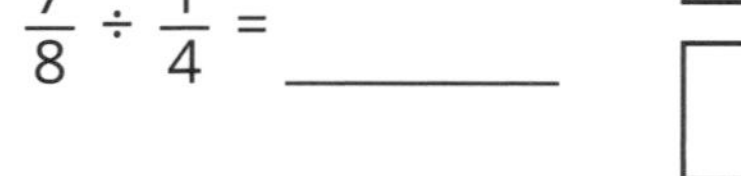

$\frac{7}{8} \div \frac{1}{4} =$ ________

$\frac{9}{10} \div \frac{2}{5} =$ ________

Learn!

Dividing by a fraction is the same as multiplying by the **reciprocal**. Try it with $\frac{3}{5} \div \frac{2}{3}$. Rewrite the division problem using multiplication. Write the divisor $\frac{2}{3}$ as its reciprocal, $\frac{3}{2}$. Then, multiply across.

$$\frac{3}{5} \div \frac{2}{3} \longrightarrow \frac{3}{5} \times \frac{3}{2} = \frac{9}{10}$$

Dividing by a whole number is also the same as multiplying by the reciprocal. Try it with $\frac{5}{6} \div 3$. Remember, 3 is the same as $\frac{3}{1}$. So, the reciprocal of $\frac{3}{1}$ is $\frac{1}{3}$.

$$\frac{5}{6} \div 3 \longrightarrow \frac{5}{6} \times \frac{1}{3} = \frac{5}{18}$$

Divide the whole number by the fraction.

$5 \div \frac{3}{4} = 6\frac{2}{3}$

$\frac{5}{1} \times \frac{4}{3} = \frac{20}{3} = 6\frac{2}{3}$

$8 \div \frac{1}{6} =$ ______

$3 \div \frac{4}{7} =$ ______

Divide the fraction by the whole number.

$\frac{1}{4} \div 6 =$ ______

$\frac{3}{8} \div 3 =$ ______

$\frac{5}{6} \div 4 =$ ______

Divide the fraction by the fraction.

$\frac{1}{3} \div \frac{7}{8} =$ ______

$\frac{4}{7} \div \frac{2}{5} =$ ______

44 Dividing fractions

Divide.

$\frac{1}{9} \div \frac{4}{5} =$ ____________

$8 \div \frac{3}{5} =$ ____________

$\frac{5}{6} \div \frac{3}{4} =$ ____________

$\frac{3}{10} \div \frac{1}{12} =$ ____________

$\frac{4}{7} \div \frac{3}{11} =$ ____________

$\frac{5}{9} \div 4 =$ ____________

$\frac{5}{8} \div \frac{1}{10} =$ ____________

$\frac{2}{3} \div \frac{7}{12} =$ ____________

$\frac{8}{9} \div \frac{5}{6} =$ ____________

$\frac{2}{5} \div \frac{7}{8} =$ ____________

$\frac{2}{7} \div \frac{6}{11} =$ ____________

$6 \div \frac{3}{7} =$ ____________

$\frac{3}{8} \div \frac{7}{10} =$ ____________

Keep going! Divide.

$\frac{3}{4} \div \frac{5}{12} =$ ______

$\frac{2}{3} \div \frac{11}{12} =$ ______

$\frac{3}{5} \div \frac{1}{10} =$ ______

$6 \div \frac{2}{7} =$ ______

$\frac{3}{8} \div \frac{3}{7} =$ ______

$\frac{1}{9} \div \frac{3}{10} =$ ______

$\frac{7}{12} \div 2 =$ ______

$\frac{5}{8} \div \frac{3}{4} =$ ______

$\frac{3}{7} \div \frac{9}{10} =$ ______

$\frac{5}{12} \div \frac{5}{8} =$ ______

$\frac{2}{5} \div \frac{7}{10} =$ ______

$\frac{5}{6} \div 15 =$ ______

TRY IT YOURSELF! Go back to pages 40–42. Instead of using models to divide, try multiplying by the reciprocal. Your answers should be the same!

Dividing fractions and mixed numbers

Learn!

You can divide fractions and mixed numbers in the same way. Start by rewriting any mixed numbers as improper fractions. Then rewrite the division problem using multiplication and solve. Try it with $\frac{4}{9} \div 2\frac{2}{3}$.

$$\frac{4}{9} \div 2\frac{2}{3} \longrightarrow \frac{4}{9} \div \frac{8}{3} \longrightarrow \frac{4}{9} \times \frac{3}{8} = \frac{12}{72} = \frac{1}{6}$$

Divide.

$2\frac{4}{5} \div 4 = \underline{\frac{7}{10}}$

$\frac{14}{5} \div \frac{4}{1} \longrightarrow \frac{14}{5} \times \frac{1}{4} = \frac{14}{20} = \frac{7}{10}$

$6 \div 1\frac{2}{3} =$ ______

$3 \div 8\frac{1}{2} =$ ______

$5\frac{1}{4} \div 3 =$ ______

$\frac{2}{5} \div 2\frac{3}{10} =$ ______

$3\frac{1}{3} \div \frac{5}{6} =$ ______

$4\frac{3}{5} \div \frac{3}{10} =$ ______

$\frac{5}{6} \div 1\frac{3}{8} =$ ______

Keep going! Divide.

$\frac{2}{3} \div 5\frac{1}{2} =$ ______

$4\frac{4}{5} \div \frac{3}{4} =$ ______

$2\frac{2}{9} \div \frac{3}{5} =$ ______

$8\frac{1}{3} \div 1\frac{1}{6} =$ ______

$\frac{11}{12} \div 2\frac{3}{4} =$ ______

$2\frac{2}{9} \div 4\frac{2}{3} =$ ______

$3\frac{1}{5} \div 1\frac{1}{3} =$ ______

$2\frac{3}{5} \div 1\frac{9}{10} =$ ______

$3\frac{7}{8} \div 5\frac{1}{6} =$ ______

IXL.com skill ID **N2B**

48 Dividing fractions and mixed numbers

Time for review! Divide.

$\frac{5}{11} \div \frac{4}{5} =$ ____________

$12 \div 3\frac{3}{7} =$ ____________

$3\frac{1}{3} \div 4\frac{1}{8} =$ ____________

$2\frac{4}{5} \div 6\frac{2}{3} =$ ____________

$5\frac{5}{8} \div 1\frac{1}{6} =$ ____________

$3\frac{1}{5} \div \frac{4}{15} =$ ____________

$7\frac{1}{3} \div 2\frac{2}{5} =$ ____________

$10 \div \frac{8}{9} =$ ____________

Keep going! Divide.

$\frac{4}{5} \div 2\frac{1}{2} =$ ____________

$3\frac{6}{7} \div 9 =$ ____________

$12 \div 2\frac{1}{4} =$ ____________

$2\frac{1}{3} \div 2\frac{5}{8} =$ ____________

$5\frac{1}{3} \div \frac{7}{12} =$ ____________

$3\frac{3}{5} \div 1\frac{7}{9} =$ ____________

Dividing fractions and mixed numbers

Divide. Use your answers to draw a path from start to finish.

START

$\frac{5}{6} \div 1\frac{1}{3}$	$\frac{5}{18}$	$\frac{9}{10} \div \frac{3}{5}$	$\frac{27}{50}$	$3\frac{1}{3} \div 6$	$1\frac{4}{5}$	$4 \div \frac{3}{7}$
$2\frac{1}{2}$	$\frac{5}{8}$	$9\frac{1}{3}$	$\frac{5}{9}$	$9\frac{5}{8}$	$1\frac{3}{11}$	$1\frac{1}{2}$
$1\frac{1}{6} \div 4$	$4\frac{2}{3}$	$7 \div \frac{10}{11}$	$7\frac{7}{10}$	$2\frac{3}{4} \div 3\frac{1}{2}$	$\frac{11}{14}$	$\frac{8}{9} \div 4$
$\frac{9}{24}$	$\frac{1}{8}$	$6\frac{4}{11}$	$\frac{10}{81}$	$\frac{11}{35}$	$\frac{2}{9}$	$3\frac{5}{9}$
$1\frac{3}{4} \div 5\frac{1}{6}$	$7\frac{1}{2}$	$5\frac{2}{5} \div \frac{2}{3}$	$\frac{35}{36}$	$\frac{7}{8} \div \frac{9}{10}$	$2\frac{1}{3}$	$5\frac{1}{3} \div 4$
$\frac{23}{24}$	$\frac{5}{8}$	$8\frac{1}{10}$	 $\frac{63}{80}$	$\frac{7}{32}$	 $\frac{3}{4}$	$7\frac{1}{3}$
$\frac{6}{7} \div 1\frac{2}{3}$	$\frac{11}{21}$	$2\frac{1}{4} \div 2\frac{1}{2}$	$\frac{9}{10}$	$\frac{3}{8} \div \frac{7}{12}$	$\frac{9}{14}$	FINISH

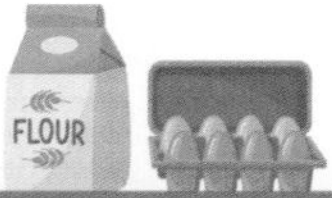

Answer each question.

Logan is making cupcakes for his sister's birthday party. He has $1\frac{1}{2}$ cups of frosting to use for 12 cupcakes. How much frosting should Logan put on each cupcake? ________________

Evan bought 3 pints of vegetable soup. Each serving is $\frac{3}{4}$ of a pint. How many servings of vegetable soup can Evan make? ________________

Sadie bought a bag of food for her hamster, Chipper. The bag contains $2\frac{1}{2}$ cups of food, and Sadie gives Chipper $\frac{1}{4}$ of a cup of food each day. How many days will the bag of food last? ________________

Allison is making bibs for her baby cousin. She has $2\frac{1}{4}$ yards of fabric, and each bib uses $\frac{3}{8}$ of a yard of fabric. How many bibs can Allison make? ________________

Mr. Rosa has a block of clay that is $12\frac{1}{2}$ inches long. He cuts it into 20 identical pieces for an art project. How long is each piece of clay? ________________

Each day, Dominic makes himself a smoothie using $\frac{3}{4}$ of a cup of juice. He has $4\frac{1}{2}$ cups of juice left in his refrigerator. If the juice is only used for smoothies, how many days will it last?

____

52 Integers and their opposites

Learn!

An **integer** is a number without a fractional part. Integers can be **positive**, **negative**, or zero. Zero is neither positive nor negative. On a number line, negative integers are to the left of zero, and positive integers are to the right.

Every nonzero integer has an **opposite**, which is the same distance from zero but on the opposite side of the number line. For example, 5 and −5 are opposites.

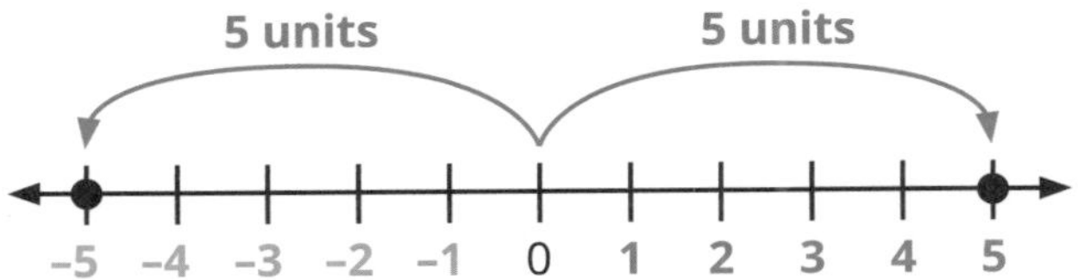

Use the number line to find the opposite of each number.

The opposite of –2 is _________.

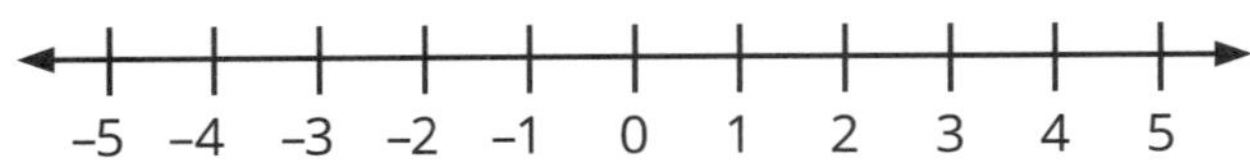

The opposite of 8 is _________.

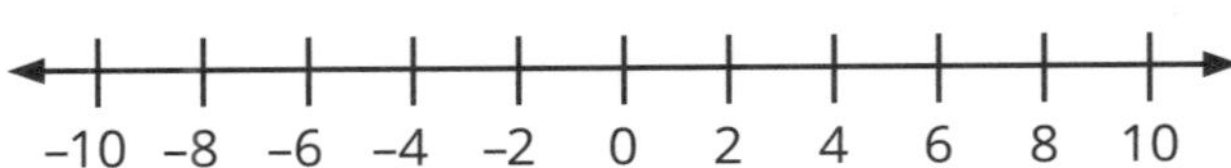

The opposite of –10 is _________.

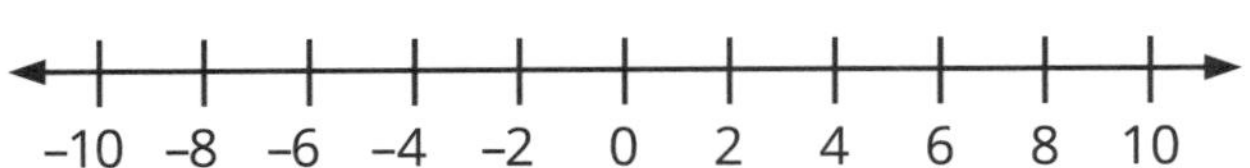

The opposite of 15 is _________.

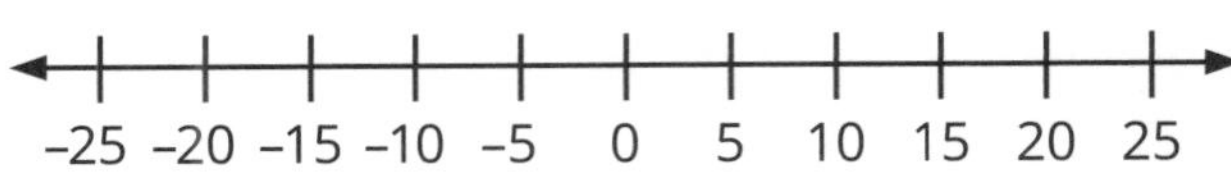

The opposite of –12 is _________.

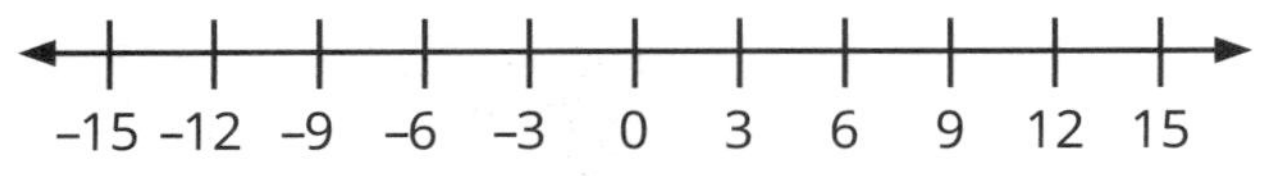

The opposite of 20 is _________.

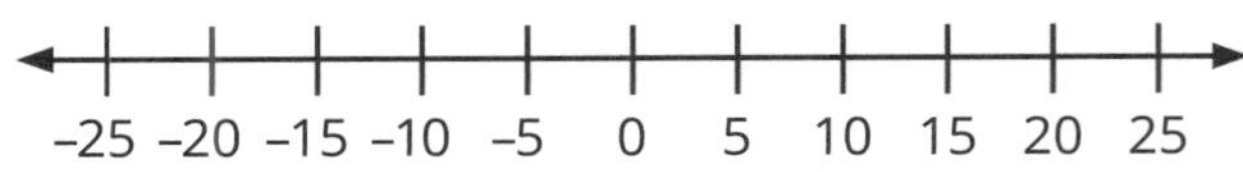

The opposite of –50 is _________.

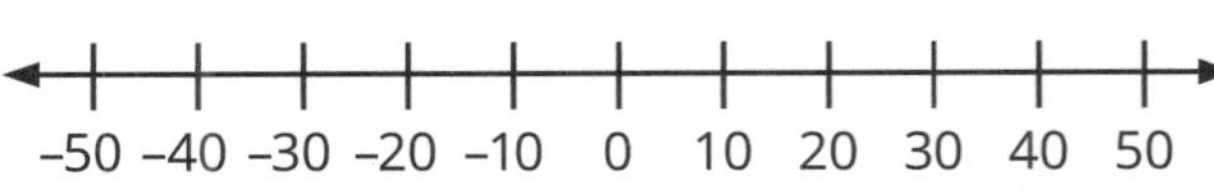

Write an integer that represents each situation.

When Maya woke up, the temperature was 7°F below zero. Write an integer to represent the temperature. __________

Kendra earned 80 points in her game by finding the key to a hidden treasure. Write an integer to represent the change in Kendra's score. __________

Jamal deposited $50 into his savings account. Write an integer to represent the change in the balance of Jamal's savings account. __________

Addison visited a city located at an elevation of 32 meters below sea level. Write an integer to represent the city's elevation. __________

The value of Goliath Electronic Company's stock rose 14 points in one day. Write an integer to represent the change in the stock's value. __________

Gabriel paid $45 for a new phone case using cash from his wallet. Write an integer to represent the change in the amount of cash in Gabriel's wallet. __________

Every smoothie at Smoothie Village is on sale for $2 off the regular price. Write an integer to represent the change in the price of a smoothie.

____

IXL.com
skill ID
8EP

54 Comparing integers

Graph each integer on the number line. Then compare the integers using < or >.

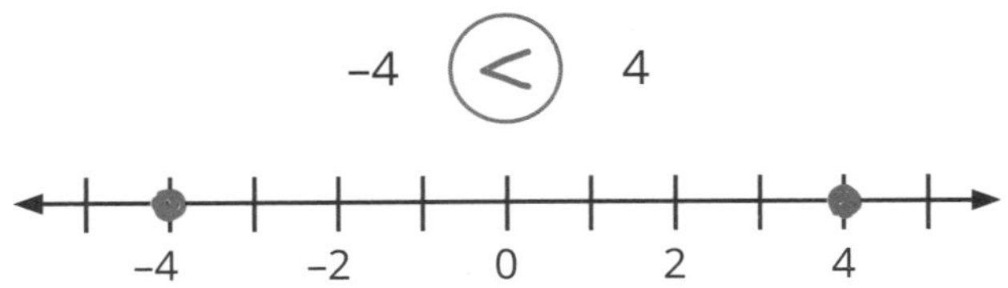

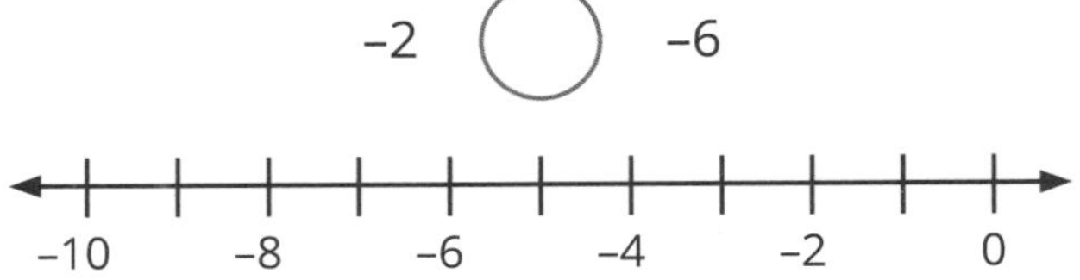

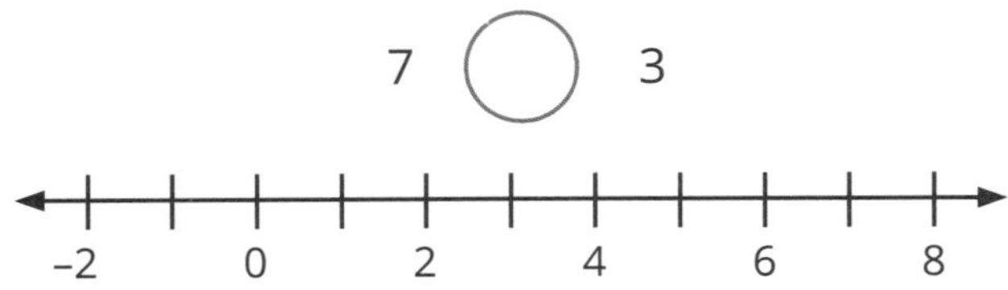

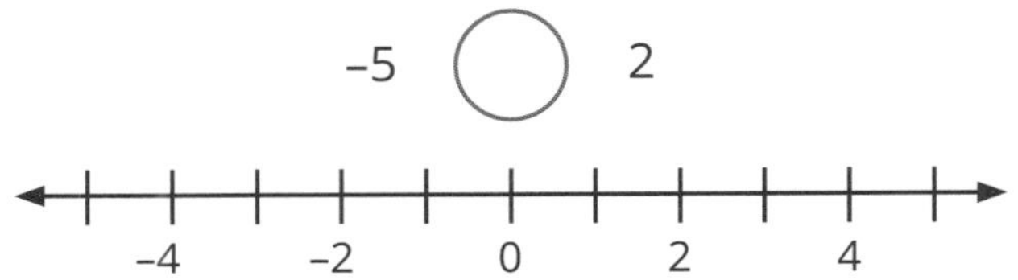

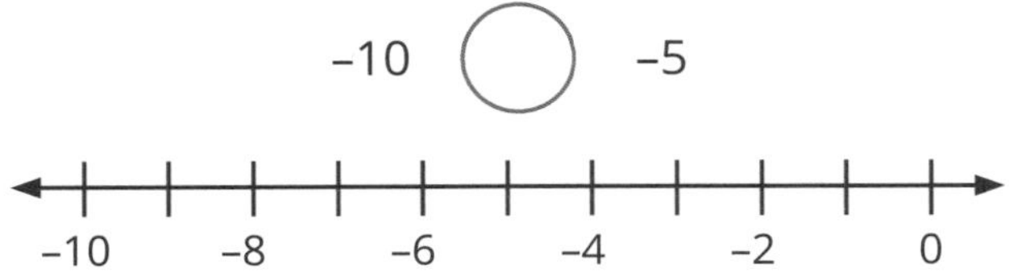

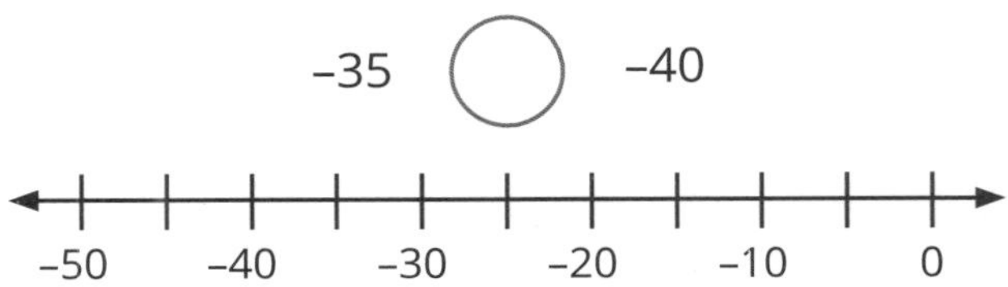

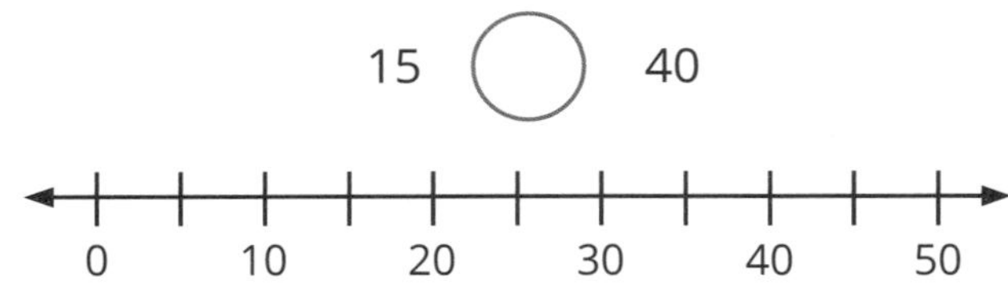

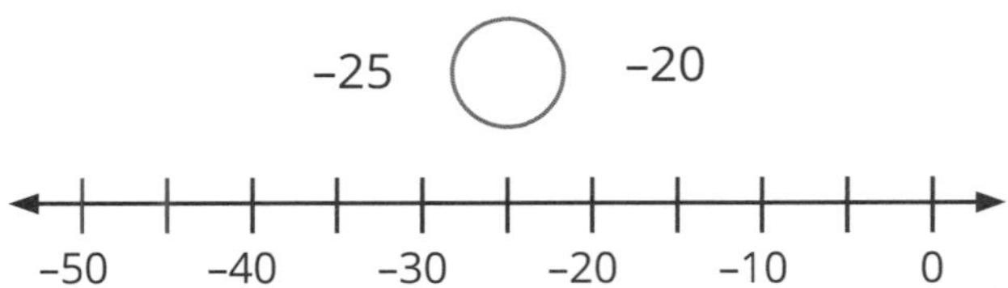

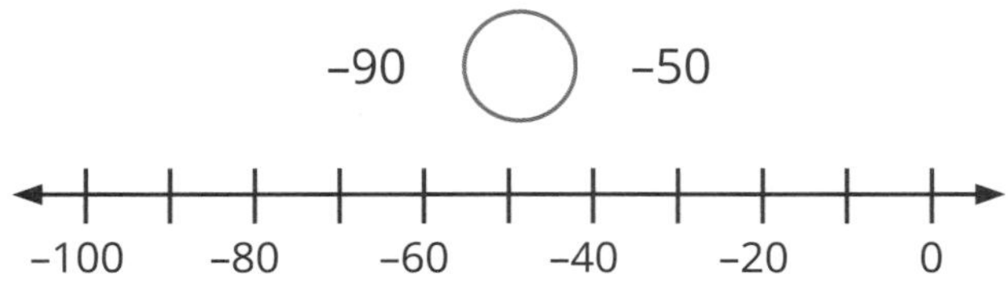

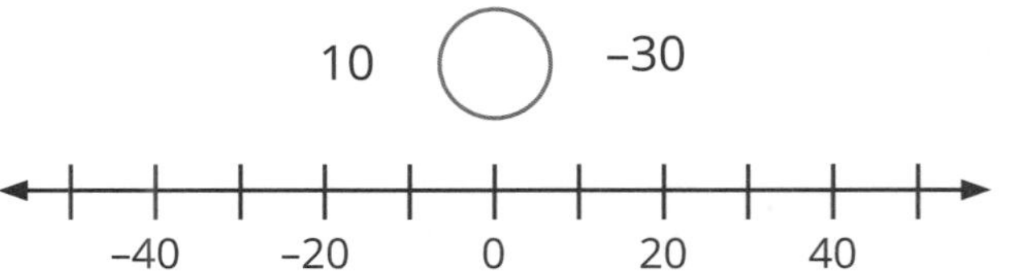

Comparing integers

Compare the integers using < or >.

–34 ◯ 33	10 ◯ –15	–25 ◯ –28
70 ◯ –60	–46 ◯ –40	76 ◯ 57
–33 ◯ 29	–99 ◯ 9	–75 ◯ –68
–6 ◯ –60	–83 ◯ –28	–54 ◯ –46
–10 ◯ –100	–89 ◯ –93	–25 ◯ –22

IXL.com
skill ID
4G6

56 Ordering integers

Graph the integers on the number line. Then order the integers from least to greatest.

4, –2, 0

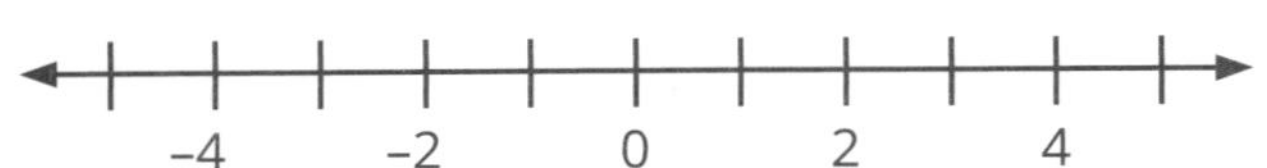

________ ________ ________

–3, 5, –1

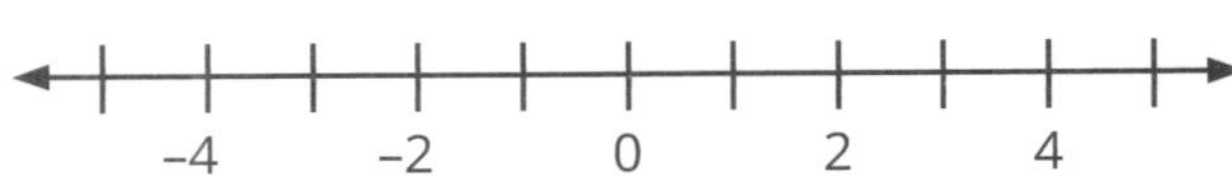

________ ________ ________

2, –2, 6

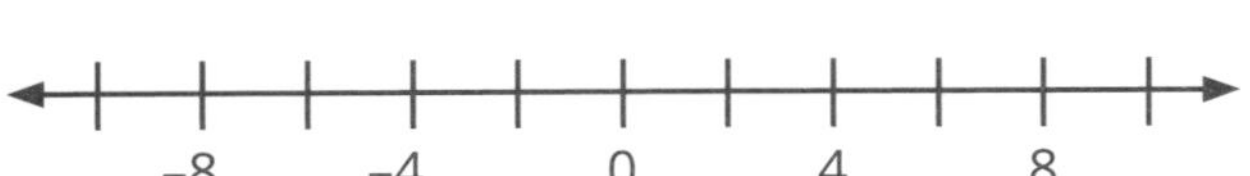

________ ________ ________

–15, –20, 10

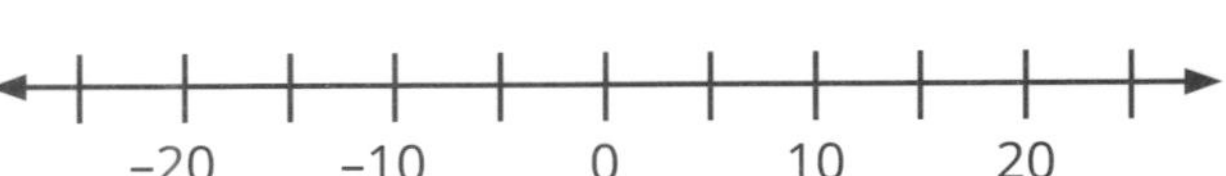

________ ________ ________

–30, 20, –10, 0

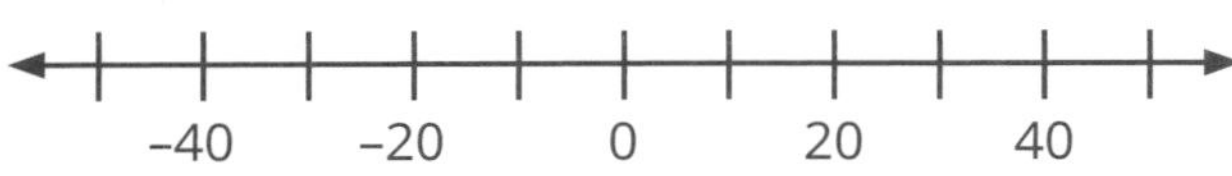

________ ________ ________ ________

–10, –70, –40, –90

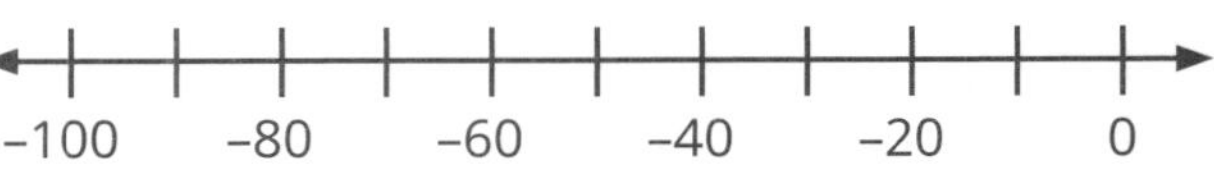

________ ________ ________ ________

Ordering integers

Order the integers from least to greatest.

17, –13, 8 ______ ______ ______

–20, –28, 25 ______ ______ ______

–53, 0, 56, –58 ______ ______ ______ ______

47, –92, –80, 12 ______ ______ ______ ______

–25, –40, –80, –55 ______ ______ ______ ______

17, –60, –32, 60, 74 ______ ______ ______ ______ ______

–41, –86, 14, 92, –29 ______ ______ ______ ______ ______

–97, –16, –33, –72, –64 ______ ______ ______ ______ ______

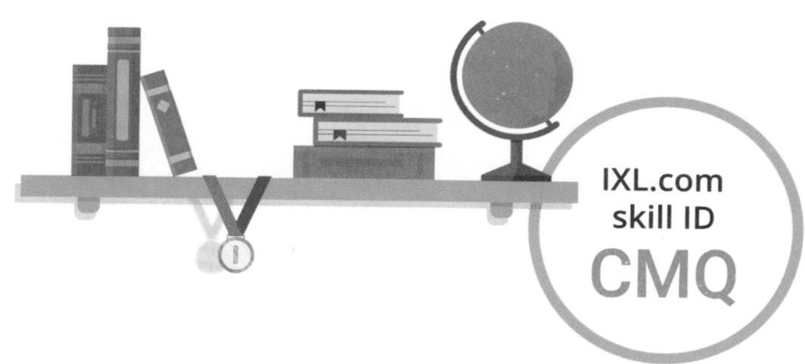

IXL.com skill ID CMQ

58 Absolute value

Learn!

The **absolute value** of a number is its distance from zero. Look at this example.

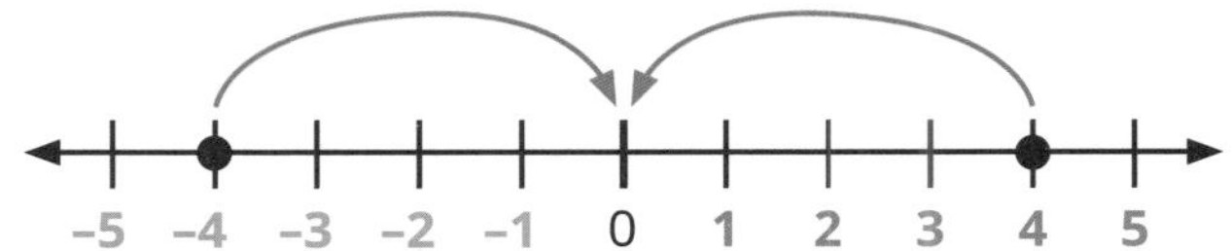

Both integers **4** and **–4** are 4 units away from zero on the number line. So, the absolute value of 4 is 4, and the absolute value of –4 is 4.

Graph each integer on the number line. Then find the absolute value.

What is the absolute value of –3? 3

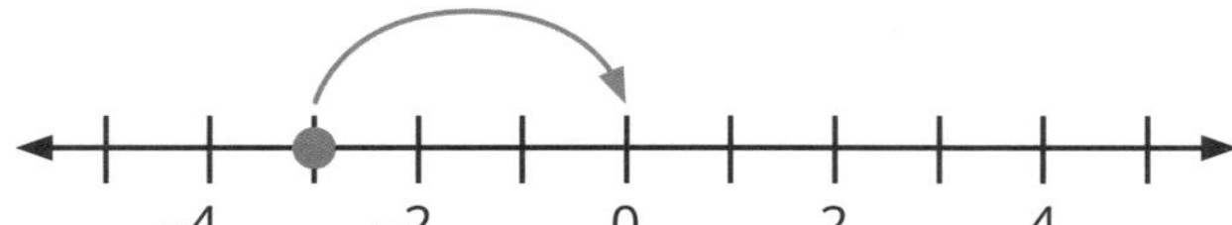

What is the absolute value of 2? ________

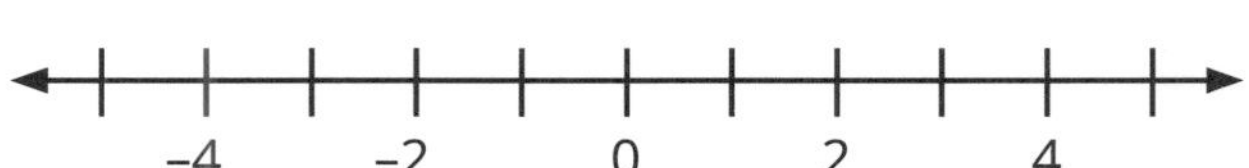

What is the absolute value of –1? ________

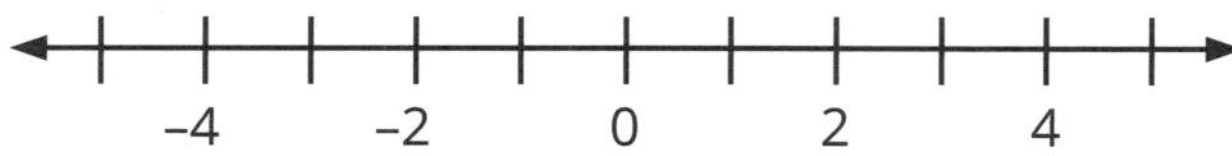

What is the absolute value of –6? ________

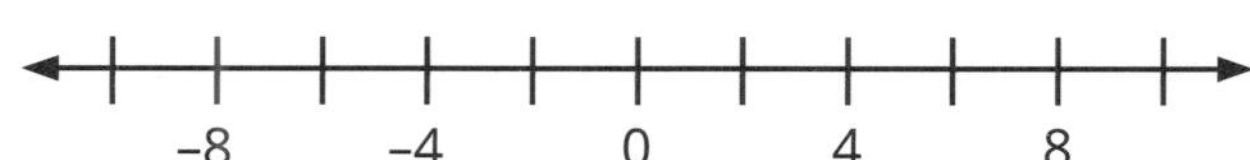

What is the absolute value of 8? ________

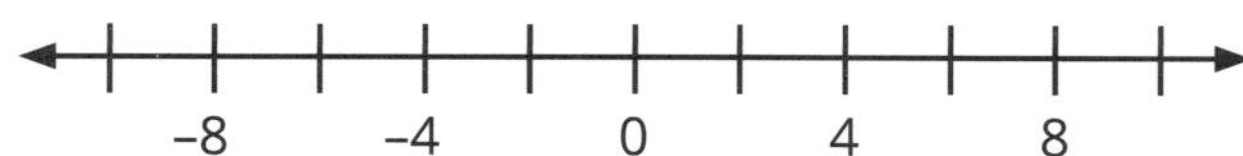

What is the absolute value of –25? ________

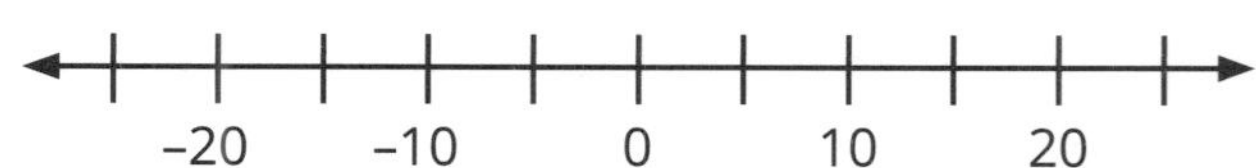

IXL.com skill ID TLR

You can use symbols to represent absolute value. For example, you can write the absolute value of –4 as |–4|.

Find the absolute value of each integer.

|–6| = 6 |9| = ____ |12| = ____

|–18| = ____ |–22| = ____ |65| = ____

|29| = ____ |–43| = ____ |52| = ____

|–30| = ____ |84| = ____ |–77| = ____

Simplify each expression.

–|–36| = –36   –|88| = ____   –|73| = ____

–|–51| = ____   –|63| = ____   –|–98| = ____

IXL.com skill ID 2YZ

60 Comparing with absolute value

Compare the numbers using <, >, or =.

$|10| \bigcirc |-10|$ $\quad$ $-25 \bigcirc |20|$ $\quad$ $|98| \bigcirc |-98|$

$|-41| \bigcirc 14$ $\quad$ $|16| \bigcirc |-62|$ $\quad$ $|6| \bigcirc -6$

$|-34| \bigcirc |34|$ $\quad$ $|25| \bigcirc |28|$ $\quad$ $|37| \bigcirc |77|$

$-76 \bigcirc |18|$ $\quad$ $53 \bigcirc |53|$ $\quad$ $|40| \bigcirc |-40|$

$5 \bigcirc |50|$ $\quad$ $|-11| \bigcirc -11$ $\quad$ $|46| \bigcirc |-42|$

IXL.com
skill ID
4A8

The table below shows the elevations of several cities. Graph and label the approximate location of each elevation on the vertical number line.

Location	Elevation (meters)
Birchstone Basin	−85
Aqua City	−2
Pine Lake	49
Lakewood Gorge	−50
Trentwood	9
Silver Falls	87

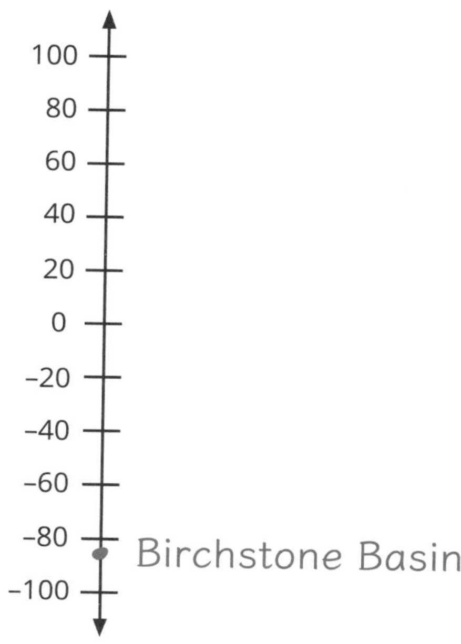

Answer each question.

Which of the locations has the lowest elevation? ____________________

What is its elevation? ____________________

Which of the locations has the highest elevation? ____________________

What is its elevation? ____________________

Is Aqua City or Trentwood closer to sea level? ____________________

Is Silver Falls or Birchstone Basin closer to sea level? ____________________

Order these locations from lowest elevation to highest elevation:
Lakewood Gorge, Aqua City, Birchstone Basin

____________________ ____________________ ____________________

Word problems

Answer each question.

The table below shows the low temperature over the past few days in Maple Hill.

Day of the week	Low temperature (°F)
Friday	5
Saturday	–2
Sunday	–4
Monday	1

On which day was the low temperature the coldest?

____

On which day was the low temperature the farthest from 0°F?

____

Order the days from coldest to warmest.

__________ __________ __________ __________

The table below shows the current elevation of four different animals compared to sea level.

Animal	Elevation (inches)
Gopher	–60
Mole	–10
Chipmunk	–36
Groundhog	–72

Which animal is the closest to sea level?

____

Which animal is at the lowest elevation?

____

Which animal is at a higher elevation: the chipmunk or the gopher?

____

IXL.com skill ID 9CW

A **rational number** is any number that can be made by dividing two integers. Rational numbers are often written as integers, fractions, or decimals.

Graph each rational number on the number line.

0.6

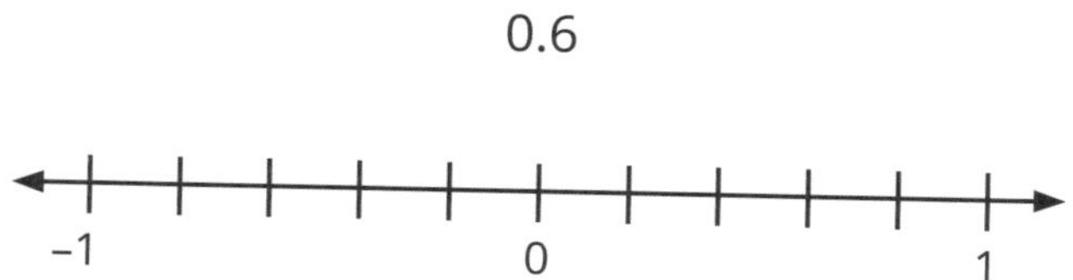

$-\frac{2}{3}$

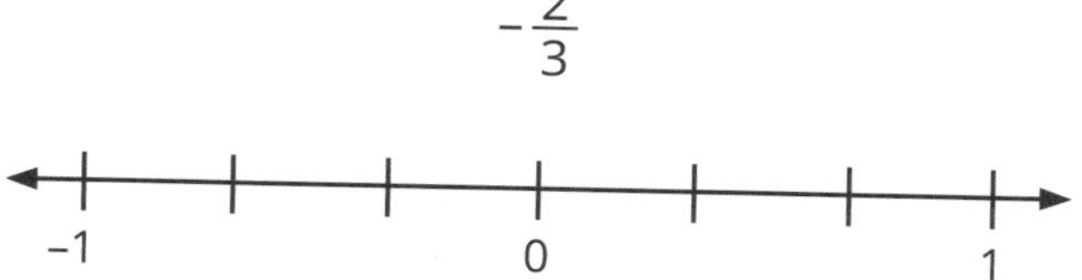

–1.25

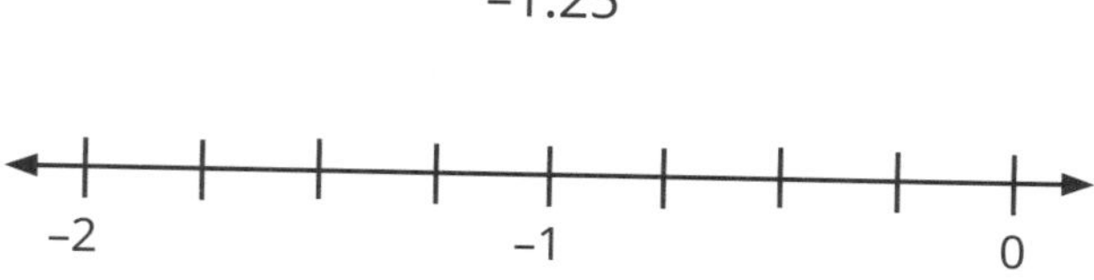

7

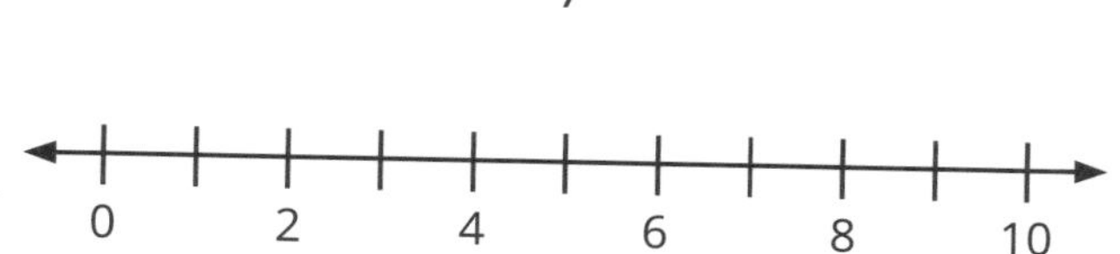

$-3\frac{1}{2}$

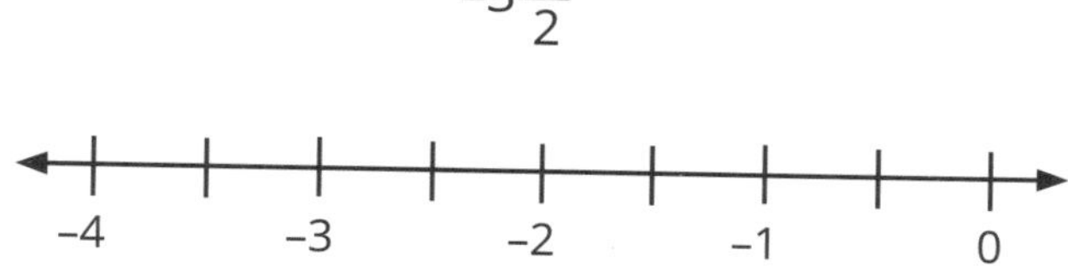

$\frac{6}{2}$

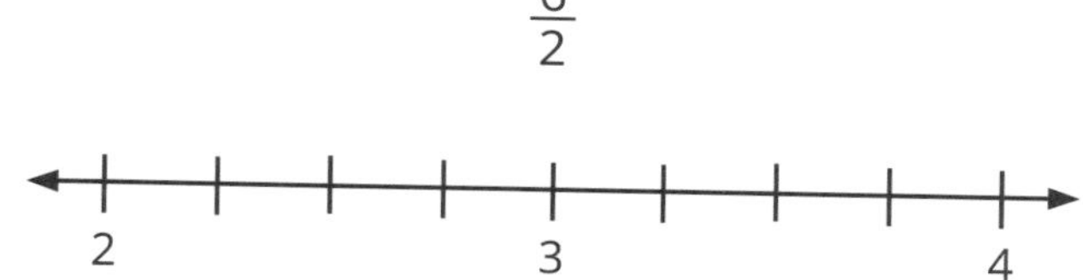

2.07

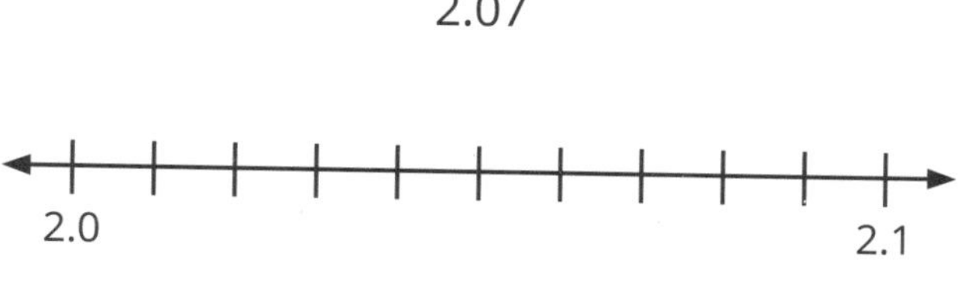

$-\frac{7}{4}$

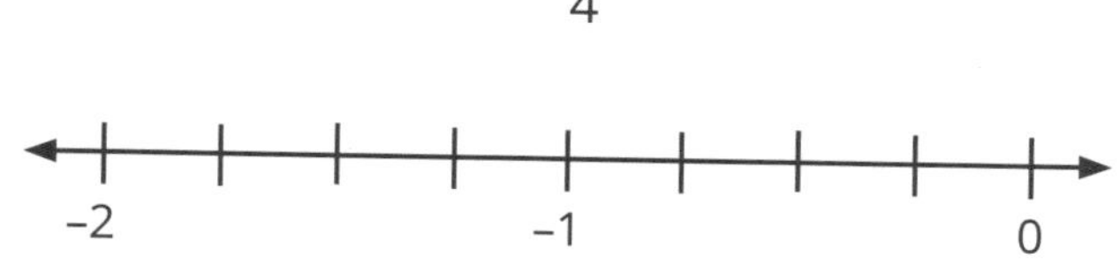

IXL.com
skill ID
DJE

64 Rational numbers and their opposites

Find the opposite of each rational number.

The opposite of $\frac{5}{9}$ is ___________.

The opposite of $-7\frac{9}{10}$ is ___________.

The opposite of 11 is ___________.

The opposite of –0.2 is ___________.

The opposite of $-\frac{20}{3}$ is ___________.

The opposite of $\frac{3}{7}$ is ___________.

The opposite of –19.75 is ___________.

The opposite of –68.4 is ___________.

The opposite of $70\frac{5}{8}$ is ___________.

The opposite of $\frac{11}{12}$ is ___________.

The opposite of 90.3 is ___________.

The opposite of $54\frac{1}{2}$ is ___________.

The opposite of $-\frac{4}{11}$ is ___________.

The opposite of –46.38 is ___________.

The opposite of $99\frac{1}{9}$ is ___________.

Find the absolute value of each rational number.

$\left|2\frac{1}{2}\right| =$ ______

$\left|-\frac{7}{12}\right| =$ ______

$|-4.55| =$ ______

$|-50.4| =$ ______

$|4.6| =$ ______

$\left|\frac{4}{9}\right| =$ ______

$|-0.08| =$ ______

$\left|-3\frac{7}{8}\right| =$ ______

$|10.9| =$ ______

$\left|-7\frac{7}{10}\right| =$ ______

$\left|-\frac{1}{6}\right| =$ ______

$\left|2\frac{3}{5}\right| =$ ______

Simplify each expression.

$-\left|49\frac{2}{7}\right| =$ ______

$-|-0.82| =$ ______

$-\left|-6\frac{1}{2}\right| =$ ______

$-|61.4| =$ ______

$-\left|-\frac{3}{4}\right| =$ ______

$-|5.01| =$ ______

66 Comparing rational numbers

Graph each rational number on the number line. Then compare the numbers using <, >, or =.

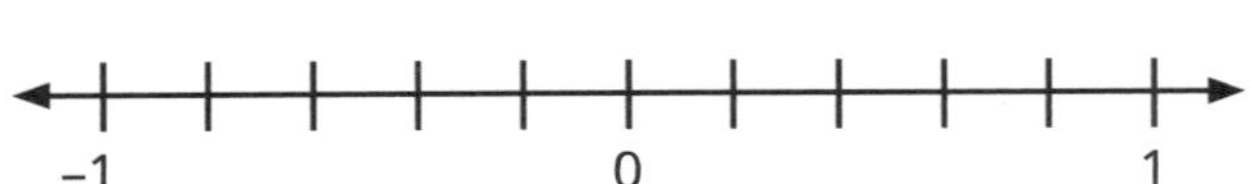

0.75 ○ 0.5

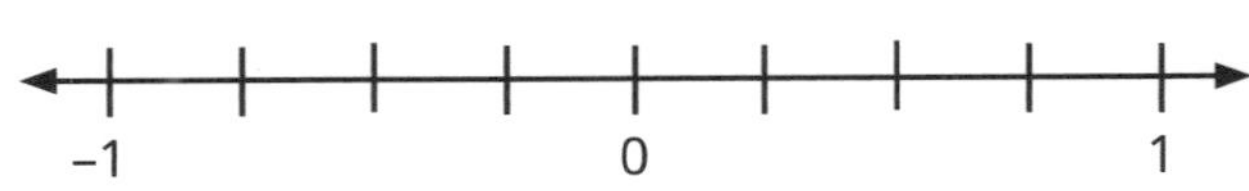

$-6\frac{1}{5}$ ○ $-7\frac{3}{5}$

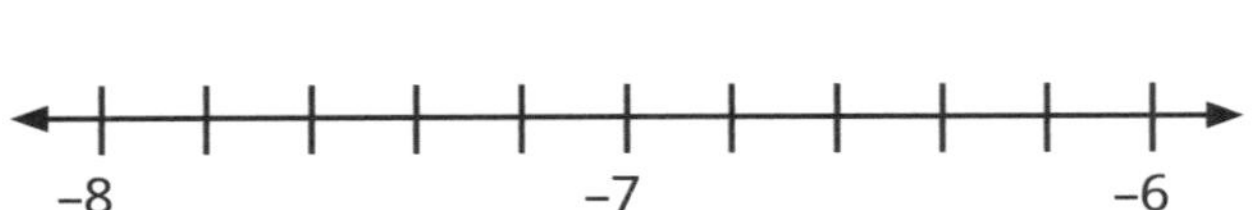

–1.5 ○ 2

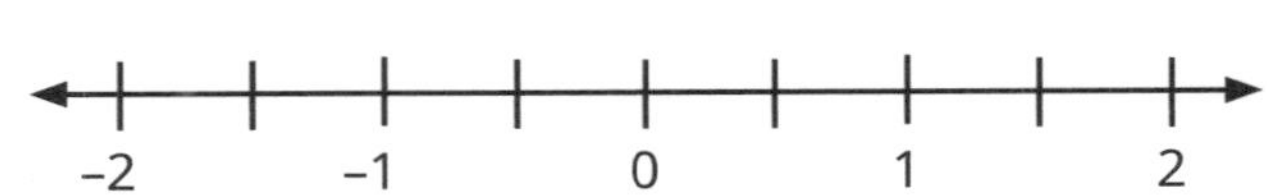

$-17\frac{3}{5}$ ○ –17.6

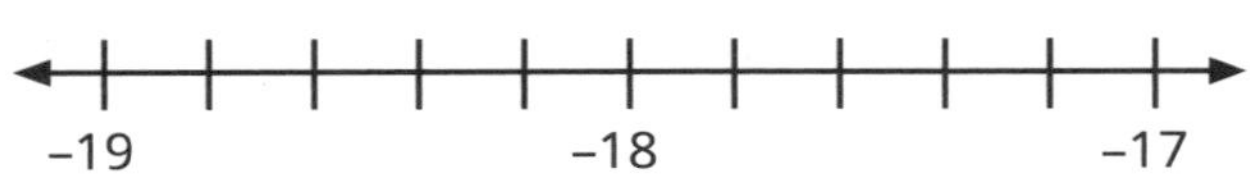

$-3\frac{1}{3}$ ○ $-2\frac{2}{3}$

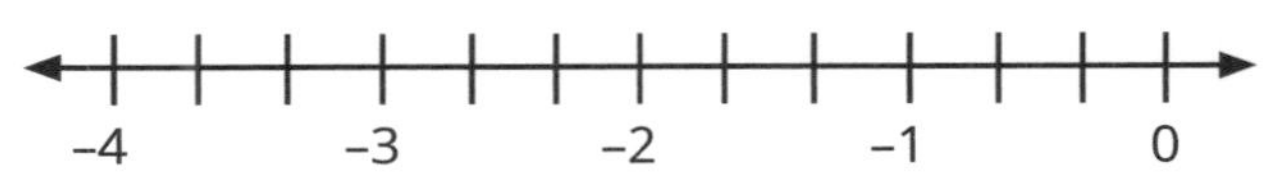

$-9\frac{3}{10}$ ○ –9.7

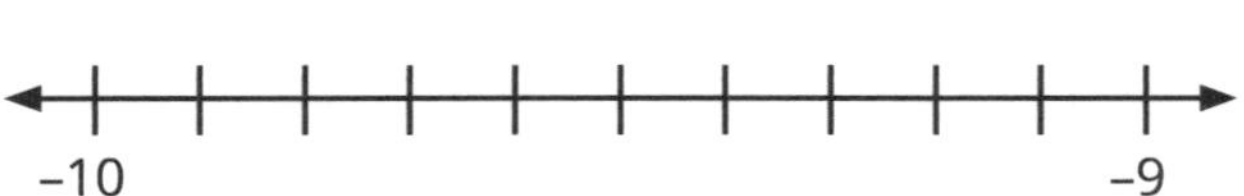

$\frac{3}{2}$ ○ 1.5

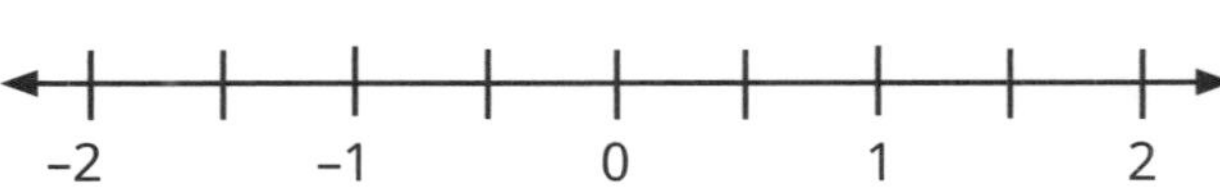

Comparing rational numbers

Compare the rational numbers using <, >, or =.

$-\frac{2}{3} \bigcirc \frac{1}{3}$

$|-5| \bigcirc -5$

$-25.1 \bigcirc -2.63$

$\frac{14}{5} \bigcirc -\frac{16}{5}$

$3\frac{5}{8} \bigcirc -4\frac{7}{8}$

$8.07 \bigcirc |-8.7|$

$-40.1 \bigcirc -40.09$

$-13\frac{3}{4} \bigcirc |-13.75|$

$15.23 \bigcirc -15\frac{2}{3}$

$\frac{19}{4} \bigcirc 4.75$

$-38\frac{4}{5} \bigcirc -38.7$

$-3\frac{5}{7} \bigcirc \frac{5}{7}$

$42.8 \bigcirc 42\frac{1}{8}$

$\frac{27}{10} \bigcirc 2.8$

$\left|-\frac{1}{20}\right| \bigcirc 0.05$

Ordering rational numbers

Graph the rational numbers on the number line. Then order the numbers from least to greatest.

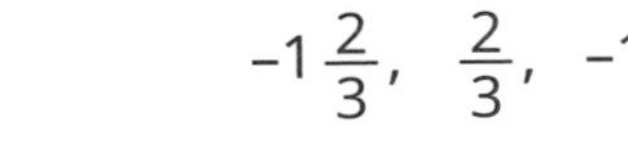

$-1\frac{2}{3}, \ \frac{2}{3}, \ -1$

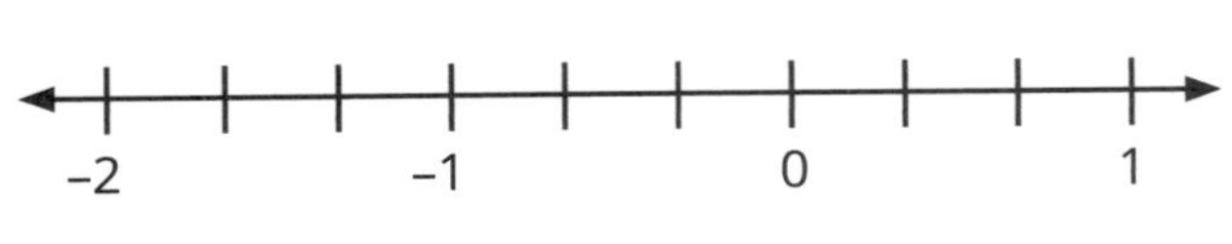

_______ _______ _______

$0.6, \ -0.4, \ 0$

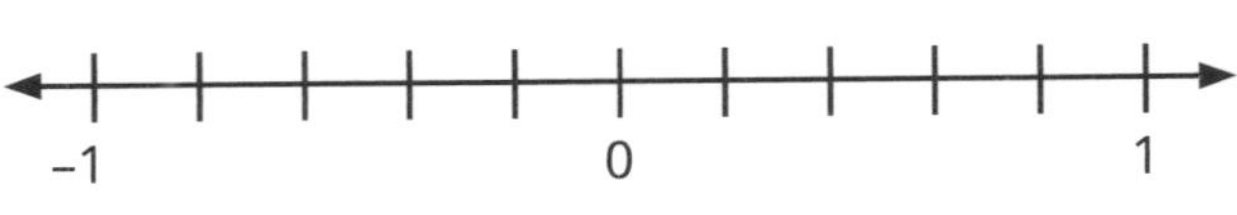

_______ _______ _______

$-\frac{3}{5}, \ -0.8, \ \frac{1}{5}$

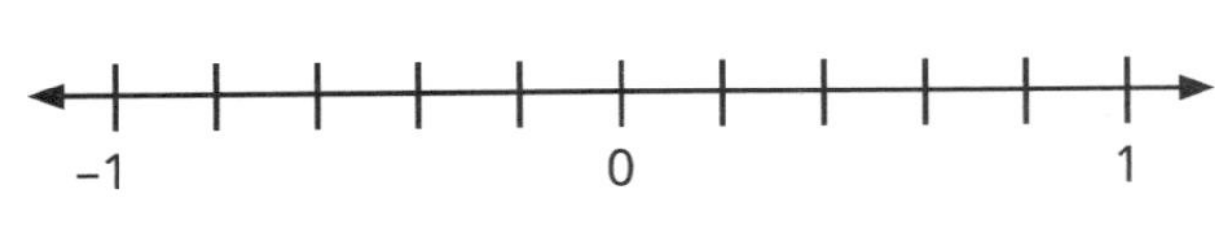

_______ _______ _______

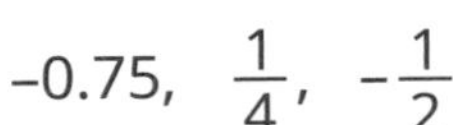

$-0.75, \ \frac{1}{4}, \ -\frac{1}{2}$

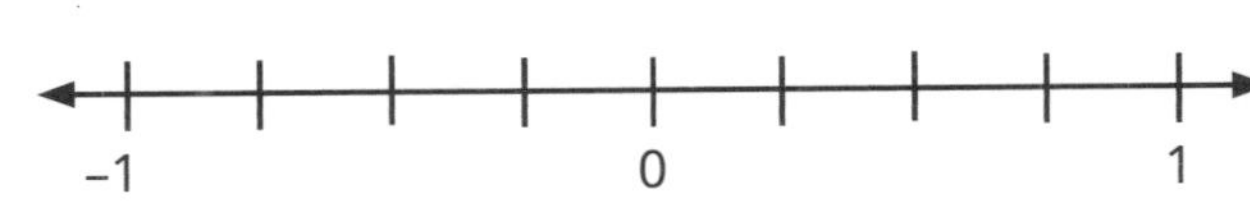

_______ _______ _______

$\frac{6}{2}, \ -3, \ -1, \ -4$

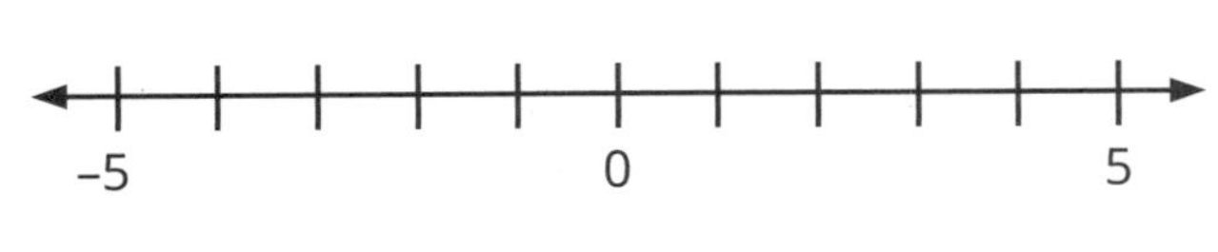

_______ _______ _______ _______

$-0.5, \ -1\frac{3}{4}, \ -\frac{3}{2}, \ -2$

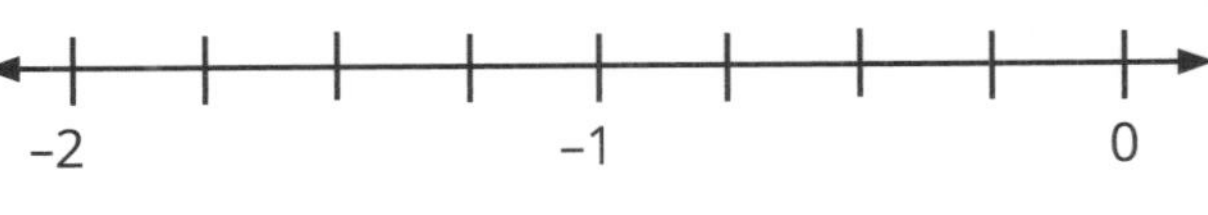

_______ _______ _______ _______

$\frac{3}{4}, \ -1, \ 0, \ -\frac{5}{4}$

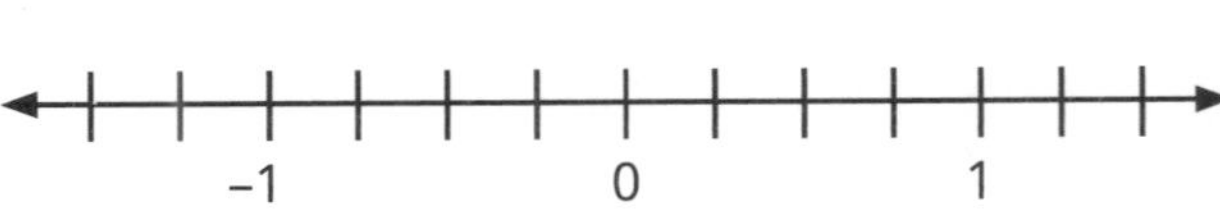

_______ _______ _______ _______

IXL.com skill ID **FMS**

Order the rational numbers from least to greatest.

$\frac{15}{2}$, -8, $\left|-8\frac{1}{2}\right|$ -8 ___ $\frac{15}{2}$ ___ $\left|-8\frac{1}{2}\right|$ ___

-30, 30.5, -30.3 ___ ___ ___

2.4, $-2\frac{1}{4}$, 0, 0.14 ___ ___ ___ ___

$-10\frac{3}{4}$, $|-10.5|$, -10, $-10\frac{1}{4}$ ___ ___ ___ ___

$\left|-16\frac{7}{10}\right|$, 16.5, $\left|16\frac{2}{5}\right|$, -16 ___ ___ ___ ___

45, $4\frac{4}{5}$, $-44\frac{1}{5}$, 44.5, -4.5 ___ ___ ___ ___ ___

$\frac{7}{3}$, 2.25, -3, $\left|-1\frac{3}{4}\right|$, -1 ___ ___ ___ ___ ___

$-5\frac{7}{8}$, -5.6, -5.75, $-5\frac{1}{2}$, -5.1 ___ ___ ___ ___ ___

IXL.com skill ID 5AX

Rational numbers

Find the path from start to finish. The rational numbers in your path should go in order from least to greatest. No diagonal moves are allowed.

START

-10.5	$-\frac{22}{2}$	$-7\frac{4}{5}$	-6.8	$-5\frac{2}{9}$
$-9\frac{7}{8}$	$-\frac{23}{3}$	-6.45	$-4\frac{4}{5}$	-6
$-\frac{11}{1}$	-7.9	$-8\frac{5}{6}$	-2.05	$-\frac{9}{4}$
$-2\frac{2}{5}$	1	$\frac{8}{9}$	$\left\lvert -\frac{1}{12} \right\rvert$	0
$\frac{13}{4}$	$\lvert -4.5 \rvert$	$-4\frac{1}{8}$	-0.05	$\frac{5}{3}$
$\left\lvert -1\frac{1}{6} \right\rvert$	$5\frac{3}{4}$	6.1	$\frac{17}{2}$	$\lvert -10 \rvert$

FINISH

The Robinson family makes and sells soap using milk from the goats on their farm.

They are collecting feedback from customers about some of their newer scents. Customers are asked to rate the scent on a scale of –3 to 3. A score of –3 means "I would not use a soap with this scent." A score of 3 means "I love it!"

The table shows the average rating for each of the new scents.

Scent	Average rating
Orange Blossom	–1.3
Lavender Sage	$2\frac{1}{4}$
Smooth Vanilla	–0.6
Bright Berry	$\frac{5}{4}$
Honey Oatmeal	1
Fresh Rose	$-\frac{3}{4}$

Use the table to answer the questions.

Which scent received the highest average rating? ______________________

Which scent received the lowest average rating? ______________________

Write the scents in order from the lowest average rating to the highest average rating.

______________________, ______________________, ______________________,

______________________, ______________________, ______________________

One of last year's scents, Fresh Balsam, had an average rating of 1.4. Which of this year's scents would that fall between?

______________________ and ______________________

IXL.com skill ID ETK

72 Coordinate plane

Learn!

The **coordinate plane** is the grid formed by the intersection of horizontal and vertical number lines. The **x-axis** is the horizontal number line. The **y-axis** is the vertical number line. The two axes intersect at the **origin**, which is at zero on both number lines.

These number lines separate the coordinate plane into four sections called **quadrants**. Quadrant I is in the upper right corner of the coordinate plane, where the coordinates are positive. The rest of the quadrants are numbered in a counterclockwise direction.

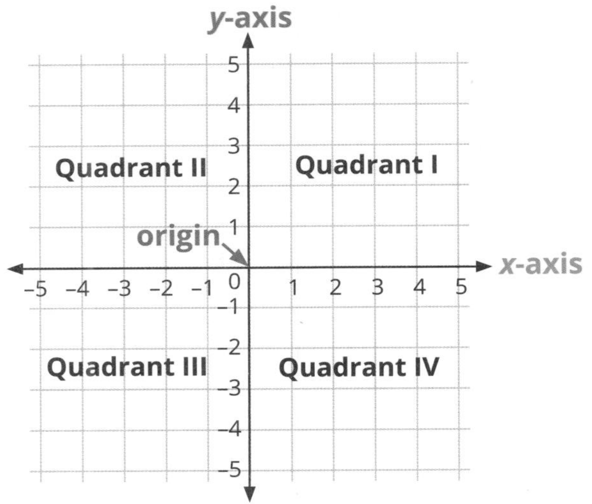

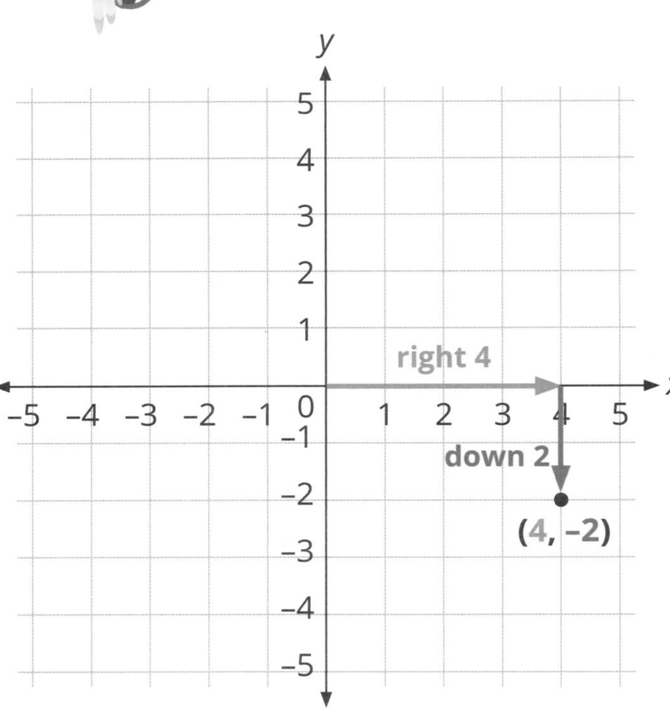

An **ordered pair** (x, y) tells the location of a point on the coordinate plane.

The first number in the ordered pair is called the ***x*-coordinate**. The second number is called the ***y*-coordinate**. The coordinates tell you where the point lies in relation to the x-axis and the y-axis.

For example, in the ordered pair (**4**, **−2**), the x-coordinate is 4 and the y-coordinate is −2. From the origin, the point is 4 units to the right and 2 units down.

Determine if each statement is always true, sometimes true, or never true.

Points graphed in Quadrant I have a positive *x*-coordinate. always true

An ordered pair with a negative *x*-coordinate will be graphed in Quadrant III. ______

The *x*-coordinate and *y*-coordinate will both be negative for a point graphed in Quadrant IV. ______

An ordered pair with a positive *x*-coordinate will be graphed above the *x*-axis. ______

Points graphed on the *x*-axis have a *y*-coordinate of 0. ______

Points graphed in Quadrant II have a positive *y*-coordinate. ______

An ordered pair graphed in Quadrant III will have a positive *y*-coordinate. ______

Points graphed below the *x*-axis have a negative *y*-coordinate.

______

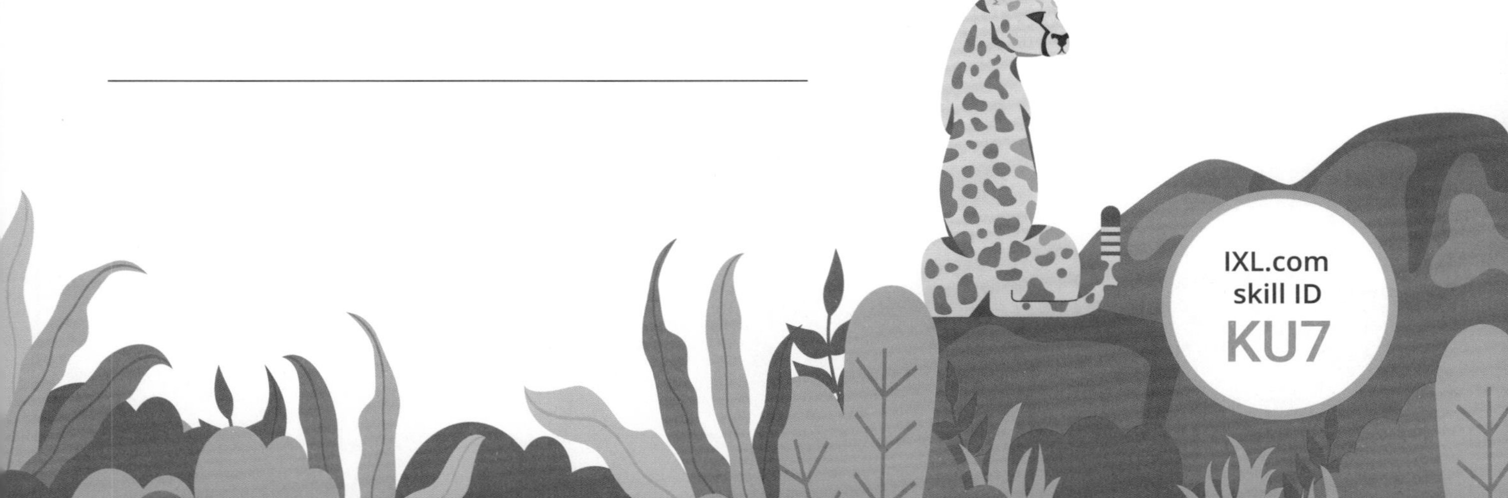

Coordinate plane

Write the ordered pair for each point on the coordinate plane.

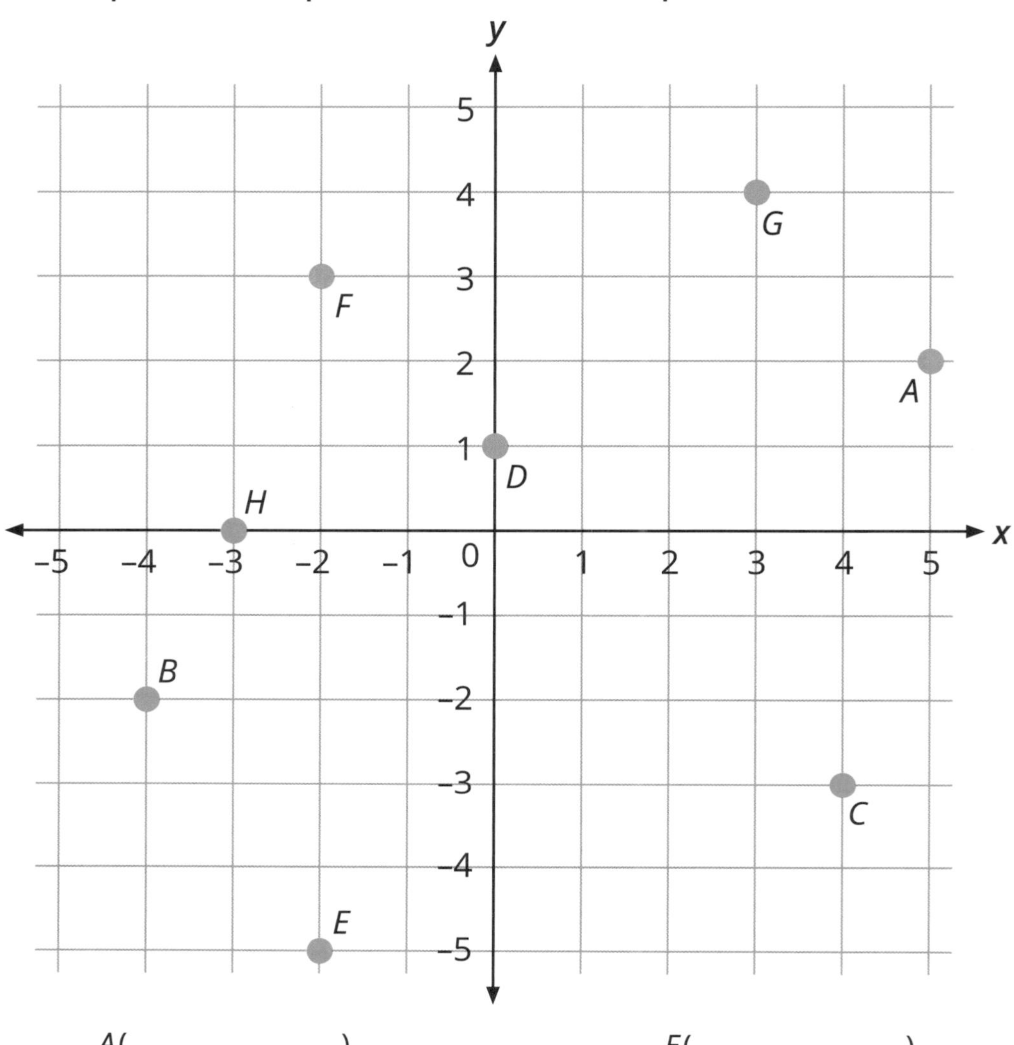

A(______ , ______)

B(______ , ______)

C(______ , ______)

D(______ , ______)

E(______ , ______)

F(______ , ______)

G(______ , ______)

H(______ , ______)

Write the ordered pair for each point on the coordinate plane.

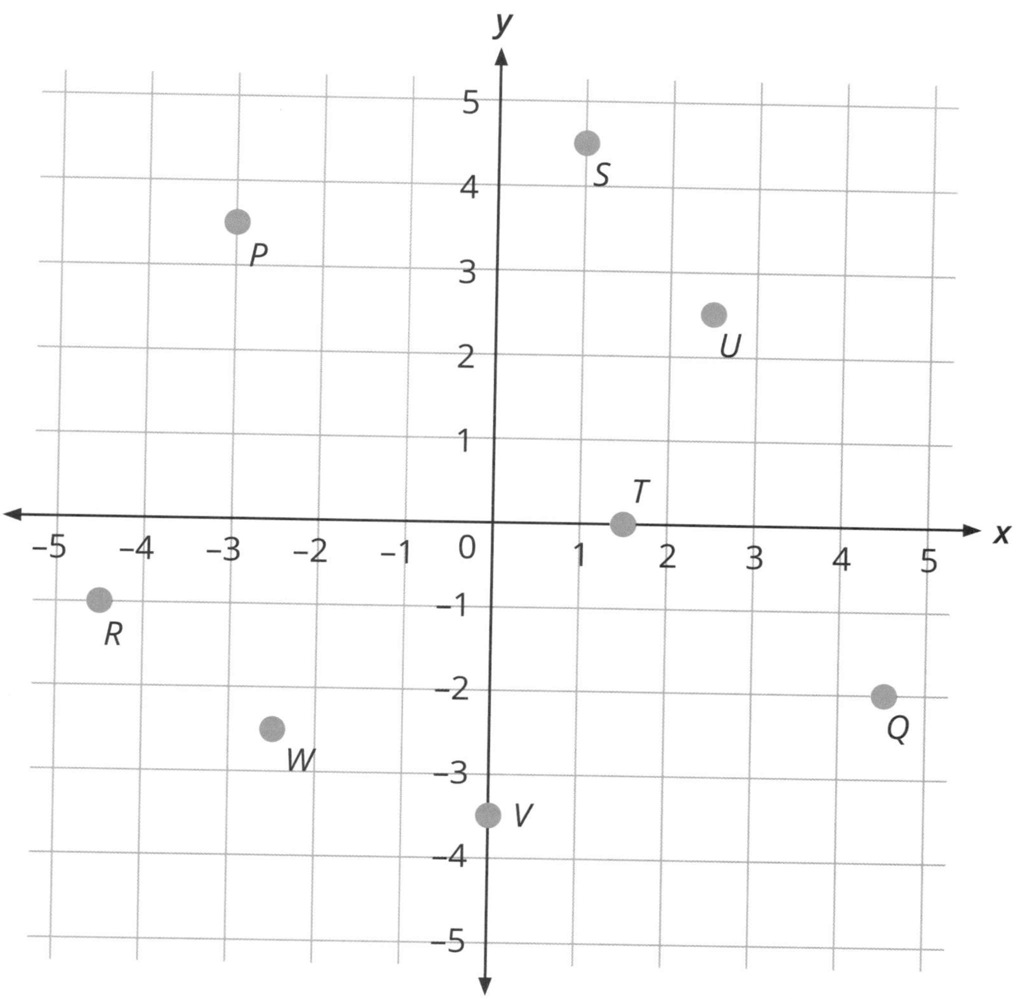

P(–3 , 3.5)

Q(______ , ______)

R(______ , ______)

S(______ , ______)

T(______ , ______)

U(______ , ______)

V(______ , ______)

W(______ , ______)

IXL.com skill ID GFN

Coordinate plane

Graph and label each point on the coordinate plane below.

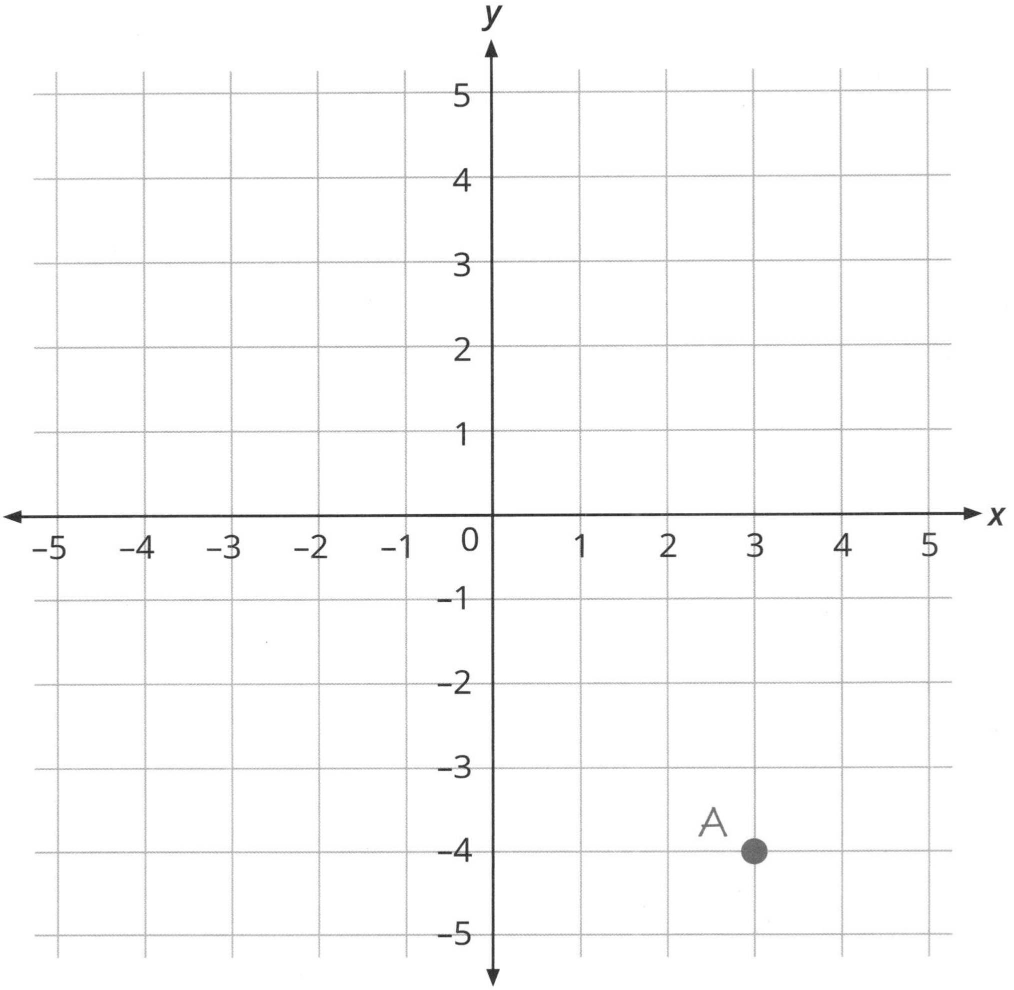

A(3, −4)	*B*(2, 0)	*C*(1, 4)	*D*(−2, 3)
E(−4, −1)	*F*(4, −1)	*G*(0, −4)	*H*(−5, 1)

Graph and label each point on the coordinate plane below.

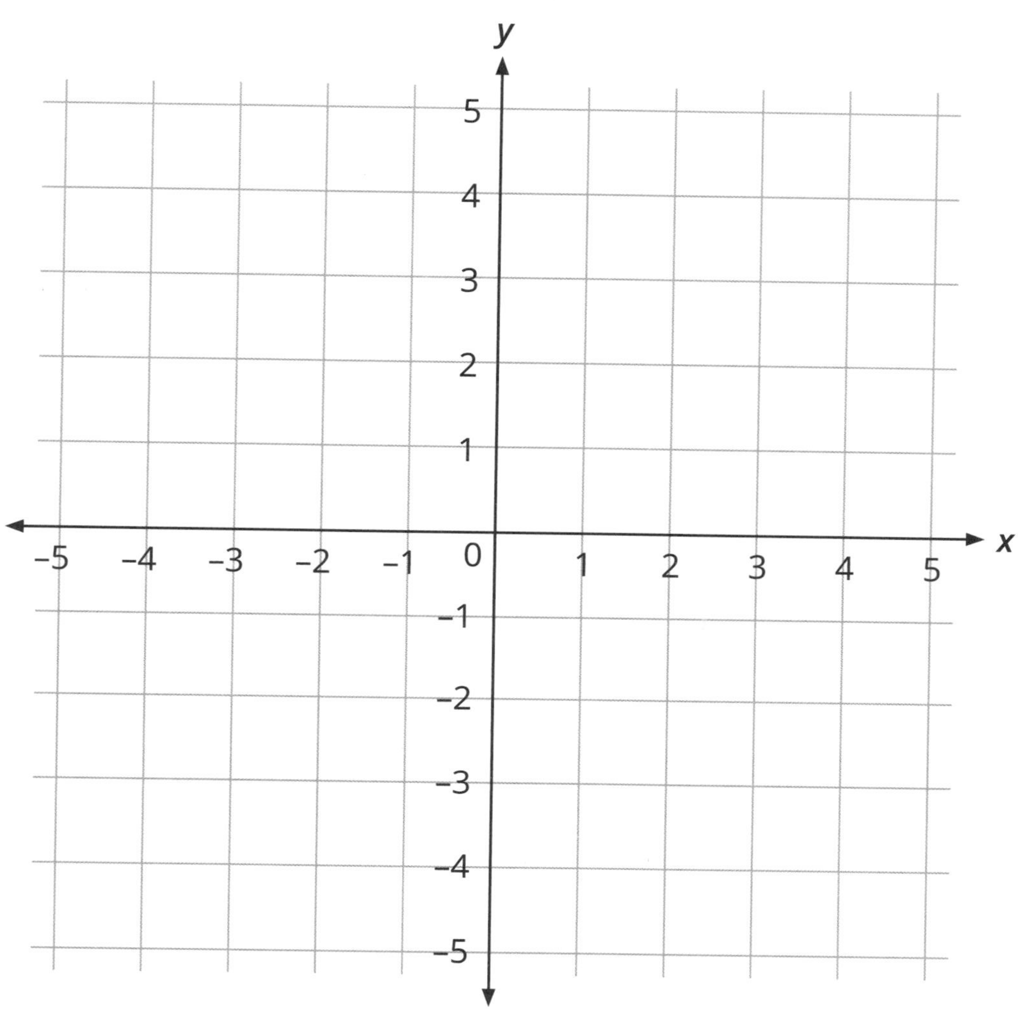

P(−3, 1.5)	*Q*(1.5, 4)	*R*(0, 3.5)	*S*(4.5, −2)
T(−3.5, 0)	*U*(−1.5, −3.5)	*V*(3.5, 0.5)	*W*(−4.5, −2.5)

78 Reflecting points over the x-axis

Learn!

You can **reflect** a point over any line. The reflected point is the same distance from the line but lies directly opposite the original point. When reflecting a point over the x-axis, the x-coordinate stays the same and the y-coordinate is the opposite. Try it with **(−4, 2)**.

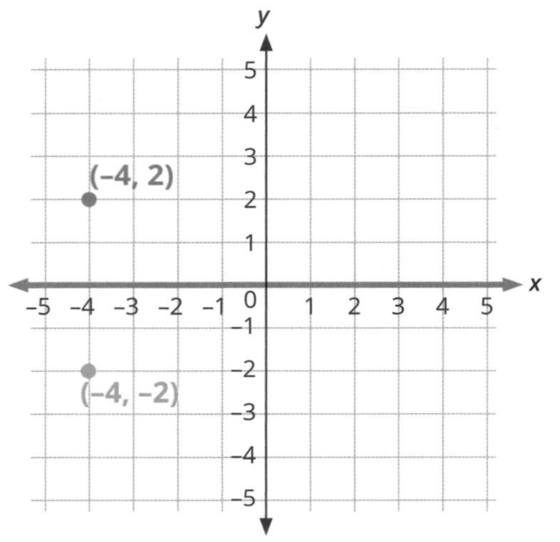

To reflect **(−4, 2)** over the *x*-axis, use the same *x*-coordinate, −4, and take the opposite of the *y*-coordinate.

The opposite of 2 is −2.

So, the reflection of **(−4, 2)** over the ***x*-axis** is **(−4, −2)**.

Reflect each point over the *x*-axis. Then, write the new ordered pair.

Reflect point *M* over the *x*-axis.

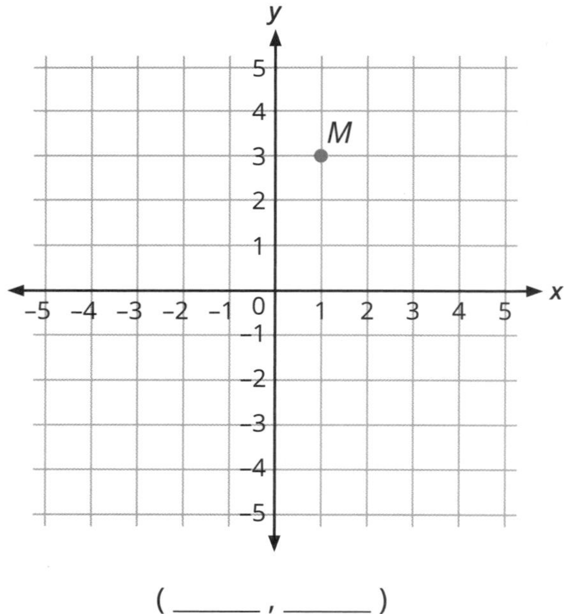

(______ , ______)

Reflect point *N* over the *x*-axis.

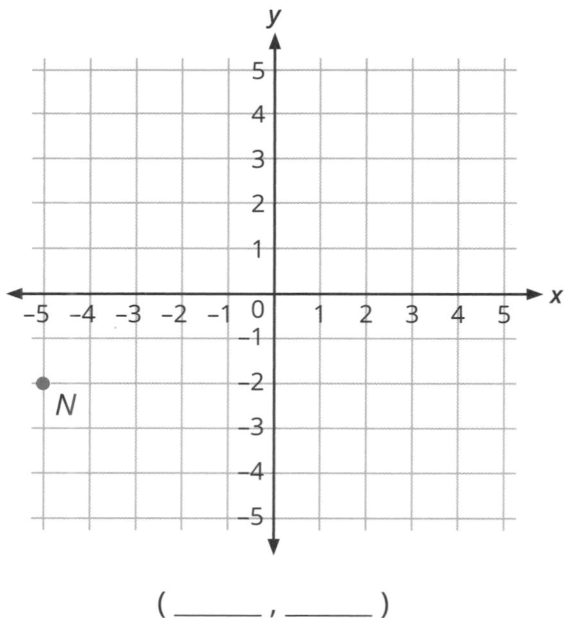

(______ , ______)

Reflecting points over the *y*-axis

Learn!

You can reflect a point over the *y*-axis, too. When reflecting a point over the *y*-axis, the *y*-coordinate stays the same and the *x*-coordinate is the opposite. Try it with **(−4, 2)**.

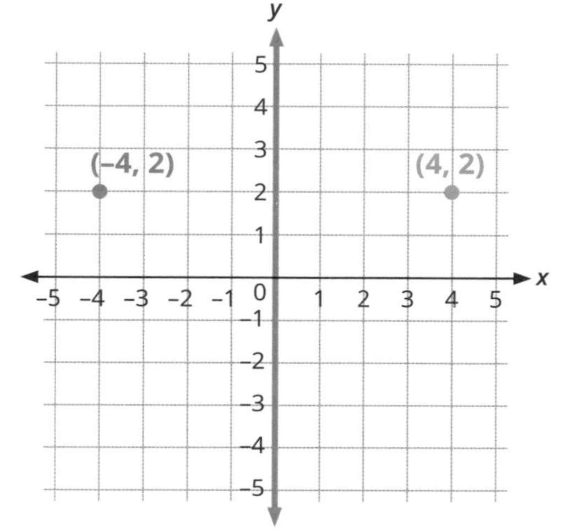

To reflect **(–4, 2)** over the *y*-axis, use the same *y*-coordinate, 2, and take the opposite of the *x*-coordinate.

The opposite of –4 is 4.

So, the reflection of **(–4, 2)** over the ***y*-axis** is **(4, 2)**.

Reflect each point over the *y*-axis. Then, write the new ordered pair.

Reflect point *A* over the *y*-axis.

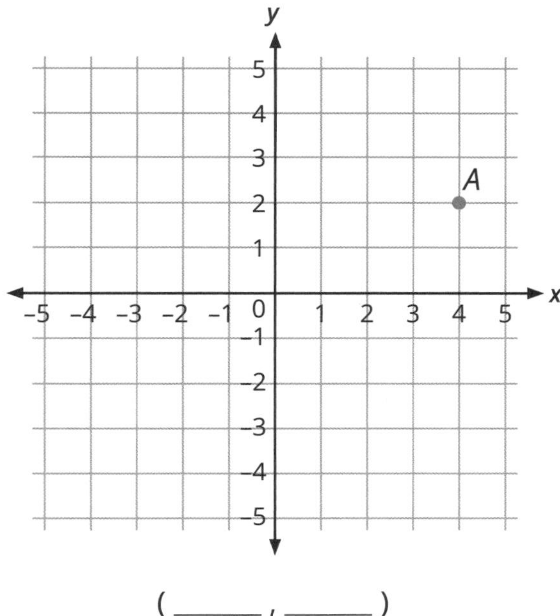

(______ , ______)

Reflect point *D* over the *y*-axis.

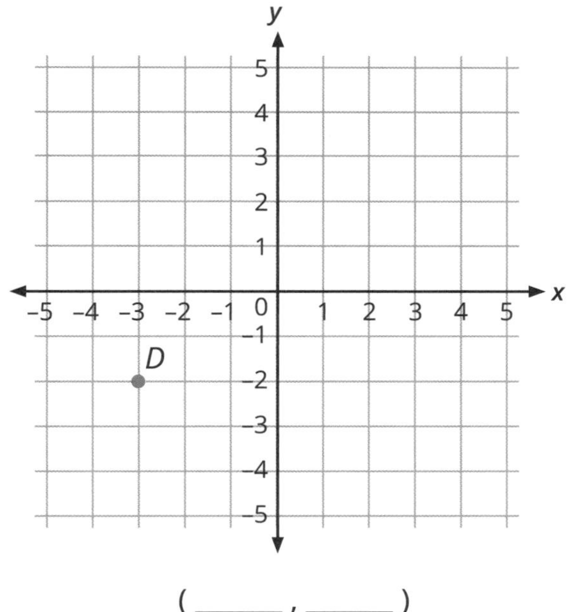

(______ , ______)

THINK ABOUT IT! What would the coordinates of the point (3, 5) be if it were reflected over the *x*-axis and then the *y*-axis? What about (–1, 4)?

IXL.com skill ID **32S**

Exploration Zone

You just practiced reflecting points over a line. You can reflect figures, too! A **reflection** flips a point or figure over a line to create a mirror image.

TRY IT YOURSELF!

Graph the image of each figure by completing the given reflection. Use what you know about reflecting points over the *x*-axis and *y*-axis to help you.

Reflect ΔCDE over the *x*-axis.

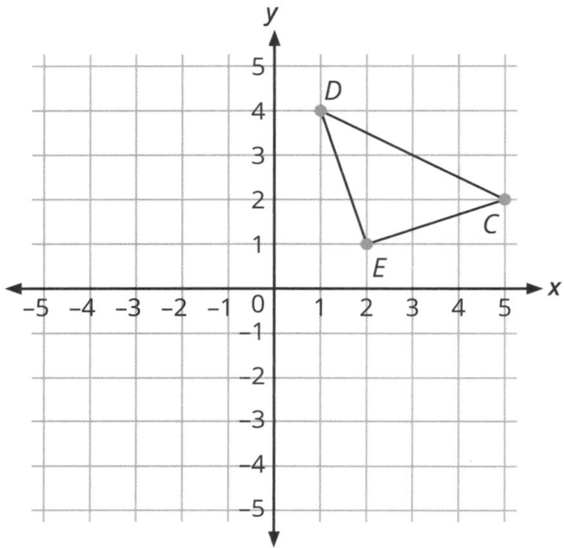

Reflect ΔRST over the *y*-axis.

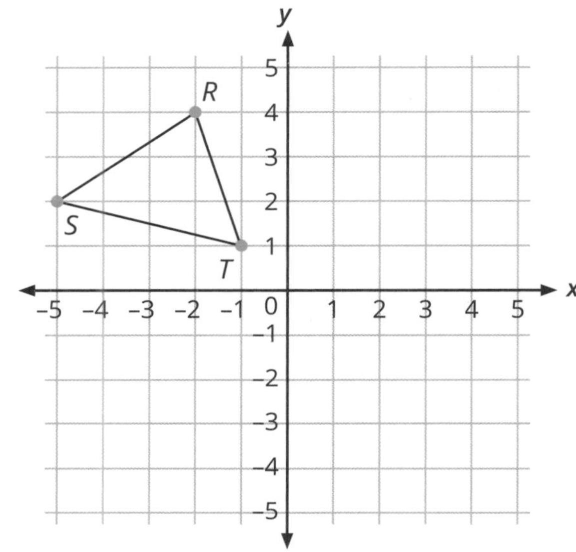

Reflect ΔXYZ over the *y*-axis.

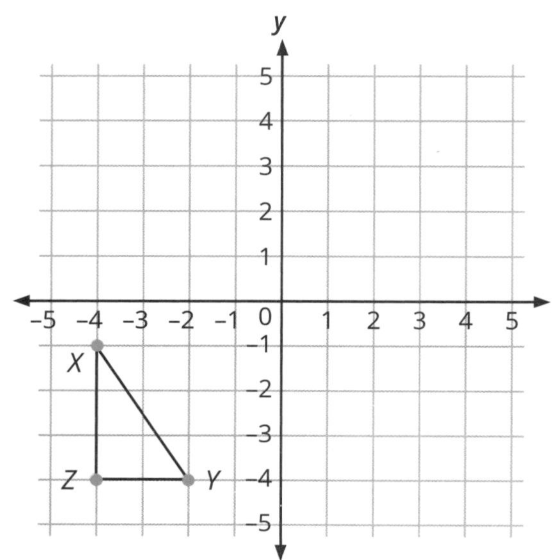

Go back and label each reflected point with its ordered pair.

A **translation** moves or slides a point or figure to a different location on the coordinate plane. A translation can move up, down, right, or left.

TRY IT YOURSELF!

Graph the image of each figure by completing the given translation.

Translate Δ*FGH* 5 units up.

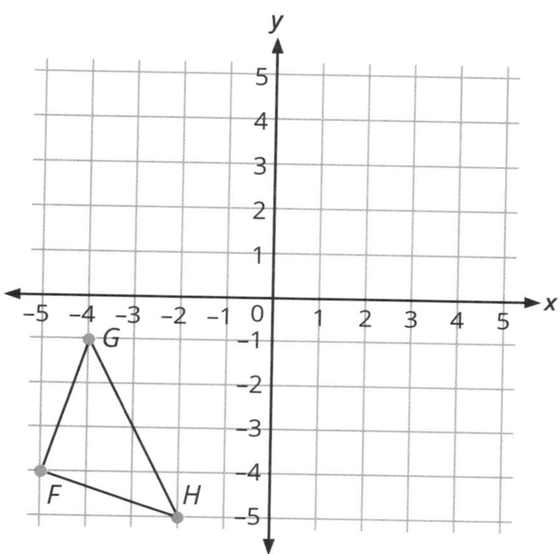

Translate Δ*PQR* 6 units left.

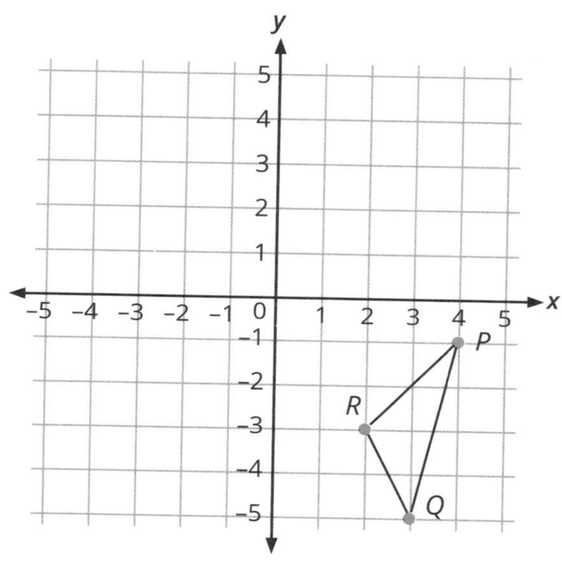

Translate Δ*JKL* 7 units right.

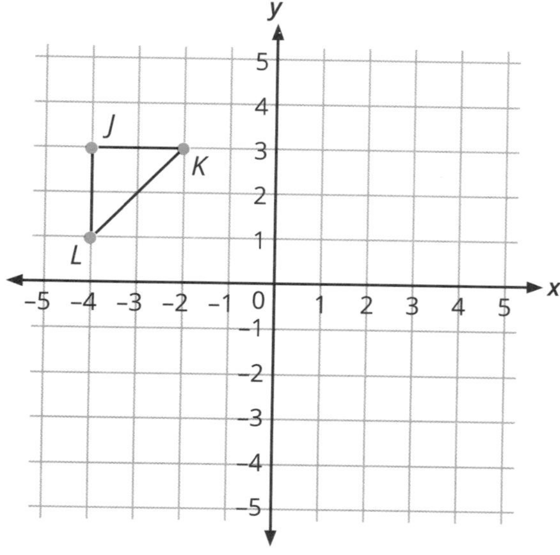

Go back and label each translated point with its ordered pair.

Distance between two points

Learn!

The distance between two points on a graph is the length of the line segment that connects them. To find vertical or horizontal distances, you can count to find the length of the line segment on the graph. Or, you can look at the distance from each point to the *x*- or *y*-axis. Try it!

Find the distance between (–3, 2) and (4, 2). Determine the distance between each point and the *y*-axis. Since the points are on opposite sides of the axis, add those distances.

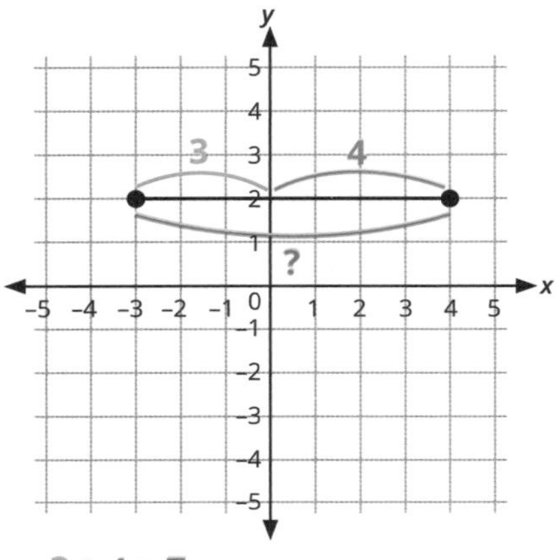

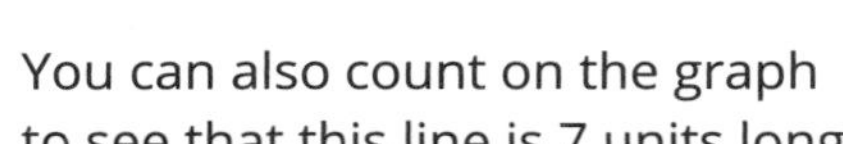

3 + 4 = 7

You can also count on the graph to see that this line is 7 units long.

Find the distance between (3, –2) and (3, –5). Determine the distance between each point and the *x*-axis. Since the points are in the same quadrant, subtract those distances.

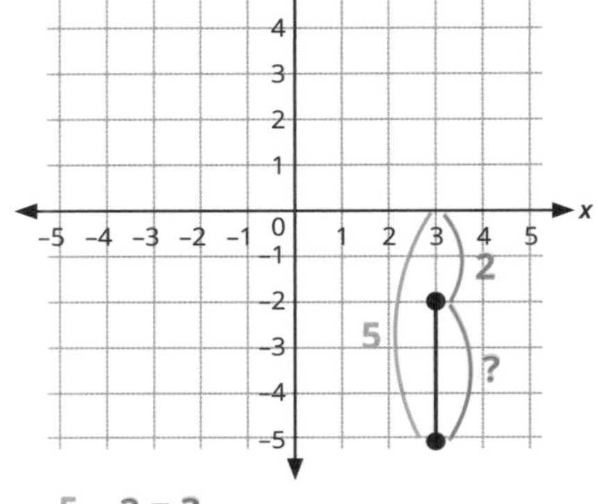

5 – 2 = 3

You can also count on the graph to see that this line is 3 units long.

Use the coordinate plane to find the distance between the points.

Find the distance between (2, 4) and (2, –5).

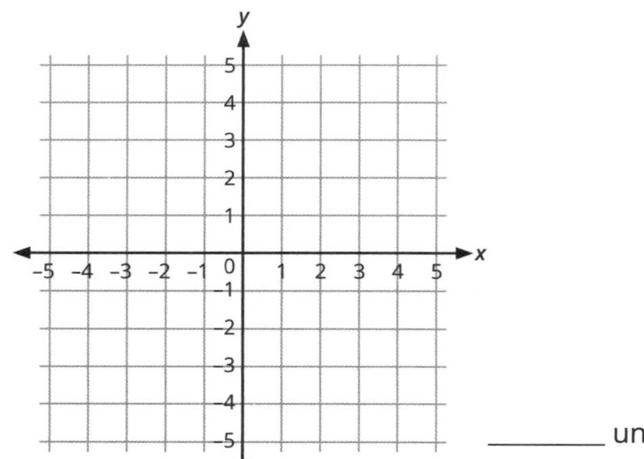

_________ units

Find the distance between (–5, 1) and (–2, 1).

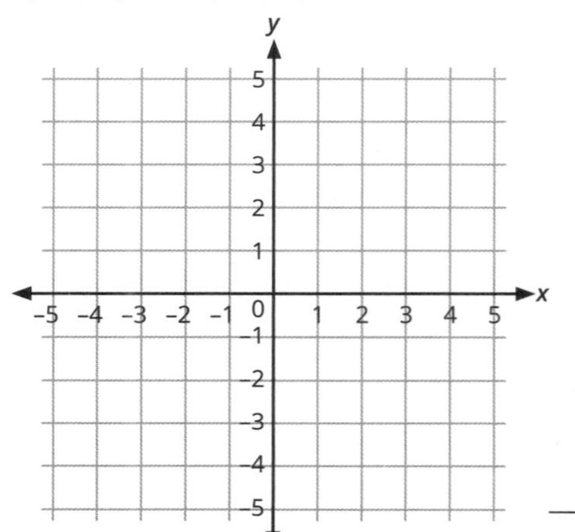

_________ units

Use the coordinate plane to find the distance between the points.

Find the distance between (–4, –1) and (2, –1).

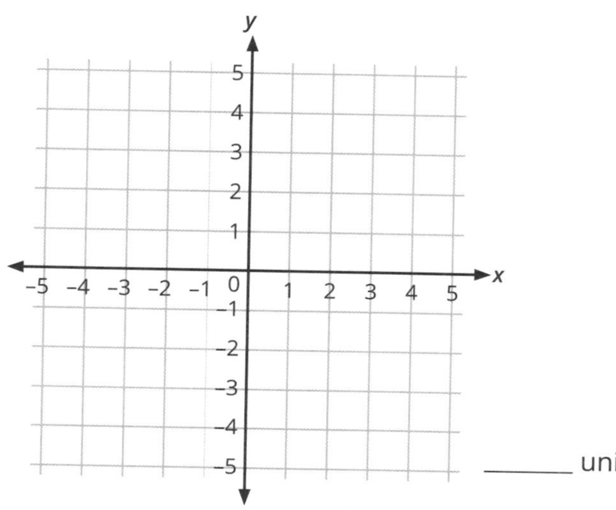

_____ units

Find the distance between (–2, 4) and (–2, 2).

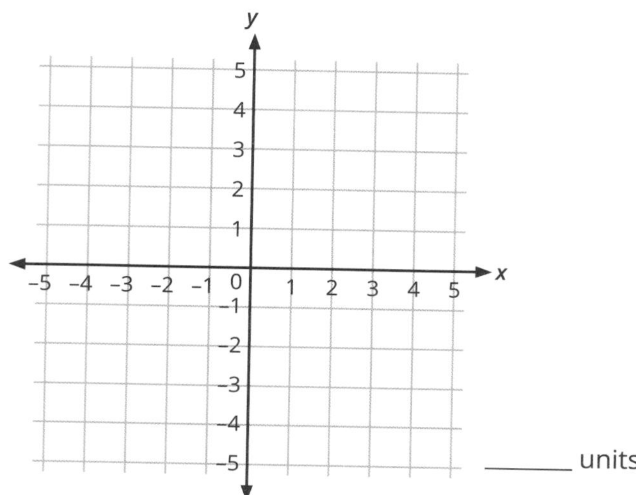

_____ units

Keep going! Find the distance between the given points.

Find the distance between (5, 1) and (5, 5). _____ units

Find the distance between (3, –4) and (3, –2). _____ units

Find the distance between $\left(-\frac{3}{4}, 5\right)$ and $\left(-\frac{3}{4}, -3\right)$. _____ units

Find the distance between (–1, 2.5) and (–1, –4.25). _____ units

Find the distance between $\left(4\frac{1}{4}, 0\right)$ and $\left(2\frac{3}{4}, 0\right)$. _____ units

For more practice, visit IXL.com or the IXL mobile app and enter this code in the search bar.

IXL.com skill ID **A7P**

Aisha and her family visit Wayside Amusement Park every summer. The park's website provides a detailed map of the attractions, and Aisha uses the map to plan her day.

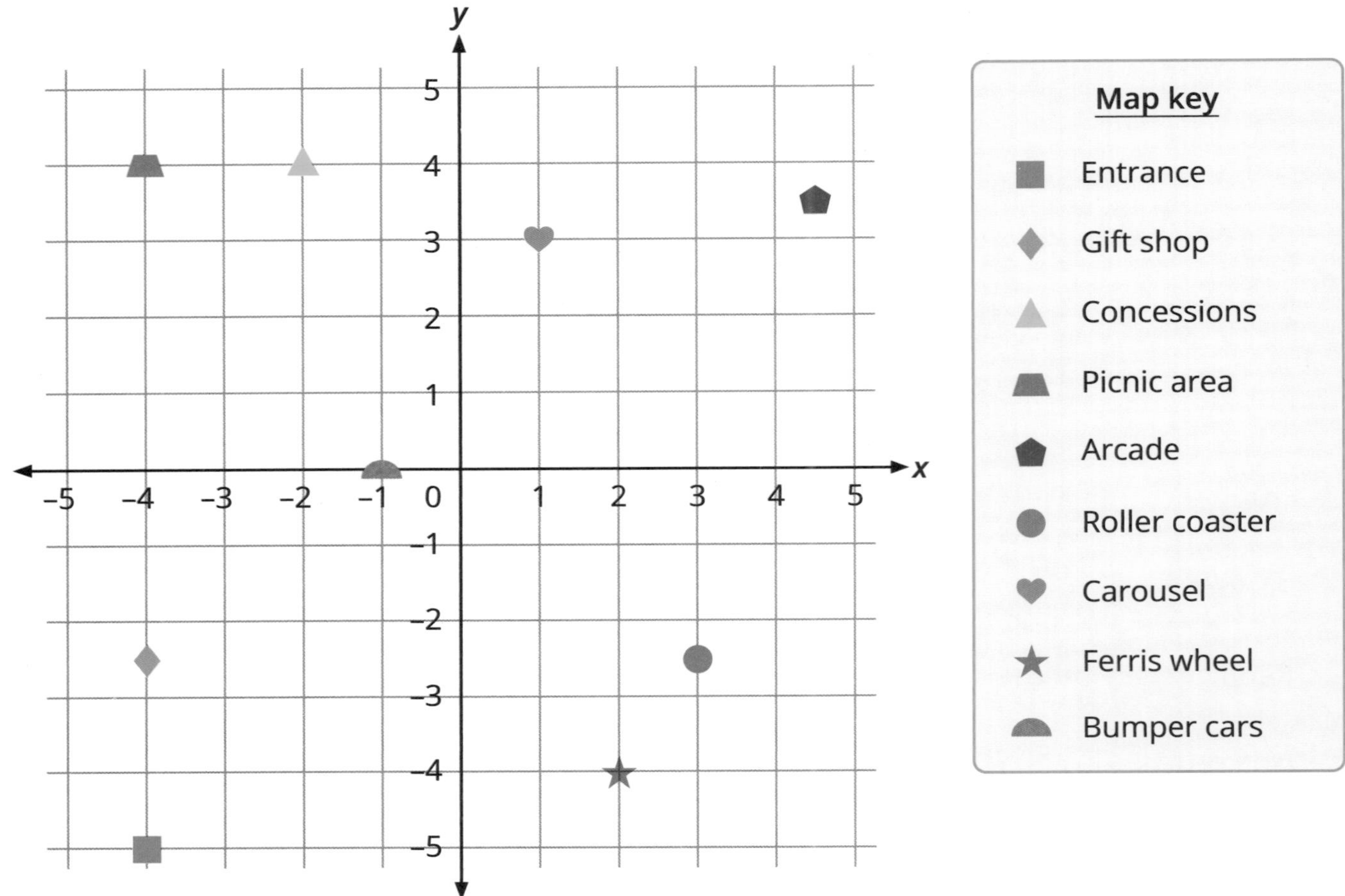

Answer each question.

What are the coordinates of the park's entrance? (______ , ______)

What attraction is located at (3, –2.5)? ____________________

What attraction is located in Quadrant III, near the entrance? ____________________

What is the distance between the picnic area and the concessions? ____________________

What are the coordinates of the carousel? (______ , ______)

What is one attraction located in Quadrant IV? ____________________

What is the distance between the entrance and the picnic area? ____________________

What attraction is located at $\left(4\frac{1}{2}, 3\frac{1}{2}\right)$? ____________________

Terrell lives in Maple Point Village. The coordinate plane shows a map of some of the locations that are important to Terrell.

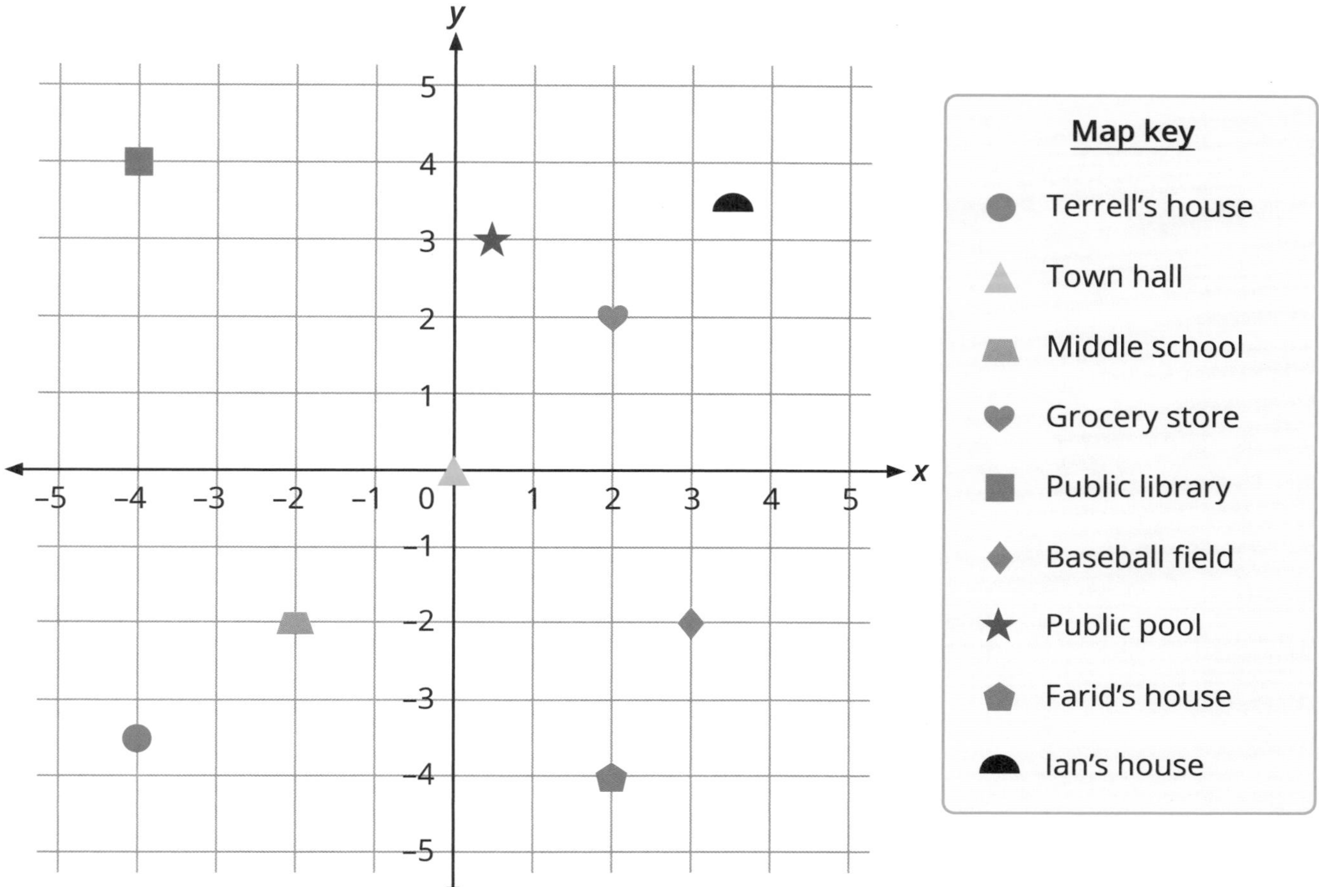

Answer each question.

What are the coordinates of Terrell's house? (______ , ______)

What is located at the origin? ________________________

How far is it from the grocery store to Farid's house? ________________________

What is located in Quadrant II? ________________________

What is located at (0.5, 3)? ________________________

What are the coordinates of the public library? (______ , ______)

What is located at (2, 2)? ________________________

How far is it from the baseball field to the middle school?

____

IXL.com skill ID N96

86 Writing ratios

Learn!

A **ratio** is a way of comparing two numbers. Ratios can be written using words, a colon, or a fraction. Try it with the pictures below.

There are 3 circles and 2 triangles.

The ratio of circles to triangles is:

3 to 2 3:2 $\frac{3}{2}$

Fill in the blanks to write each ratio using a colon.

What is the ratio of squares to triangles?

_____ : _____

What is the ratio of hearts to squares?

_____ : _____

What is the ratio of circles to total shapes?

_____ : _____

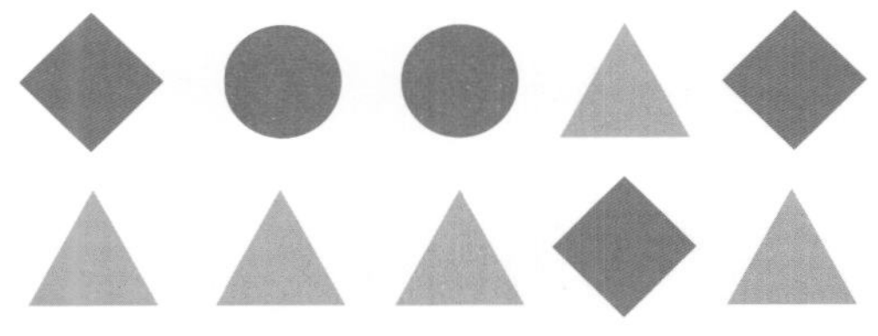

What is the ratio of triangles to circles?

_____ : _____

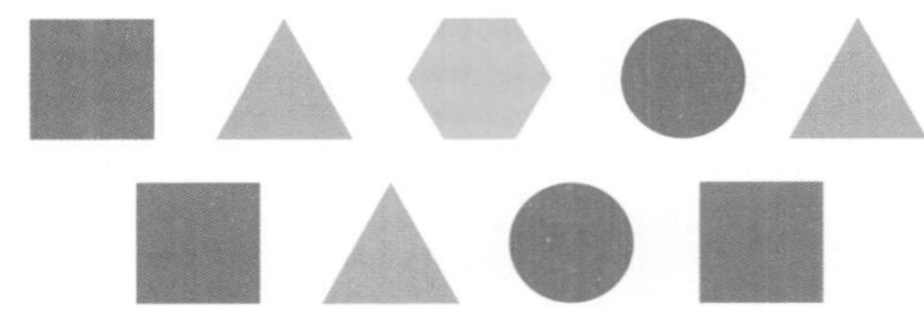

What is the ratio of total shapes to hexagons?

_____ : _____

Write a ratio for each problem.

Levi bought a bouquet of flowers for his grandmother. There were 5 white flowers and 7 pink flowers. What is the ratio of white flowers to pink flowers in the bouquet?

_______ : _______

There are 25 students in Rosa's class, and 2 of the students are left-handed. What is the ratio of left-handed students to total students in Rosa's class?

_______ : _______

Of the 30 days in April, it rained on 11 of them. What is the ratio of days it rained in April to days it did not rain?

_______ : _______

There are 45 seats at Lake Street Theater. For the most recent performance, 28 of the seats were filled. What is the ratio of empty seats to filled seats at the most recent performance?

_______ : _______

Keenan ordered 8 chocolate chip scones and 15 blueberry scones. What is the ratio of chocolate chip scones to total scones that Keenan ordered?

_______ : _______

Zoe bought balloons to decorate for a surprise party. She bought 14 gold balloons and 11 silver balloons. What is the ratio of total balloons to gold balloons?

_______ : _______

88 Equivalent ratios

Learn!

Equivalent ratios are ratios that show the same relationship. You can find equivalent ratios the same way you find equivalent fractions. First, write the ratio as a fraction. Then, multiply or divide the numerator and the denominator by the same number. Try it with the ratio 6:15.

You can divide the numerator and the denominator by 3.

$$\frac{6}{15} \overset{\div 3}{=} \frac{2}{5}$$

You can also multiply the numerator and denominator by a number, like 2.

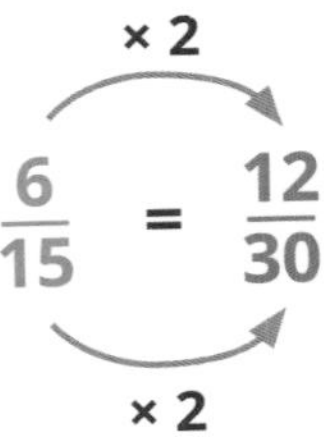

So, the ratios **6:15**, **2:5**, and **12:30** are all equivalent.

Circle all of the equivalent ratios in each set.

(3:5) 12:9 (15:25)	10:7 20:14 4:1
24:18 4:3 12:9	3:8 9:24 15:6
2:9 3:10 6:27	9:15 18:30 3:5
8:2 16:4 4:1 48:3	2:10 1:9 5:45 3:27

IXL.com skill ID 2LM

Fill in the blanks to write an equivalent ratio.

2:5 = ______ : ______

6:1 = ______ : ______

7:3 = ______ : ______

18:12 = ______ : ______

8:14 = ______ : ______

2:8 = ______ : ______

Fill in the blank to complete each equivalent ratio.

18:20 = ______:10

42:14 = ______:2

32:48 = 4:______

30:12 = 10:______

4:20 = 8:______

50:40 = ______:8

______:9 = 44:99

______:50 = 3:2

45:______ = 5:2

60:______ = 5:7

18:______ = 54:81

______:36 = 6:18

Word problems

Determine if the ratios are equivalent.

Kaylee is sending a fruit basket to her aunt and uncle. The small basket has 6 apples and 12 oranges. The medium basket has 9 apples and 20 oranges. Are the ratios of apples to oranges equivalent?

Yes No

Evelyn bought a shrimp appetizer that had 4 jumbo shrimp and 8 regular shrimp. Miguel bought a shrimp appetizer that had 3 jumbo shrimp and 6 regular shrimp. Are the ratios of jumbo shrimp to regular shrimp equivalent?

Yes No

Every month, Tiana volunteers 12 hours at the library and 16 hours at the food pantry. Chen volunteers 9 hours at the library and 12 hours at the food pantry every month. Are the ratios of hours at the library to hours at the food pantry equivalent?

Yes No

Camilla used 9 stars and 4 hearts in her painting for art class. Kendra used 10 stars and 5 hearts in her painting. Are the ratios of stars to hearts equivalent?

Yes No

Steven has 8 blue shirts and 20 white shirts in his closet. Jayce has 6 blue shirts and 15 white shirts in his closet. Are the ratios of blue shirts to white shirts equivalent?

Yes No

At the 12 o'clock showing of *Dinosaur Expedition*, there were 48 children and 24 adults. At the 4 o'clock showing, there were 75 children and 30 adults. Are the ratios of children to adults equivalent?

Yes No

Ratio tables

You can use a **ratio table** to organize equivalent ratios. Complete each ratio table by filling in the missing values.

1	2	3	4	5
7	14	21	28	35

7	8	9	10	11
		99	110	121

3	6	9	12	15
12		36		60

5	10	15	20	25
1			4	5

2	4	6	8	10
10	20			

4	8	12	16	20
12		36		

3	4	5	6	7
36		60		

6	18	30	42	54
	3		7	

12	14	16	18	20
			9	10

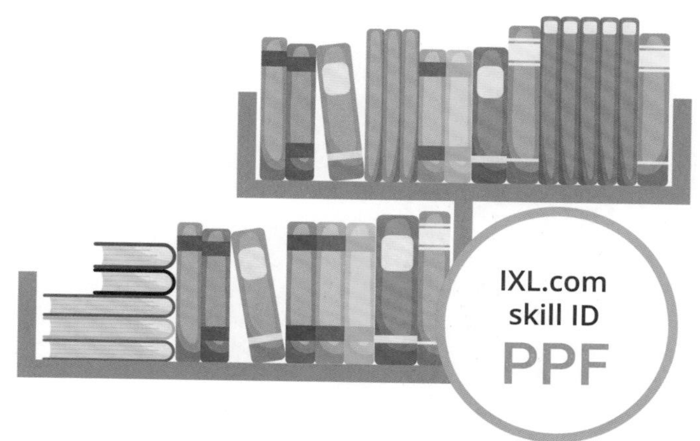

Ratio tables

Use the information to fill in the missing values for each ratio table.

Each T-shirt at the concert costs $15.

T-shirts	1	2		4
Cost	$15		$45	$60

Tex's Taco Truck sells 2 tacos for $7.

Tacos	2		6	8
Cost	$7	$14		

It takes Kelly 15 minutes to ride her bike 2 miles.

Minutes	15	30	45	
Miles	2		6	8

Elise uses 4 lemons to make 1 quart of lemonade.

Lemons	4	8	12	
Quarts	1		3	4

Tanvi plants 3 tulips for every 5 daffodils in her garden.

Tulips	3	9		27
Daffodils	5		30	

Ariel uses 5 balls of yarn for every 4 hats she knits.

Balls of yarn	5	10	15	
Hats	4			16

Complete each ratio table. Then, plot the points on the graph.

Reagan kayaks 2 miles every hour.

Hours	1	2	3	4
Miles	2	4		

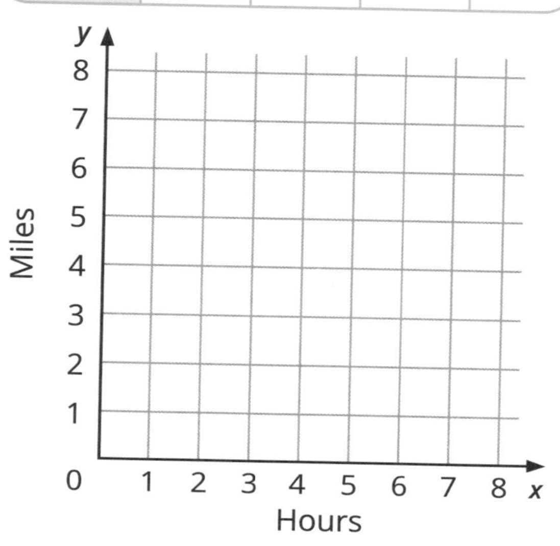

Aqua Lake Cafe charges $5 for 2 wraps.

Wraps	2	6	10	
Cost ($)	5	15		35

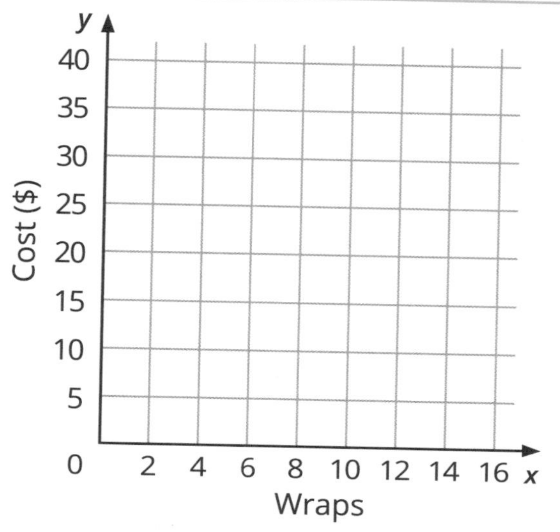

Chef Mark mixes 3 cups of yogurt for every 2 cups of sour cream in his vegetable dip.

Cups of sour cream	2	4	6	
Cups of yogurt	3			12

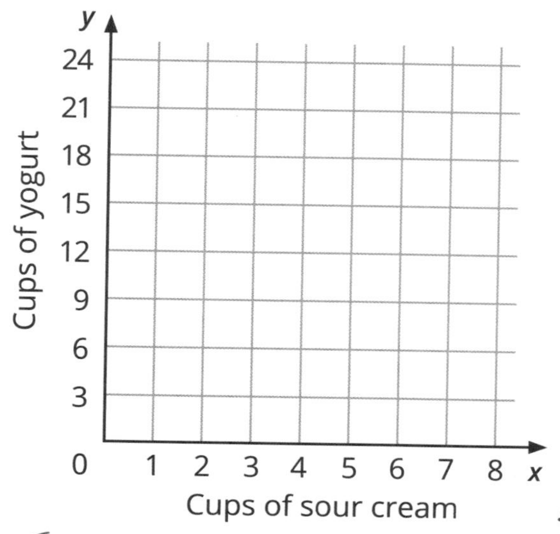

IXL.com skill ID **6Z2**

Exploration Zone

Ratios apply to many math concepts, including scaled copies. A **scaled copy** of a figure has the same shape but is a different size. It can be larger or smaller than the original figure. The original figure and its scaled copy have **corresponding parts**, which are parts in one figure that match up with parts in the other. For example, side *AB* in the original figure below corresponds to side *PQ* in the scaled copy.

Use your knowledge of ratios to better understand the relationship between corresponding sides. Fill in the table with the side lengths of each polygon.

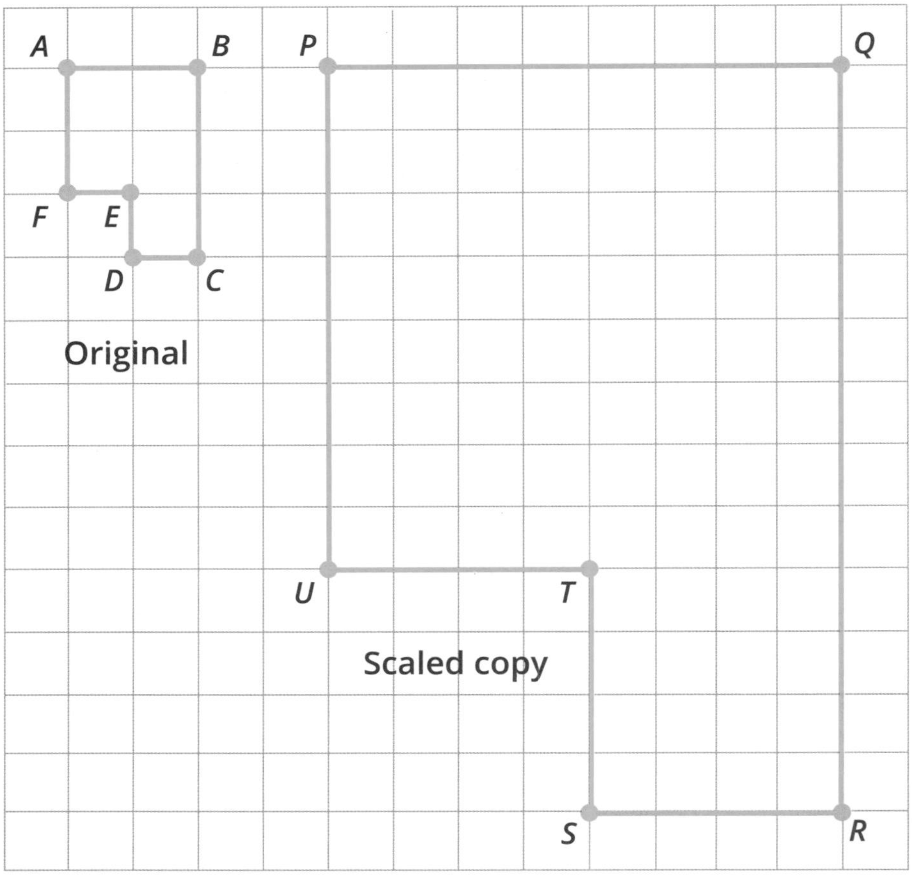

A B P Q
F E
D C
Original
U T
Scaled copy
S R

Original	*AB*	*BC*	*CD*	*DE*	*EF*	*FA*
	2					
Scaled copy	*PQ*	*QR*	*RS*	*ST*	*TU*	*UP*
	8					

Keep going! Fill in the table with the side lengths of each polygon.

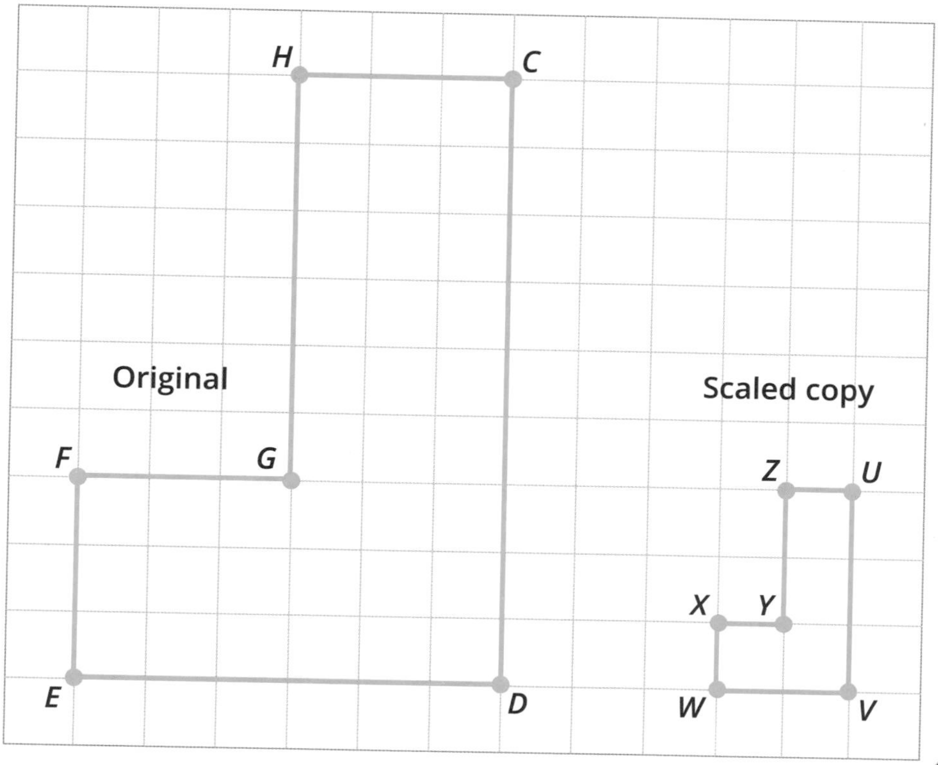

H C
Original
Scaled copy
F G
Z U
X Y
E D W V

	CD	DE	EF	FG	GH	HC
Original	9					
	UV	VW	WX	XY	YZ	ZU
Scaled copy	3					

In both tables, what do you notice about the ratios between the side lengths of the original figure and the corresponding side lengths of the scaled copy?

____

____

____

96 Unit rates

Learn!

A **rate** is a comparison of two quantities that have different units, such as 120 miles every 2 hours. A **unit rate** is a special type of rate where the second amount is 1, such as 60 miles every 1 hour, or 60 miles per hour. To find a unit rate, you can divide.

Try it! There are 24 people sitting at 3 tables. How many people are there per table?

$$24 \div 3 = 8$$

The unit rate is 8 people per table.

Find the unit rate.

135 miles in 3 hours ________ miles per hour

48 mailboxes in 4 rows ________ mailboxes per row

90 pencils in 5 packs ________ pencils per pack

16 apples in 2 bags ________ apples per bag

3 shelves hold 45 books ________ books per shelf

58 fluid ounces of juice in 8 glasses ________ fluid ounces per glass

12 seconds to travel 78 meters ________ meters per second

165 pages in 15 days ________ pages per day

IXL.com skill ID JSZ

The **unit price** tells you how much one unit of something costs. When you compare two prices, you can use unit prices to find the better deal.

Find the unit price.

$10.50 for 2 boxes of popsicles $ ________ per box

$11 for 4 pounds of peaches $ ________ per pound

3 square feet of fabric for $10.20 $ ________ per square foot

5 jars of applesauce for $10.95 $ ________ per jar

$8.96 for 4 boxes of tissues $ ________ per box

Circle the better buy.

16-pack of markers for $3.52	12-pack of markers for $2.28
5 gallons of gas for $21.55	$47.30 for 11 gallons of gas
$3.75 for a 3-pack of socks	8-pack of socks for $10.40
4 boxes of cat treats for $15.80	$11.25 for 3 boxes of cat treats

IXL.com
skill ID
UKD

Answer each question.

Roy scored 72 points in a trivia game. He correctly answered 24 questions during the game. How many points did Roy score per question? __________

Tisha earned $144 working as a referee in a youth soccer league last spring. She was a referee in 6 games. How much money did Tisha earn per game? __________

Diane bought 7 feet of braided rope to make a fishing net. She paid $6.86. How much money did Diane pay per foot of braided rope? __________

A chef makes his own garlic butter to serve with warm bread at his restaurant. The recipe calls for 6 tablespoons of fresh garlic for every 4 cups of butter. How much garlic does the chef use per cup of butter? __________

Lanette bought 4 Greek yogurt cups for $4.76. How much did Lanette pay per Greek yogurt cup? __________

Find each unit rate. Use your answers to draw a path from start to finish.

START

65 pages in 5 days

7 pages per day

112 pieces in 14 pies

10 pieces per pie

$11.13 for 7 notebooks

$0.63 per notebook

$3.40 for 2 pounds of grapes

13 pages per day

26 pages per day

12 pieces per pie

$1.60 per T-shirt

$1.79 per notebook

$2.20 per pound

$0.59 per pound

96 fluid ounces of juice in 3 quarts

32 fluid ounces per quart

14 T-shirts for $87.50

$6.25 per T-shirt

80 pens in 5 packages

16 pens per package

9 gallons of gas for $37.62

45 fluid ounces per quart

41 miles per hour

$7 per T-shirt

12 pens per package

26 pens per package

$4.18 per gallon

$4.28 per gallon

4 packages of yarn to knit 5 hats

50 miles per hour

2 hours to drive 110 miles

17 papers per hour

3 hours to grade 51 papers

6 papers per hour

3 sandwiches for $14.37

$2.32 per quart

0.45 hats per package

55 miles per hour

0.8 meters per second

$0.22 per battery

$2.08 per sandwich

$4.39 per sandwich

$3.44 for 8 quarts of potting soil

$0.86 per quart

40 seconds to swim 50 meters

1.25 meters per second

20-pack of batteries for $9.20

$0.46 per battery

FINISH

100 Word problems

Answer each question.

Maggie has two cats. She feeds Bongo 6 cups of food over the course of 8 days, while Daisy gets 3 cups over the course of 6 days. Which cat gets more food per day?

Polly and Emir are training for a bike race. Polly biked 30 miles in 4 hours. Emir biked 24 miles in 3 hours. Assuming they each traveled at a constant speed, who biked at a faster rate?

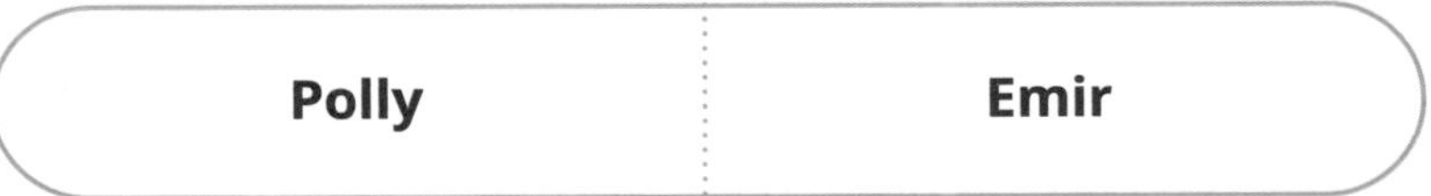

Ariana and Jared are each entering their homemade tomato sauce in a cooking contest. Ariana's recipe uses 15 tablespoons of fresh basil for 6 quarts of sauce. Jared's recipe uses 9 tablespoons of fresh basil for 4 quarts of sauce. Who uses more basil per quart of sauce?

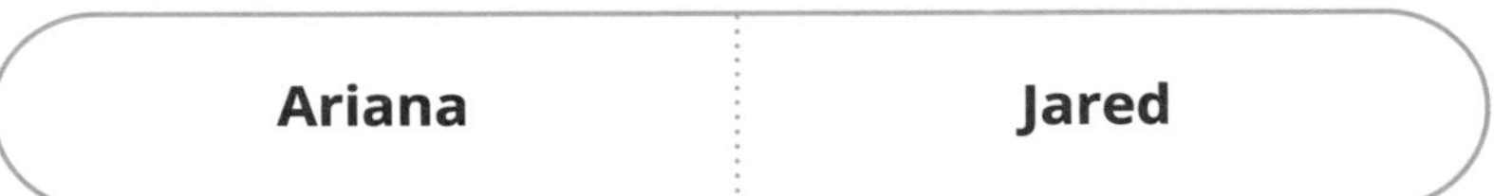

Employees at Scrumptious Smoothies use 4 cups of strawberries to make 8 strawberry-banana smoothies. To make 4 kiwi-strawberry smoothies, they use 3 cups of strawberries. Which flavor uses more cups of strawberries per smoothie?

strawberry-banana | **kiwi-strawberry**

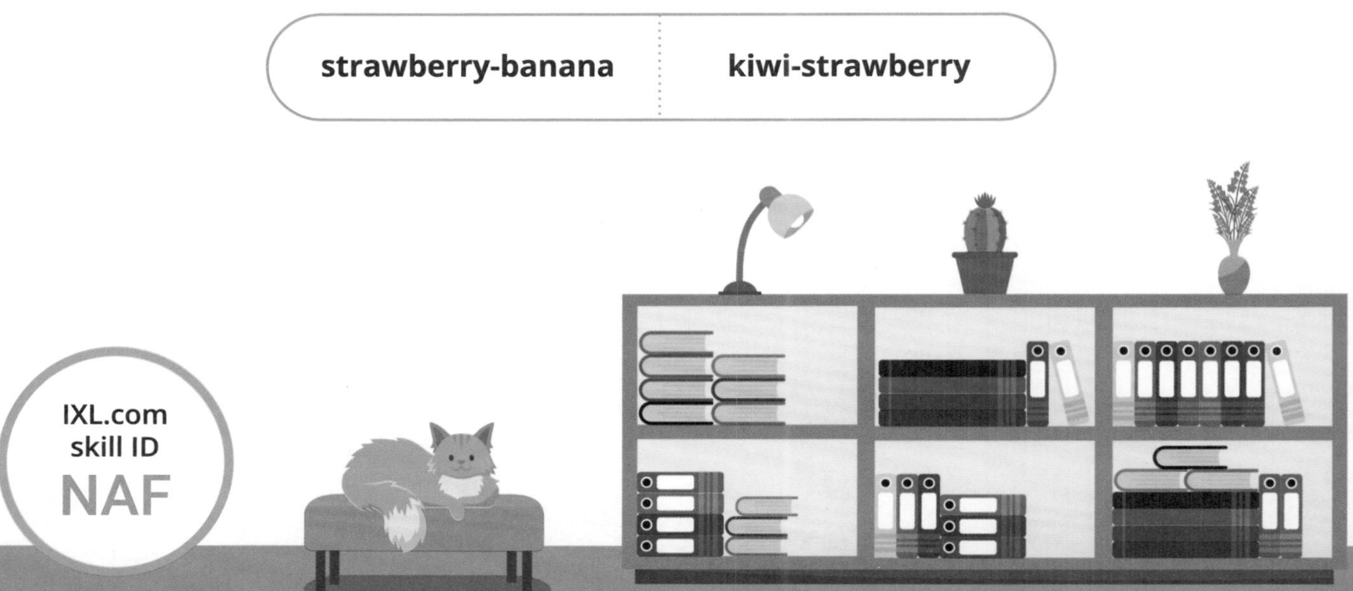

For each problem, complete the table. Then answer the question.

Mateo goes cross-country skiing every weekend during the winter. Last weekend, he skied 12 miles in 4 hours. This weekend, he skied for 5 hours at the same pace. How many miles did Mateo ski this weekend?

Miles	12		
Hours	4	1	5

____

Eddie works as a math tutor at Stonebridge Community Center after school on Wednesdays. He earns $67.50 for 3 hours of tutoring. How much would Eddie earn for 2 hours of tutoring?

Money	$67.50		
Hours	3	1	2

____

To warm up before the first soccer game in the tournament, Darius did 110 jumping jacks in 2 minutes. Before today's game, he will do jumping jacks for 3 minutes. If he does them at the same rate, how many jumping jacks will Darius do today?

Jumping jacks	110		
Minutes	2	1	3

____

Jayda is ordering signs to advertise for the neighborhood yard sale. Instant Print charges $59.65 for 5 printed signs. Jayda is ordering 13 signs. How much will Jayda pay?

Cost	$59.65		
Signs	5	1	13

____

102 Converting customary units

Learn!

You can use the information in these tables to convert between measurements within the customary system.

Length
1 foot (ft.) = 12 inches (in.) 1 yard (yd.) = 3 ft. 1 mile (mi.) = 1,760 yd.

Weight
1 pound (lb.) = 16 ounces (oz.) 1 ton = 2,000 lb.

Capacity
1 tablespoon (tbsp.) = 3 teaspoons (tsp.) 1 cup (c.) = 16 tbsp. 1 c. = 8 fluid ounces (fl. oz.) 1 pint (pt.) = 2 c. 1 quart (qt.) = 2 pt. 1 gallon (gal.) = 4 qt.

Convert each measurement.

5 ft. = ____________________ in.

32 oz. = ____________________ lb.

4 yd. = ____________________ ft.

3 c. = ____________________ tbsp.

1.5 gal. = ____________________ qt.

24 tsp. = ____________________ tbsp.

0.25 ton = ____________________ oz.

3 pt. = ____________________ fl. oz.

48 pt. = ____________________ gal.

1,320 ft. = ____________________ mi.

Comparing customary units

Compare each pair of measurements using <, >, or =.

2 ft. ◯ 30 in.

2 tbsp. ◯ 6 tsp.

4 c. ◯ 24 fl. oz.

3 lb. ◯ 50 oz.

2.5 tons ◯ 5,000 lb.

72 in. ◯ 6 ft.

9 yd. ◯ 30 ft.

4.5 lb. ◯ 64 oz.

3.5 gal. ◯ 7 qt.

2,640 yd. ◯ 1.5 mi.

30 tbsp. ◯ 3 c.

4 pt. ◯ 8 c.

3.5 yd. ◯ 120 in.

3,200 oz. ◯ 1 ton

16 pt. ◯ 0.5 gal.

Converting metric units

Learn!

You can use the information in these tables to convert between measurements within the metric system.

Length
1 centimeter (cm) = 10 millimeters (mm) 1 meter (m) = 100 cm 1 kilometer (km) = 1,000 m

Mass
1 gram (g) = 1,000 milligrams (mg) 1 kilogram (kg) = 1,000 g

Capacity
1 liter (L) = 1,000 milliliters (mL)

Convert each measurement.

100 cm = ____________________ mm

2,400 mL = ____________________ L

0.5 m = ____________________ cm

380 g = ____________________ mg

3.2 L = ____________________ mL

3,500 mm = ____________________ cm

1,250 g = ____________________ kg

450,000 mg = ____________________ kg

200 m = ____________________ km

0.75 m = ____________________ mm

Comparing metric units

Compare each pair of measurements using <, >, or =.

650 m ○ 6.5 km

200 m ○ 0.02 km

245 g ○ 2.4 kg

95 m ○ 9,500 cm

13.4 cm ○ 13,500 mm

0.25 km ○ 250 m

8,200 cm ○ 8.2 km

0.46 kg ○ 45,000 mg

2.8 kg ○ 280 g

40 L ○ 4,000 mL

7,999 mg ○ 0.8 g

415 g ○ 40.5 kg

1,250 g ○ 1.25 kg

85,000 mm ○ 8.45 m

0.83 km ○ 83,000 cm

IXL.com
skill ID
FDH

106 Converting between units

Learn!

You can use the information in these tables to convert measurements between the customary and metric systems. Most of these conversion factors are approximate.

Length
1 in. = 2.54 cm
1 ft. ≈ 0.3 m
1 cm ≈ 0.39 in.
1 m ≈ 3.28 ft.

Weight / Mass
1 oz. ≈ 28.35 g
1 lb. ≈ 0.45 kg
1 g ≈ 0.04 oz.
1 kg ≈ 2.2 lb.

Capacity
1 qt. ≈ 0.95 L
1 gal. ≈ 3.79 L
1 L ≈ 1.06 qt.
1 L ≈ 0.26 gal.

Convert each measurement. Round your answer to the nearest tenth, if needed.

2 L ≈ ____________ gal.

8 qt. ≈ ____________ L

5 ft. ≈ ____________ m

10 in. = ____________ cm

9 L ≈ ____________ qt.

40 cm ≈ ____________ in.

4 m ≈ ____________ ft.

6 lb. ≈ ____________ kg

12 gal. ≈ ____________ L

65 g ≈ ____________ oz.

IXL.com skill ID 5CF

32 oz. ≈ ____________ g

Exploration Zone

You have learned about converting between customary and metric units. Temperature is also measured in different units around the world. The most commonly used units are Fahrenheit (°F) and Celsius (°C). You can convert between Fahrenheit and Celsius by following these steps:

To go from °F to °C, use the formula $\boldsymbol{C = (F - 32) \times \frac{5}{9}}$. Try converting 50°F to °C.

$C = (\mathbf{50 - 32}) \times \frac{5}{9}$	First, subtract 32 from 50.
$C = 18 \times \frac{5}{9}$	Then, multiply by $\frac{5}{9}$.
$C = 10$	So, 50°F = 10°C.

To go from °C to °F, use the formula $\boldsymbol{F = \left(C \times \frac{9}{5}\right) + 32}$. Try converting 20°C to °F.

$F = \left(\mathbf{20 \times \frac{9}{5}}\right) + 32$	First, multiply 20 by $\frac{9}{5}$.
$F = 36 + 32$	Then, add 32.
$F = 68$	So, 20°C = 68°F.

TRY IT YOURSELF!

Convert each temperature.

15°C = ______________ °F

32°F = ______________ °C

25°C = ______________ °F

Percents

A **percent** is a part out of 100 and is written with the % sign. Percents, fractions, and decimals each represent the relationship between a part and a whole. In the models below, each large square represents one whole and is divided into 100 parts.

Express the shaded area in each model as a percent, a fraction, and a decimal.

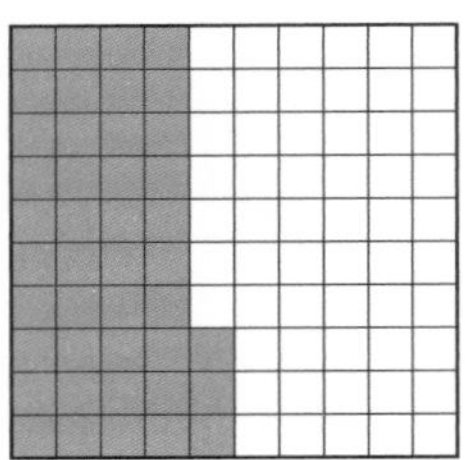

Percent: 43% ______ Fraction: ______ Decimal: ______

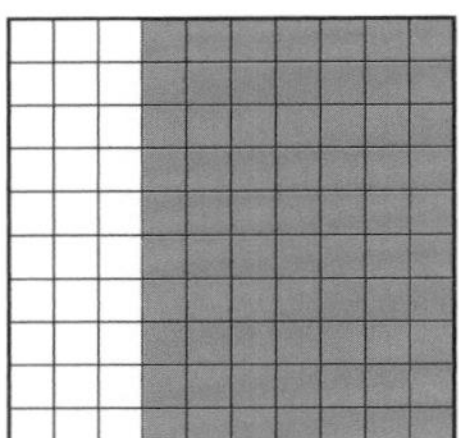

Percent: ______ Fraction: ______ Decimal: ______

Percent: ______ Fraction: ______ Decimal: ______

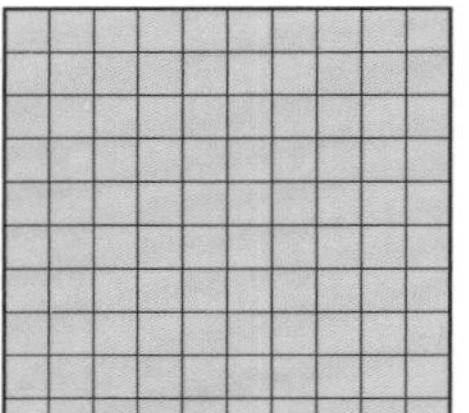
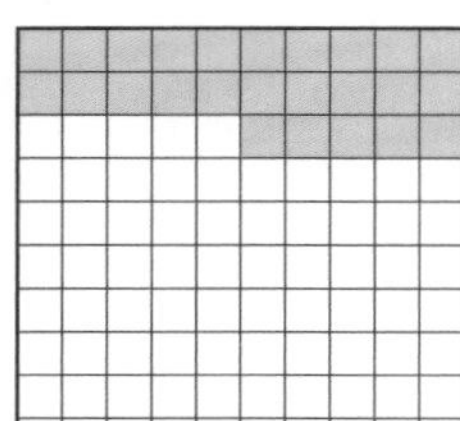

Percent: ______ Fraction: ______ Decimal: ______

Complete the table by filling in the missing numbers.

Fraction	Decimal	Percent
$\frac{23}{100}$	0.23	23%
$\frac{57}{100}$		
	0.79	
		90%
	0.4	
$\frac{3}{4}$		
	0.01	
		12.5%
$1\frac{7}{100}$		
	0.003	
		120%

IXL.com skill ID ZAV

Word problems

Answer each question.

Malik and Bryce are each saving money to buy a new tablet. Malik has saved 40% of the money he needs. Bryce has saved $\frac{3}{10}$ of the money he needs. Who has saved a greater percentage of the money needed to buy a new tablet?

Candace and Lucia checked out the same book from the library last week. Candace has finished reading 70% of the book, and Lucia has finished reading $\frac{13}{20}$ of the book. Who has read a greater percentage of the book?

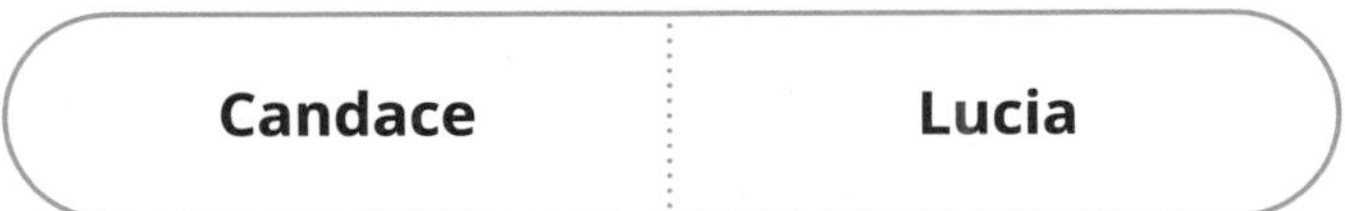

At Prime Pizza, $\frac{37}{50}$ of the pizzas ordered were pepperoni. At City Pizza, 65% of the pizzas ordered were pepperoni. At which restaurant did pepperoni pizzas make up a greater percentage of the pizzas sold?

Prime Pizza | **City Pizza**

Sally sold 35% of the pumpkins at her stand last weekend, while Gina sold 11 out of 25 pumpkins at her stand. Who sold a greater percentage of pumpkins?

Sally | **Gina**

This season, the Cougars won 5 out of 8 of their soccer games, and the Lions won 75% of their soccer games. Which team won a greater percentage of their soccer games?

Cougars | **Lions**

Learn!

In percent problems, there is a relationship between the **percent**, the **whole**, and the **part**. To solve a percent problem, you will need to find one of those three.

Sometimes you will need to find the percent. To do this, divide the part by the whole.

Try it! What **percent** of **40** is **14**? The part is 14, and the whole is 40.

$\frac{14}{40}$ **= 0.35 or 35%**

So, 35% of 40 is 14.

Find each percent.

20 % of 75 = 15

$\frac{15}{75} = 0.2$ or 20%

_____% of 30 = 18

_____% of 50 = 17

_____% of 30 = 9

_____% of 84 = 21

_____% of 80 = 26

_____% of 60 = 87

_____% of 125 = 80

_____% of 50 = 60

_____% of 200 = 175

_____% of 120 = 6

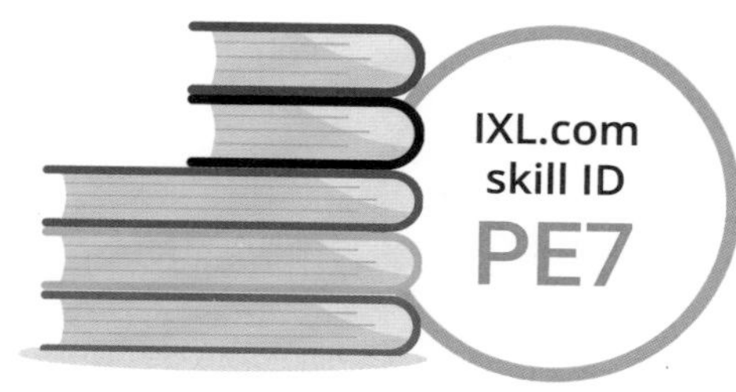

112 Percent problems

Learn!

Sometimes you will need to find the part. This is the same as finding the percent of a number. To do this, write the percent as a fraction or a decimal and multiply by the whole.

Try it! **15%** of 60 is **what number**? The percent is 0.15 or $\frac{3}{20}$, and the whole is 60.

0.15 × 60 = 9 **So, 15% of 60 is 9.**

Find each part.

50% of 70 = ________ 20% of 25 = ________ 5% of 20 = ________

30% of 40 = ________ 44% of 100 = ________ 76% of 50 = ________

105% of 60 = ________ 86% of 175 = ________ 12.5% of 120 = ________

130% of 40 = ________ 0.1% of 160 = ________

IXL.com skill ID **8N4**

Learn!

You found the part by multiplying the percent and the whole. Sometimes you will need to find the whole. To do this, use a related division problem. Divide the part by the percent. Remember to write the percent as a fraction or decimal.

Try it! **20%** of **what number** is **30**? The part is 30, and the percent is 0.2 or $\frac{1}{5}$.

30 ÷ 0.2 = 150

So, 20% of 150 is 30.

Find each whole.

10% of ________ = 3

50% of ________ = 32

25% of ________ = 10

90% of ________ = 45

20% of ________ = 17

125% of ________ = 150

5% of ________ = 4

95% of ________ = 19

10.5% of ________ = 21

0.5% of ________ = 2

160% of ________ = 96

IXL.com
skill ID
D6L

114 Percent problems

Answer each percent problem. Use your answers to draw a path from start to finish.

START
What percent of 36 is 9?
25%
20% of 40 is what number?
8
40% of what number is 18?
45
25% of 84 is what number?
720
40%
50
36
72
21
63
75% of what number is 54?
57%
What percent of 140 is 105?
50%
What percent of 80 is 16?
37
20% of 75 is what number?
18
133
147%
20%
68%
22%
150
40% of what number is 15?
400
40% of 30 is what number?
120
What percent of 50 is 43?
24
48% of what number is 12?
20%
6
12
22
40
36
30
What percent of 75 is 27?
63%
80% of what number is 28?
35
18% of 50 is what number?
9
FINISH
IXL.com skill ID
ELY

Answer each question.

Isaiah's baseball team played 20 games last summer. Isaiah hit a home run in 2 of the games. In what percentage of the games did Isaiah hit a home run? ____________

There are 25 students in Charlotte's class, and 8% of the students have blonde hair. How many students in Charlotte's class have blonde hair? ____________

At the Oak Valley Conservation Center, 30% of the penguins are macaroni penguins. If there are 15 macaroni penguins, how many penguins are at Oak Valley Conservation Center? ____________

Tamir wants to buy a new phone case for $40. He has already saved 35% of the money needed. How much money has Tamir already saved? ____________

Addison has completed 18 levels in *Toppling Towers*, which is 45% of all the levels in the game. How many total levels are in *Toppling Towers*? ____________

Maureen is running for student council. Of the 95 students who voted, 76 of the students voted for her. What percentage of the students voted for Maureen? ____________

Order of operations

Learn!

You should follow the **order of operations** when you evaluate an expression with multiple operations.

1. Grouping symbols, such as parentheses
2. Exponents
3. Multiplication and division, from left to right
4. Addition and subtraction, from left to right

Note: If your expression does not have one of these steps, move on to the next one!

Evaluate each expression using the order of operations.

$25 - 3^2 \cdot 2 =$ 7

$25 - 9 \cdot 2$

$25 - 18$

7

$2^3 \div (6 - 2) =$ ________

$18 + 4^2 \div 2 =$ ________

$14 + 6 \cdot 2^2 =$ ________

$9^2 \div 3 - (17 - 8) =$ ________

$45 \div 3^2 + 4 \cdot 5 =$ ________

Keep going! Evaluate each expression using the order of operations.

$5 + 40 \div 2^3 \cdot 3 =$ _________

$17 + 5^2 \cdot (11 - 3^2) =$ _________

$49 - (30 - 2^4 + 6) \cdot 2 =$ _________

$8 + [(7^2 - 4) \div 9] \cdot 3 =$ _________

$11 + 3^3 \div 9 \cdot 6 - 5 =$ _________

$50 - [13 + 6^2 \div (25 - 7)] =$ _________

$47 - 2 \cdot [13 + 4^2 - (7 + 8)] =$ _________

Order of operations

In each problem below, a student tried to evaluate an expression but made an error. Identify the error in each student's work and correctly evaluate the expression.

Farid's work:	Show the correct work.
$5 + 2 \cdot 3^2$ $5 + 2 \cdot 9$ $7 \cdot 9$ 63	

What error did Farid make?

Madelyn's work:	Show the correct work.
$40 - (8 + 7) + 4^2$ $40 - 15 + 4^2$ $40 - 15 + 8$ $25 + 8$ 33	

What error did Madelyn make?

IXL.com skill ID
V46

Evaluate each expression using the order of operations.

$2 + 1.5 \cdot 3 =$ ________

$8 \div 0.4 + 3^2 =$ ________

$(4.8 + 1.2) \cdot 4 \div 3$ ________

$4^2 \cdot 0.2 \div 1.6 =$ ________

$3.7 + 2.4 \cdot 5 - 2^3 =$ ________

$1.6 + (5^2 - 3.5) \cdot 0.2 =$ ________

$7.5 \cdot 0.8 - 0.3 \cdot 2^4 =$ ________

IXL.com skill ID YEE

Order of operations

Keep going! Evaluate each expression using the order of operations.

$7 + 4 \cdot \frac{1}{2} =$ ______

$3 - \frac{3}{4} \cdot \frac{2}{3} =$ ______

$\frac{1}{6} \div \frac{1}{4} - \left(\frac{1}{3}\right)^2 =$ ______

$\frac{5}{6} \div 3 \cdot \left(\frac{7}{8} + \frac{5}{8}\right) =$ ______

$\frac{2}{3} \div \left(\frac{5}{6} + \frac{1}{2}\right) + \frac{1}{4} =$ ______

$\frac{1}{4} + \left(\frac{3}{5} - \frac{3}{10}\right) \div 2 =$ ______

$\left(\frac{1}{2}\right)^3 \cdot 6 + \left(\frac{2}{3} - \frac{1}{6}\right) =$ ______

Make each equation true by adding parentheses.

$6^2 \div (3 \cdot 4) + 7 = 10$

$6^2 \div 12 + 7$

$36 \div 12 + 7$

$3 + 7$

10

$50 - 2^3 \cdot 5 - 2 = 26$

$3^2 \cdot 11 - 8 + 16 = 43$

$2^4 + 8 \div 2 \cdot 4 = 48$

$4 + 8 - 6 \cdot 4^2 = 36$

$6^2 \div 2 + 4 \cdot 4 = 24$

$3 + 5^2 - 8 + 6 \div 2 = 21$

$8 + 2^3 \cdot 3^2 - 5 + 10 = 50$

Parts of an expression

Learn!

An **expression** is a mathematical phrase that contains numbers, variables, or both. An expression does *not* have an equal sign.

An expression is made up of different parts. Look at the example.

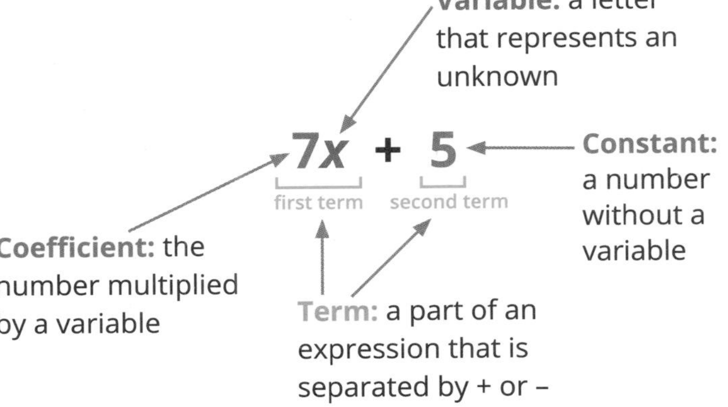
Variable: a letter that represents an unknown
7x + 5
first term
second term
Constant: a number without a variable
Coefficient: the number multiplied by a variable
Term: a part of an expression that is separated by + or –

Answer the questions about each expression.

$5d + 7f - 6$	
How many terms does this expression have?	3
What are the variables?	d and f
What is the coefficient of the first term?	5

$2.5 + 0.3a - 4.8b$	
What is the constant term in this expression?	______
What are the variables?	___ and ___
What is the coefficient of the second term?	______

$9 - 2t + 12u$	
What is the constant term in this expression?	______
What are the variables?	___ and ___
What is the coefficient of the third term?	______

$\frac{5}{8}h + \frac{2}{3} - 4\frac{1}{2}k$	
How many terms does this expression have?	______
What is the constant term?	______
What are the variables?	___ and ___

IXL.com skill ID **9KE**

Learn!

To translate a verbal expression into an algebraic expression, look for keywords that tell you whether the expression involves addition, subtraction, multiplication, or division. The table below shows some examples of these keywords.

Addition Phrases	Subtraction Phrases	Multiplication Phrases	Division Phrases
Plus Sum Total Increased by More than	Minus Difference Subtracted from Decreased by Less than	Times Multiplied by Product of Twice	Quotient Divided by

Write each phrase as an expression.

5 times w

$5w$

8 divided by h

______

10 less than b

______

k decreased by 17

______

6 increased by r

______

12 multiplied by q

______

the quotient of d and 20

______

c decreased by $\frac{7}{8}$

______

the product of 14 and u

______

the sum of $3\frac{1}{6}$ and n

______

t divided by 6.3

______

IXL.com skill ID F5B

Writing expressions

Learn!

Sometimes an expression can have more than one operation. Think about the order of operations, and use parentheses if needed. Look at the example.

3 times the total of 6 and *x* → $3(6 + x)$

Write each phrase as an expression.

3 times the difference of *j* and 4

____

add 4 to the quotient of *c* and 2

____

divide *h* by the sum of 10 and *u*

____

16 minus the quotient of *v* and 7

____

the product of *p* and *z* increased by 15

____

multiply the difference of *d* and 1.5 by 6

____

$\frac{4}{5}$ times the sum of *m* and 18

____

divide *x* by *n*, then increase the result by 0.9

____

divide *t* by 4, then decrease the result by $\frac{7}{10}$

____

twice the sum of $3\frac{2}{3}$ and *k*

____

Write an expression for each story.

Eva has a bag containing t dog toys. She shares them equally among the 3 dogs at the dog park. Write an expression showing how many toys Eva gave each dog. ______________

Lamar has a collection of snow globes from places he has visited with his family. He had s snow globes in his collection and bought 3 more last week. Write an expression showing how many snow globes Lamar has now. ______________

Abdul had n songs downloaded on his tablet. He deleted 5 of them to free up storage space on the tablet. Write an expression showing how many songs Abdul has on his tablet now. ______________

Destiny bought a pack of d sports drinks for basketball camp. She kept 3 for herself and split the rest equally among her 4 friends. Write an expression to show how many sports drinks Destiny gave to each friend. ______________

A total of a adult tickets and c student tickets to the Valley View School Fair have been sold. Each adult ticket costs \$5 and each student ticket costs \$2. Write an expression showing the total value of the tickets that have been sold. ______________

126 Evaluating expressions

Learn!

To evaluate an expression with a variable, you will need to replace the variable with the given value. This is called **substitution**. Then simplify using the order of operations.

Try it with the expression $5n - 8$.
Evaluate the expression for $n = 6$.

$$5n - 8$$
$$5(6) - 8$$
$$30 - 8$$
$$22$$

Evaluate each expression using the given value.

$f - 11$ for $f = 17$

$7d$ for $d = 2$

$c + 9$ for $c = 12$

$\frac{20}{a}$ for $a = 4$

$9h + 7$ for $h = \frac{1}{3}$

$0.3(2 + n)$ for $n = 8$

IXL.com
skill ID
Q8Z

Evaluate each expression using the given values.

$n + p$ for $n = 8$ and $p = 5$

$5x - r^2$ for $x = 6$ and $r = 3$

$2qt$ for $q = 4$ and $t = 10$

$u(11 - m)$ for $u = 9$ and $m = 7$

$\frac{v}{3} + c$ for $v = 18$ and $c = 2$

$\frac{p}{4} - s$ for $p = 16$ and $s = 3$

$z^3 + 8b$ for $z = 3$ and $b = \frac{1}{4}$

$1.5t - 2.2y$ for $t = 16$ and $y = 5$

IXL.com skill ID HC9

Evaluating expressions

Evaluate each expression for $h = 3$, $k = 5$, $j = 0.2$, and $m = \frac{1}{4}$.

$\frac{5}{8} + m$	$2k - h$	$\frac{18}{j^2}$
$16m + k$	$\frac{20h}{k}$	$kj + 4$
$h^3 - \frac{k}{10} + m$	$j(k^2 - 4h)$	$4(12m + h - k)$

Evaluate the expression to answer each question.

Mya likes to ride her scooter to her friend Jade's house. The total time for n trips to Jade's house and back is $30n$ minutes. Last week, Mya took 4 trips to Jade's house. How many minutes did Mya ride her scooter last week to Jade's house and back? ________________

Felix is making chocolate mousse for his family. In order to serve p people, he must make $\frac{p}{2}$ cups of mousse. Felix expects to serve 8 people. How many cups of chocolate mousse should Felix make? ________________

Juan is building a scale model of an actual boat. A part that is a inches long on the actual boat will be $0.05a$ inches long on the model boat. The mast of the actual boat is 240 inches long. How long is the mast on the model boat? ________________

An object that travels a distance d in time t has an average speed of $\frac{d}{t}$. Liam read an article about a cheetah that ran 100 meters in 8 seconds. What was the cheetah's average speed in meters per second? ________________

The Farfield Amusement Park allows customers to order tickets online. The amusement park charges a service fee in addition to the cost of the tickets. The total price for a adults and c children is $25a + 12.5c + 5$ dollars. Samantha's dad ordered tickets for their family of 2 adults and 3 children. What price will Samantha's dad pay for the tickets? ________________

Properties of addition

Learn!

The table shows three important properties of addition.

Commutative property: You can change the order of the addends and get the same sum.	$a + b = b + a$
Associative property: You can group the addends in different ways and get the same sum.	$(a + b) + c = a + (b + c)$
Identity property: You can add 0 and it does not change a number.	$a + 0 = a$

Determine which property of addition is shown.

$9 + 5 = 5 + 9$

Commutative property
____

$8 = 8 + 0$

____

$m + (n + p) = (m + n) + p$

____

$x + y = y + x$

____

Complete the equivalent expressions using the properties listed.

$11 + k + 5$

$= k +$ _______ $+ 5$ ← Commutative property

$= k +$ _______

$(4w + 6) + 5$

$= 4w + ($ _______ $+$ _______ $)$ ← Associative property

$= 4w +$ _______

$9 + 7b + 8$

$= 7b +$ _______ $+ 8$ ← Commutative property

$= 7b +$ _______

IXL.com skill ID **JRM**

Properties of multiplication

Learn!

The table shows four important properties of multiplication.

Commutative property: You can change the order of the factors and get the same product.	$a \cdot b = b \cdot a$
Associative property: You can group the factors in different ways and get the same product.	$(a \cdot b) \cdot c = a \cdot (b \cdot c)$
Identity property: You can multiply by 1 and it does not change a number.	$a \cdot 1 = a$
Zero property: You can multiply by 0 and the product will always be 0.	$a \cdot 0 = 0$

Determine which property of multiplication is shown.

$4 \cdot 9 = 9 \cdot 4$

____

$0 = 7 \cdot 0$

____

$3 \cdot (q \cdot r) = (3 \cdot q) \cdot r$

____

$d \cdot 1 = d$

____

Complete the equivalent expressions using the properties listed.

$6 \cdot n \cdot 4$

$= 6 \cdot$ _____ $\cdot\ n$ ← Commutative property

$=$ _____ n

$10 \cdot (7 \cdot m)$

$= (10 \cdot$ _____ $) \cdot m$ ← Associative property

$=$ _____ m

$3 \cdot 1 \cdot k$

$=$ _____ k ← Identity property

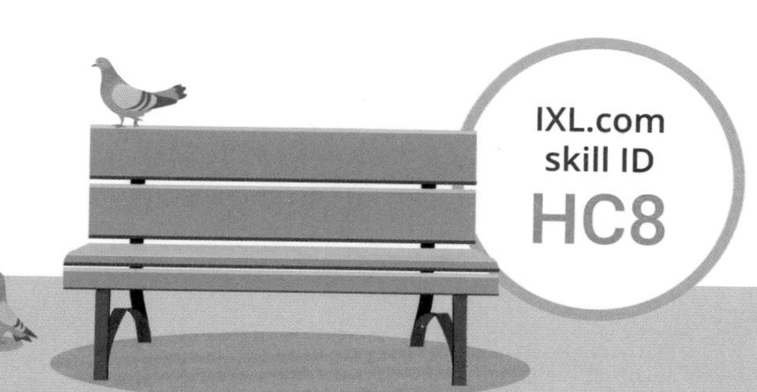

Distributive property

Learn!

The table shows the distributive property across addition and subtraction.

Distributive property across addition: Multiply the number outside the parentheses by each term inside the parentheses. Then add those products.	$a(b + c) = a(b) + a(c)$
Distributive property across subtraction: Multiply the number outside the parentheses by each term inside the parentheses. Then subtract those products.	$a(b - c) = a(b) - a(c)$

Complete the equivalent expressions using the distributive property.

$7(c + 2)$

$= 7($ ______ $) + 7($ ______ $)$

$=$ ______ $+$ ______

$3(5 - n - t)$

$= 3($ ______ $) - 3($ ______ $) - 3($ ______ $)$

$=$ ______ $-$ ______ $-$ ______

Simplify each expression using the distributive property.

$4(7 + k) =$ 28 + 4k

$9(w + 6) =$ ______

$5(2g - 6) =$ ______

$\frac{1}{6}(18 - 12b) =$ ______

$0.5(16y + 20) =$ ______

$3\left(4a - b + \frac{2}{3}\right) =$ ______

$10(2f + 0.6 - 5t) =$ ______

Time for review! Simplify each expression using the properties of operations.

$3 + (12 + n) =$ ______________

$4(w - 5) =$ ______________

$7 + k + 2 =$ ______________

$5c \cdot 1.7 =$ ______________

$14 + 16v + 3 =$ ______________

$16(3a) =$ ______________

$13(2 + f - s) =$ ______________

$4\left(9x - \frac{3}{4} + y\right) =$ ______________

$(2p + 13) + 0.4 =$ ______________

$\frac{1}{4}(12q - 16z + 8d) =$ ______________

$1.5(6d + 4a + 10) =$ ______________

$0.2(1.5y + 3.5f + 5) =$ ______________

$\frac{2}{3}(3 + 18b + 6w) =$ ______________

Combining like terms

Learn!

Like terms are terms that have the same variables raised to the same powers. You can simplify an expression by combining any like terms. To combine like terms, add or subtract their coefficients. Note that if no coefficient is written with a variable, the coefficient is 1. Try it! Simplify $4n + 6p + n + 2p$.

$4n + 6p + n + 2p$	Identify like terms.
$(4n + n) + (6p + 2p)$	Group like terms.
$\mathbf{5n + 8p}$	Combine like terms.

Simplify each expression by combining like terms.

$7h + 6h =$ ____________________

$q + q =$ ____________________

$5j - j =$ ____________________

$9w - 8w =$ ____________________

$11k + k + 4 =$ ____________________

$13c - c + 5c =$ ____________________

$9t + 2r - 3t + 5r =$ ____________________

$11u + 8v - 3u - v =$ ____________________

$9d + 5 + 3f - 2d - f =$ ____________________

$14p - p + 8n + 9 - 2 =$ ____________________

IXL.com skill ID **CN9**

Keep going! Simplify each expression by combining like terms.

$10t^2 + 6t^2 =$ $16t^2$

$9a^3 - 2a^3 =$ ____________

$j^3 + 8j^3 - 4j^3 =$ ____________

$16u^2 - u^2 + 3u^2 =$ ____________

$3b^2 + 9c - b^2 =$ ____________

$11w^3 + 16v - 7w^3 =$ ____________

$9u + 3u^3 - u + u^3 =$ ____________

$12d^2 + 7d - 3d^2 + 8d - d =$ ____________

$y + 5.9z^2 - 3z^2 + 2.4y =$ ____________

$\frac{1}{4}q^2 - \frac{1}{5} + r^3 + \frac{1}{2}q^2 =$ ____________

Equivalent expressions

Draw a line between each pair of equivalent expressions.

$4(5x - 3)$	$5(x - 4)$
$6x + 5x$	$20x - 12$
$5x - 20$	$3x + 8x$
$16x + 3x - 5x$	$2(7x)$
$6(2x + 3)$	$4x - 9 + 7x$
$7x + 9x$	$18x - 2x$
$11x - 9$	$12x + 1 - 9x$
$3x + 1$	$12x + 18$

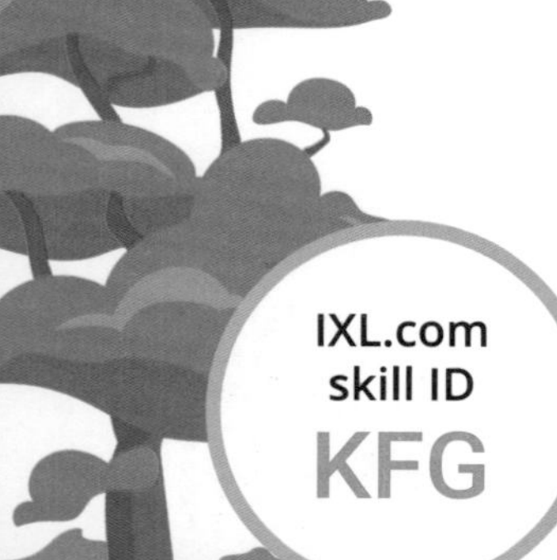

IXL.com
skill ID
KFG

Simplify each expression.

$7(n - 5) =$ ______

$6a + 5 - 2a =$ ______

$9 + 2b + 8b =$ ______

$5(3c + 5) - 15 =$ ______

$7t - 6 - 5t =$ ______

$5g + 13 + g - 4 =$ ______

$10(z - 5y) =$ ______

$16k - k + 11m - 8k =$ ______

$4d + 6(5 + 3d) =$ ______

$11p + 3(8p - 1) =$ ______

$30k + 16w - 4k - 5w =$ ______

$18h + 6(2 + h) - 7 =$ ______

$14 + 2(5u - 4) - 3u =$ ______

IXL.com skill ID **HTG**

138 Writing equations

An **equation** is a mathematical statement that says two expressions are equal. Equations always have an equal sign.

Write the words as an equation.

17 plus n is 32

$17 + n = 32$

63 divided by k is 7

____

h decreased by 11 is the same as 14

____

40 equals the product of 8 and b

____

x increased by 28 is 51

____

58 equals p divided by 3

____

81 subtracted from b is 14

____

f plus 61 is the same as 80

____

the quotient of r and 8 is 5.6

____

twice v equals $\frac{7}{8}$

____

$\frac{1}{2}$ increased by m is $\frac{9}{10}$

____

8 is the same as 2.2 subtracted from c

____

IXL.com skill ID **AN8**

A **solution** to an equation is a value for the variable that makes the equation true. Circle the solution to each equation.

$n - 8 = 17$	$s + 37 = 52$	$9g = 27$
$n = 25$ (circled) $n = 9$	$s = 15$ $s = 89$	$g = 18$ $g = 3$
$41 = 26 + b$	$f - 33 = 8$	$\frac{u}{6} = 7$
$b = 67$ $b = 15$	$f = 25$ $f = 41$	$u = 42$ $u = 13$
$3.5 = \frac{q}{2}$	$h - \frac{3}{5} = \frac{1}{5}$	$12 = 30 - c$
$q = 1.5$ $q = 7$	$h = \frac{4}{5}$ $h = \frac{2}{5}$	$c = 22$ $c = 18$
$\frac{1}{3}d = 21$	$\frac{j}{1.5} = 3$	$14.2 + p = 32.6$
$d = 7$ $d = 63$	$j = 2$ $j = 4.5$	$p = 18.4$ $p = 46.8$

IXL.com skill ID **VG8**

140 One-step equations

Learn!

You can solve one-step equations using **inverse operations**. Addition and subtraction are inverse operations. To solve a one-step addition or subtraction equation, use the inverse operation on both sides of the equation to get the variable alone. Look at the examples.

$$x + 6 = 15$$
$$x + 6 - 6 = 15 - 6$$
$$x = 9$$

Subtract 6 from both sides of the equation.

$$y - 8 = 13$$
$$y - 8 + 8 = 13 + 8$$
$$y = 21$$

Add 8 to both sides of the equation.

Use inverse operations to solve each equation.

$b - 11 = 6$

$b =$ ________

$h + 17 = 19$

$h =$ ________

$r + 20 = 36$

$r =$ ________

$5 = m - 7$

$m =$ ________

$9 + c = 32$

$c =$ ________

$z - 31 = 8$

$z =$ ________

$d - 19 = 33$

$d =$ ________

$38 = 15 + g$

$g =$ ________

Keep going! Use inverse operations to solve each equation.

$d + 15 = 19$

$d =$ ____________

$h - 33 = 20$

$h =$ ____________

$29 = p - 14$

$p =$ ____________

$k - 12.4 = 2.9$

$k =$ ____________

$a - \frac{1}{5} = \frac{3}{5}$

$a =$ ____________

$17 + m = 44$

$m =$ ____________

$r + \frac{2}{3} = \frac{5}{6}$

$r =$ ____________

$11.5 + u = 27.8$

$u =$ ____________

$g - \frac{1}{4} = \frac{5}{12}$

$g =$ ____________

$16.1 = c - 3.7$

$c =$ ____________

$f + 16.5 = 42.3$

$f =$ ____________

$\frac{4}{5} = \frac{1}{10} + t$

$t =$ ____________

$s - 16 = 1\frac{4}{7}$

$s =$ ____________

$w + 4\frac{1}{4} = 13\frac{5}{8}$

$w =$ ____________

One-step equations

Learn!

Multiplication and division are also inverse operations. To solve a one-step multiplication or division equation, use the inverse operation on both sides of the equation to get the variable alone. Look at the examples.

$4x = 36$

$\frac{4x}{4} = \frac{36}{4}$ **Divide** both sides of the equation **by 4**.

$x = 9$

$\frac{y}{7} = 5$

$\frac{y}{7} \cdot 7 = 5 \cdot 7$ **Multiply** both sides of the equation **by 7**.

$y = 35$

Use inverse operations to solve each equation.

$\frac{b}{2} = 8$

$b =$ ______

$7u = 42$

$u =$ ______

$50 = 5z$

$z =$ ______

$\frac{k}{5} = 9$

$k =$ ______

$33 = 11h$

$h =$ ______

$\frac{a}{8} = 4$

$a =$ ______

$3w = 48$

$w =$ ______

$81 = \frac{x}{9}$

$x =$ ______

IXL.com skill ID **JUA**

Keep going! Use inverse operations to solve each equation. Remember, dividing by a fraction is the same as multiplying by its reciprocal.

$6y = 30$

$y =$ ________

$\frac{a}{3} = 13$

$a =$ ________

$\frac{c}{0.6} = 8$

$c =$ ________

$7 = \frac{h}{4}$

$h =$ ________

$15u = 60$

$u =$ ________

$\frac{3}{5}b = 9$

$b =$ ________

$56 = 8m$

$m =$ ________

$\frac{2}{3}r = \frac{2}{5}$

$r =$ ________

$0.4w = 3.4$

$w =$ ________

$\frac{1}{3} = \frac{5}{6}k$

$k =$ ________

$\frac{z}{0.05} = 32$

$z =$ ________

$1.1p = 18.7$

$p =$ ________

$\frac{1}{2}t = 1\frac{1}{5}$

$t =$ ________

$\frac{x}{2.1} = 13.4$

$x =$ ________

IXL.com skill ID **T53**

One-step equations

Time for review! Solve each equation.

$19 + c = 26$

$c =$ __________

$24 = 3k$

$k =$ __________

$5 = \frac{u}{6}$

$u =$ __________

$r - 11 = 40$

$r =$ __________

$\frac{t}{7} = 10$

$t =$ __________

$m + 22 = 36$

$m =$ __________

$14n = 42$

$n =$ __________

$x - 6 = 31$

$x =$ __________

$2.8 = p - 4.6$

$p =$ __________

$\frac{1}{6} + h = \frac{2}{3}$

$h =$ __________

$\frac{g}{3} = 2.1$

$g =$ __________

$\frac{3}{4}y = 15$

$y =$ __________

$\frac{z}{29} = 17$

$z =$ __________

$14j = 826$

$j =$ __________

IXL.com
skill ID
WLR

Draw a line connecting each equation to its solution.

$n - 17 = 24$	$n = 9$
$8n = 32$	$n = 22$
$\frac{n}{6} = 12$	$n = 41$
$6n = 54$	$n = 18$
$\frac{n}{2} = 11$	$n = 4$
$9 = n - 33$	$n = 72$
$22 + n = 40$	$n = 42$

One-step equations

Crack the code by solving each equation! Then, look for any places where that solution appears in the code at the bottom of the page, and write the corresponding letter on the line. Use the code to reveal the rest of the joke! Not every letter will be used in the code at the bottom.

E	$14x = 56$	L	$37 = 24 + x$
P	$\frac{x}{6} = 3$	U	$x - 8 = 6$
I	$35 = 5x$	R	$x + 18 = 30$
S	$x - 5 = 14$	A	$\frac{x}{2} = 8$
M	$17 + x = 26$	T	$8x = 48$

What tool is best suited for math?

___ ___ ___ ___ ___ – ___ ___ ___ ___ ___ ___!

9 14 13 6 7 18 13 7 4 12 19

Equations with like terms

CHALLENGE ZONE

Learn!

When solving an equation with like terms, you can combine like terms first. Then use inverse operations to isolate the variable. Try it! Solve $m + 11m = 60$.

$m + 11m = 60$

Combine like terms, paying attention to the signs. Here, m and $11m$ are like terms.

$12m = 60$

$\frac{12m}{12} = \frac{60}{12}$

Next, use inverse operations to solve. Divide both sides by 12. Then simplify.

$m = 5$

Solve each equation.

$5k + 2k = 56$

$k =$ ________

$12c - 8c = 40$

$c =$ ________

$8b + 3b = 66$

$b =$ ________

$63 = 10x - x$

$x =$ ________

$2z + 3z + z = 54$

$z =$ ________

$12w + 5w - w = 48$

$w =$ ________

$18g + 5g - 11g = 24$

$g =$ ________

$64 = 4a + a + 2a + a$

$a =$ ________

IXL.com skill ID W82

Word problems

Circle the equation that represents each word problem.

Ms. Arnold opened a package of *p* pencils. She split the pencils evenly among 24 students, giving 2 pencils to each student.

$\frac{p}{24} = 2$	$p + 24 = 2$

Jenna read 36 pages of her book last weekend. She read *c* pages on Saturday and 12 pages on Sunday.

$c + 12 = 36$	$12c = 36$

Leo walked 2 laps around the track. Each lap is *m* meters long. Leo walked a total of 800 meters.

$\frac{m}{2} = 800$	$2m = 800$

Mr. Jay coaches a softball team. Yesterday, he brought a bag of *s* softballs to practice and took 10 of the softballs out. There were still 15 softballs in the bag.

$10 - s = 15$	$s - 10 = 15$

Suzie earns $21.50 per hour as a hostess at Burrito Junction. Yesterday, she worked for *h* hours and earned a total of $75.25.

$21.50 + h = 75.25$	$21.50h = 75.25$

Write an equation for each problem. Then solve the equation to answer the question.

Shawna spent d dollars on pens and $8 on pencils at the office supply store this morning. She spent a total of $21 before tax. How much did Shawna spend on pens?

$d + 8 = 21$

$\$13$

$$d + 8 = 21$$
$$d + 8 - 8 = 21 - 8$$
$$d = 13$$

Mimi saved up b dollars to spend at City Books. After spending $15 on a mystery novel, she had $25 left. How much money did Mimi originally save up?

____

____

While playing a board game with his friends, Brian answered 7 questions correctly. Each question was worth p points. Brian earned a total of 21 points. How many points was each question worth?

Anthony took his dog on a long walk yesterday. They walked m miles to the playground and another 1.25 miles to the dog park for a total distance of 2.75 miles. How far did Anthony and his dog walk to get to the playground?

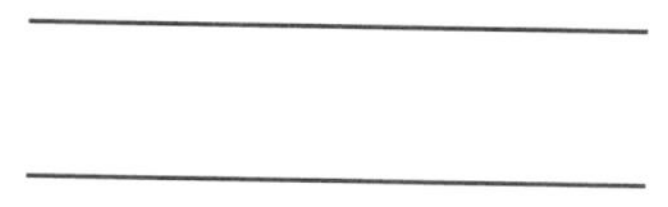

Kim is making friendship bracelets out of yarn. For each bracelet, Kim starts with a piece of yarn that is y feet long and cuts it into 4 smaller pieces that are each 1.5 feet long. What is the length of the starting piece of yarn?

____

____

IXL.com skill ID **BXY**

Writing inequalities

Learn!

An **inequality** is a comparison statement. The table below shows symbols you might see in an inequality and some of their possible meanings.

Symbol	<	>	≤	≥
Meaning	Less than Fewer than	Greater than More than	Less than or equal to At most No more than	Greater than or equal to At least No less than

Write the words as an inequality.

n is greater than 15

$n > 15$

b is less than or equal to 33

____

5 is fewer than *g*

____

–28 is greater than or equal to *y*

____

14.5 is more than *c*

____

$2\frac{1}{2}$ is no more than *x*

____

the sum of *p* and 7 is less than 19

____

4 times *h* is at least 36

____

a minus 6 is greater than 22

____

15 increased by *w* is at most 9

____

Learn!

A **solution** to an inequality is a value for the variable that makes the inequality true. Look at the inequality $n > 3$.

$n = 8$ is a solution because $8 > 3$ is true.

$n = 10$ is also a solution because $10 > 3$ is true.

$n = 1$ is **not** a solution because $1 > 3$ is not true.

Circle all of the solutions to each inequality.

$f < 13$				$u \geq 4$			
$f = 6$	$f = 10$	$f = 14$	$f = 18$	$u = 0$	$u = 3$	$u = 4$	$u = 6$
$k > 41$				$y \leq 37$			
$k = -60$	$k = -40$	$k = 40$	$k = 60$	$y = 30$	$y = 35$	$y = 40$	$y = 45$
$z > 6.8$				$d < \frac{3}{4}$			
$z = 5.9$	$z = 6.4$	$z = 6.8$	$z = 7.4$	$d = 0$	$d = \frac{1}{3}$	$d = \frac{2}{3}$	$d = 1$
$5n \geq 35$				$p + 8 < 16$			
$n = 1$	$n = 5$	$n = 7$	$n = 10$	$p = 0$	$p = 6$	$p = 18$	$p = 20$

IXL.com skill ID P9N

Graphing inequalities

Learn!

The graph of an inequality shows all possible solutions to the inequality on a number line. Look at the examples below.

Graph $n > 1$.

Start by graphing a circle at 1. Since $n = 1$ is not a solution, the circle will not be filled in. Then, draw an arrow pointing to the right to show numbers greater than 1.

$n > 1$

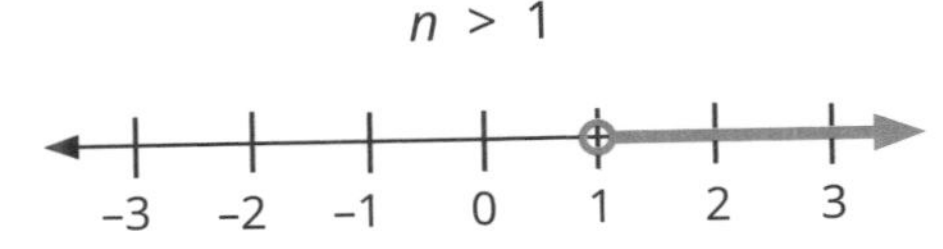

Graph $n \leq 2$.

Start by graphing a circle at 2. Since $n = 2$ is a solution, the circle will be filled in. Then, draw an arrow pointing to the left to show numbers less than 2.

$n \leq 2$

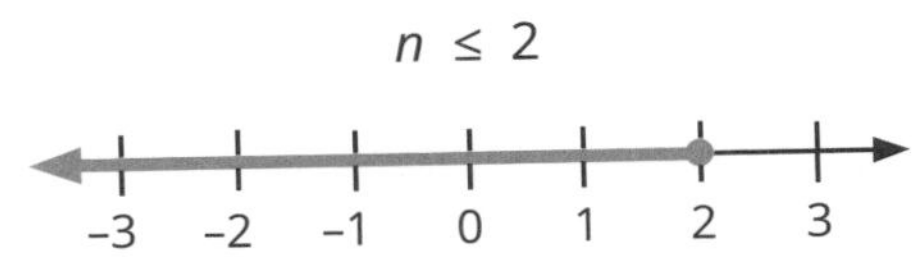

Graph each inequality on the number line.

$h < 7$

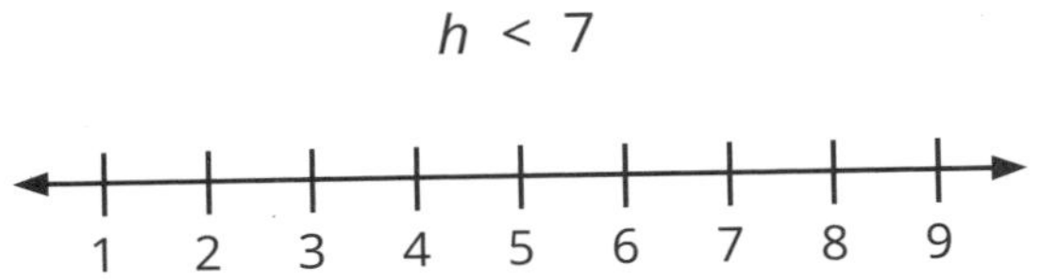

$a > \frac{1}{2}$

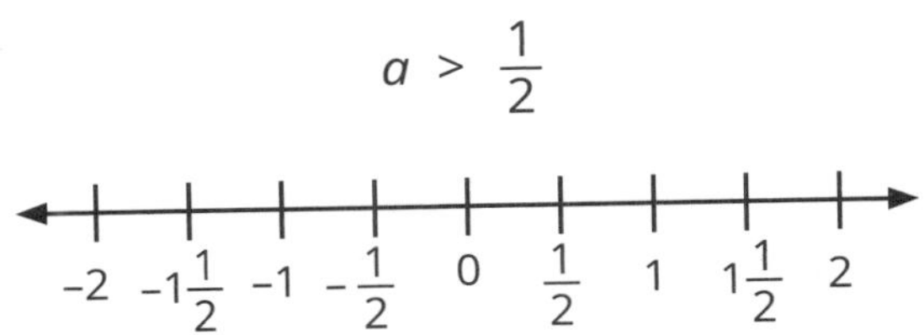

$m > 17$

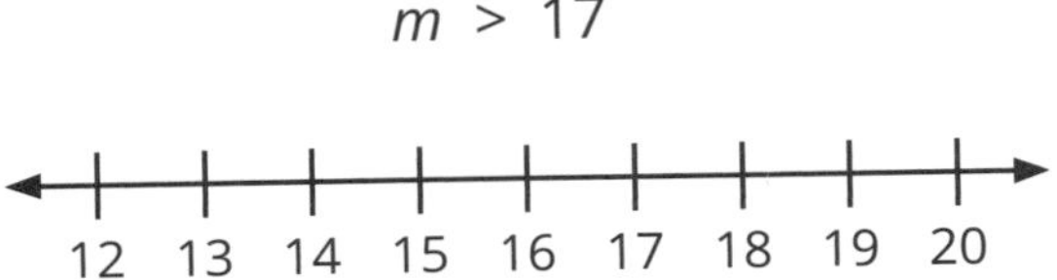

$w \geq -2$

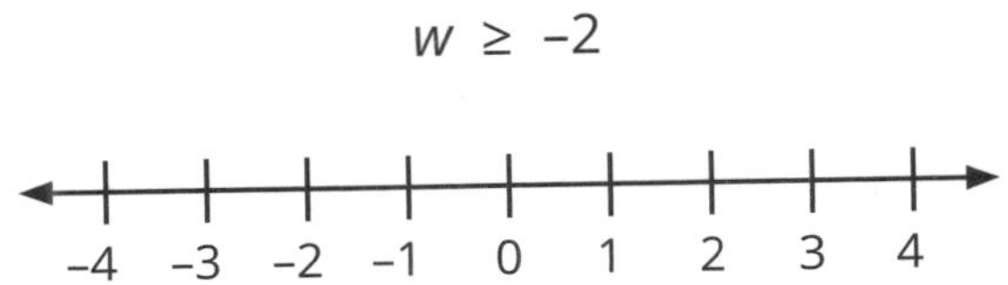

$u \leq 1.5$

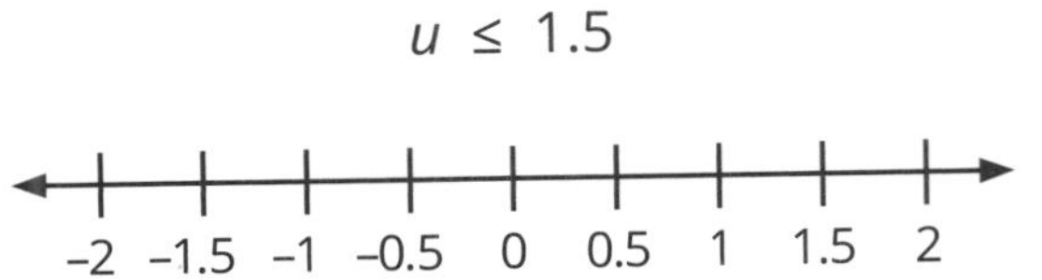

Write the inequality shown on each graph.

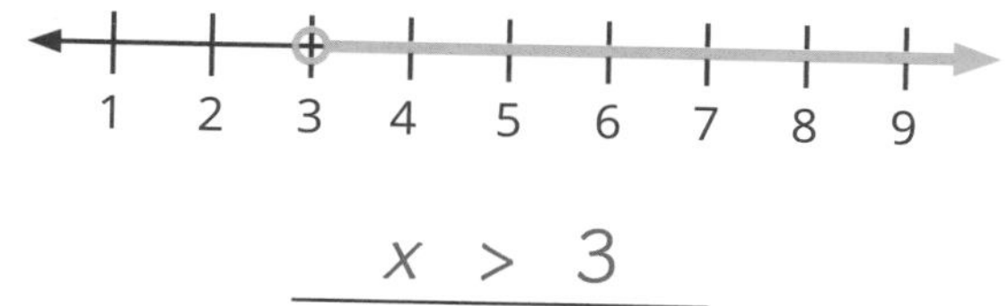

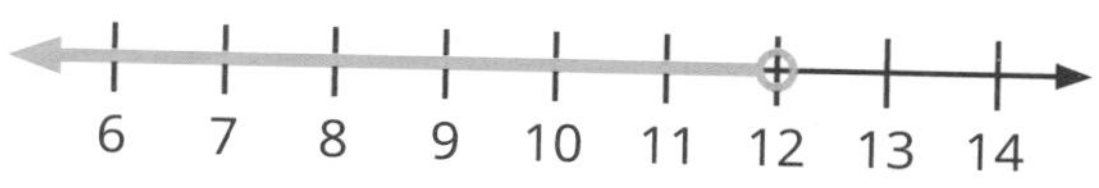

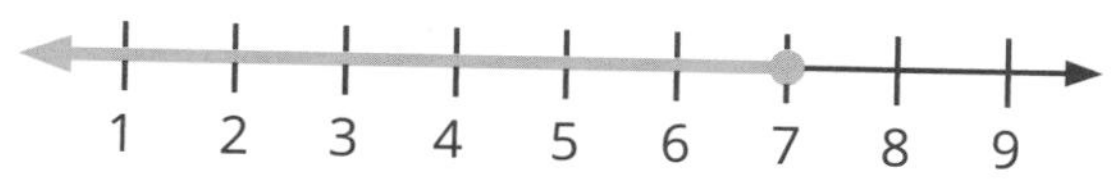

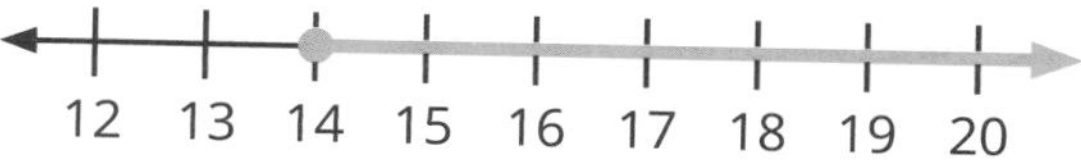

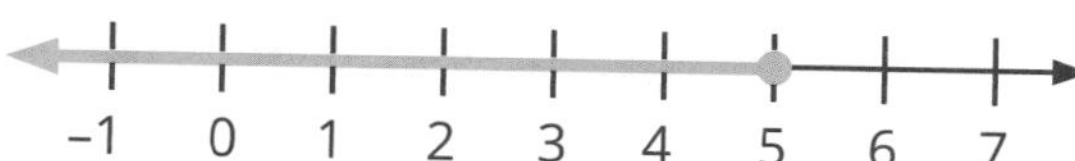

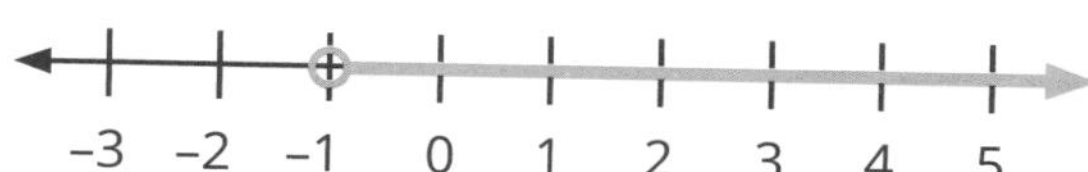

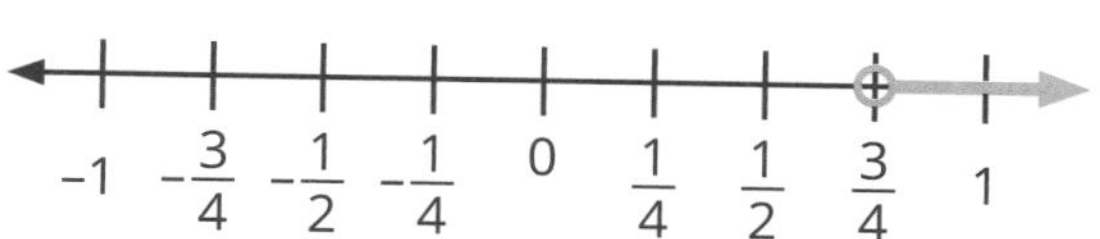

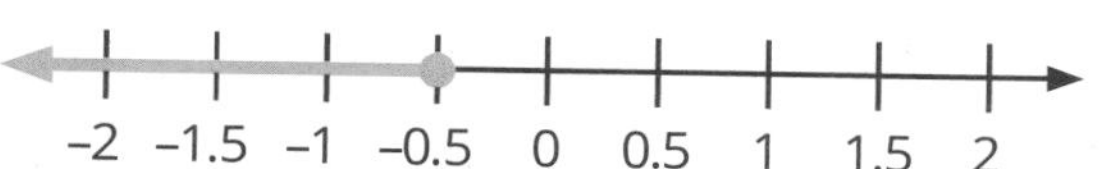

IXL.com
skill ID
N99

Graphing inequalities

Draw a line between each inequality and its graphed solution.

$x \leq -6$

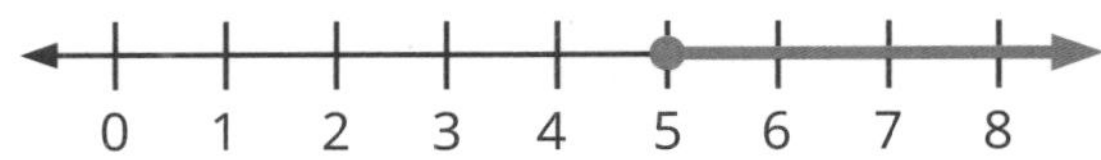

$x \geq -2$

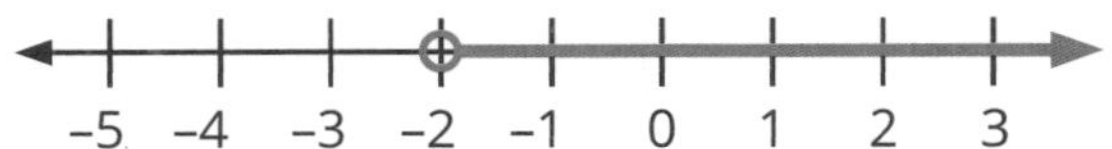

$x \geq 5$

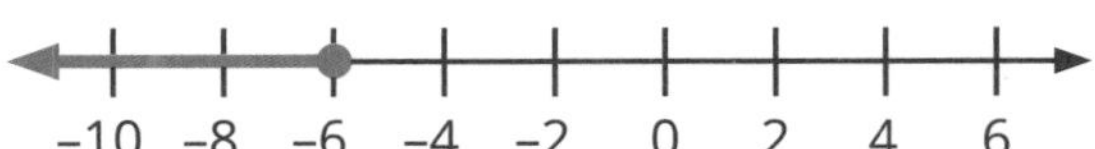

$x \leq 5$

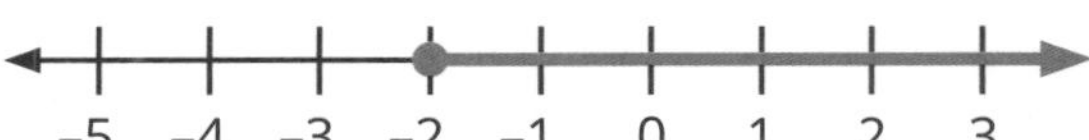

$x > -2$

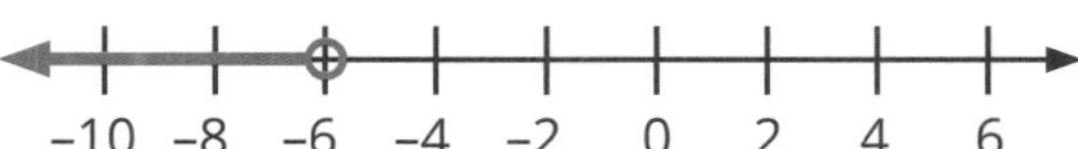

$x < -6$

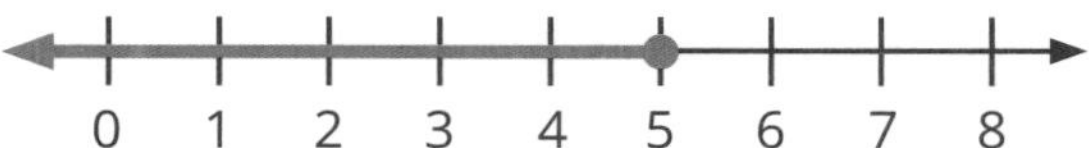

Write and graph an inequality that represents each word problem.

Sophie is going to the movies and plans to spend no more than $10 on snacks. Let *a* represent the amount Sophie will spend on snacks at the movies.

$a \leq 10$

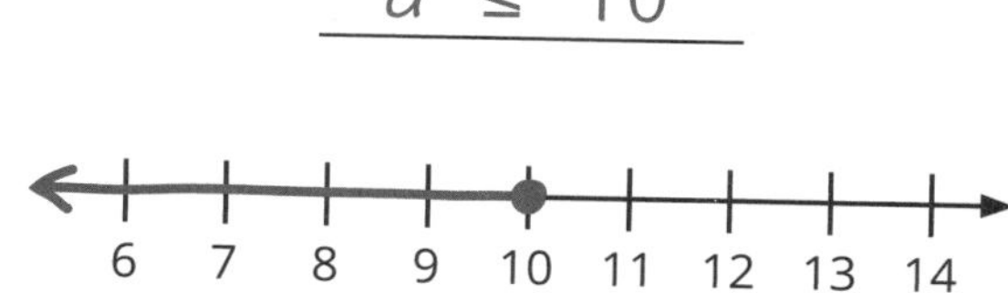

Marco is taller than his brother, who is 49 inches tall. Let *y* represent Marco's height in inches.

____

Alexa has fewer than 30 pages left in the book she is reading. Let *p* represent the number of pages Alexa has left to read.

____

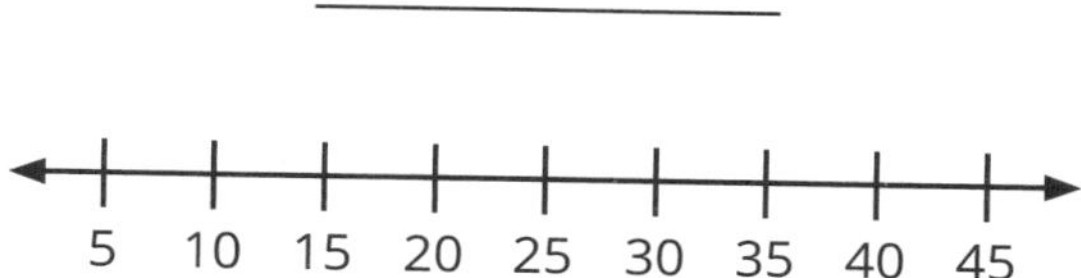

Eric walks at least 15 minutes on the treadmill every day. Let *t* represent the number of minutes Eric walks on the treadmill every day.

____

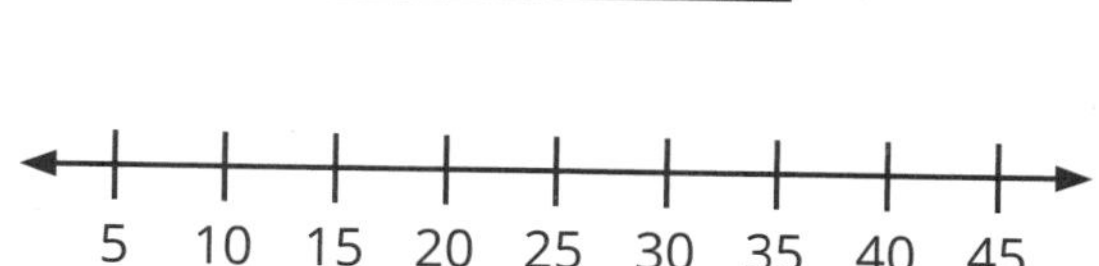

Jay gives his dog, Bruno, at most 5 treats a day. Let *b* represent the number of treats Jay gives Bruno today.

____

2 3 4 5 6 7 8 9 10

For more practice, visit IXL.com or the IXL mobile app and enter this code in the search bar.

Identifying solutions

Learn!

You can show a relationship between two quantities by using an equation with two variables. A solution to an equation with two variables is an ordered pair that makes the equation true. Look at the examples.

Is (3, 7) a solution to $y = x + 4$?

$\mathbf{7 = 3 + 4}$	Substitute (3, 7) into the equation for x and y.
$\mathbf{7 = 7}$	Check if the equation is true. Since 7 is equal to 7, (3, 7) is a solution to the equation.

Is (5, 6) a solution to $y = 2x - 3$?

$\mathbf{6 = 2(5) - 3}$	Substitute (5, 6) into the equation for x and y.
$\mathbf{6 = 10 - 3}$	Simplify.
$\mathbf{6 \neq 7}$	Check if the equation is true. Since 6 does not equal 7, (5, 6) is not a solution to the equation.

Determine whether the ordered pair is a solution to the equation.

Is (0, 8) a solution to $y = x - 8$?

Yes No

Is (5, 16) a solution to $y = x + 11$?

Yes No

Is (4, 12) a solution to $3x = y$?

Yes No

Is (15, 1) a solution to $y = \frac{x}{5} - 2$?

Yes No

Is (11, 22) a solution to $y = 2x + 10$?

Yes No

Learn!

When an equation with two variables models a real-world situation, one variable is **independent** and the other variable is **dependent**. To find the dependent variable, think about which quantity depends on the other. Look at the example.

Joey is buying grapes at the grocery store. The total cost of the grapes, c, depends on the number of pounds of grapes he decides to buy, p. So, c is the dependent variable and p is the independent variable.

Identify the independent and dependent variables in each situation.

The number of tickets Ms. Singh buys, n, and the total cost of the tickets, t

Independent variable: ______ Dependent variable: ______

The number of pieces of bread Tessa has, p, and the number of sandwiches she can make, s

Independent variable: ______ Dependent variable: ______

The amount of money Vinny earns, a, and the number of hours he works, r

Independent variable: ______ Dependent variable: ______

The number of gallons of gas Cameron uses, g, and the number of miles he drives, d

Independent variable: ______ Dependent variable: ______

The number of players on a basketball team, k, and the number of uniforms needed, u

Independent variable: ______ Dependent variable: ______

IXL.com
skill ID
9UJ

Two-variable equations

Evaluate each equation using the given value.

Use the equation $y = 3x$ to find the value of y when $x = 4$. $y =$ ________

Use the equation $x + 9 = y$ to find the value of y when $x = 7$. $y =$ ________

Use the equation $y = \frac{x}{6}$ to find the value of y when $x = 18$. $y =$ ________

Use the equation $y = x - 11$ to find the value of y when $x = 15$. $y =$ ________

Use the equation $y = \frac{x}{5} + 3$ to find the value of y when $x = 20$. $y =$ ________

Use the equation $y = 7x - 10$ to find the value of y when $x = 5$. $y =$ ________

IXL.com
skill ID
46Q

Complete each table using the equation provided.

$y = 5x$

x	y
1	5
2	10
3	15
4	20

$5 \cdot 1 = 5$

$5 \cdot 2 = 10$

$5 \cdot 3 = 15$

$5 \cdot 4 = 20$

$y = x + 2$

x	y
1	
3	
5	
7	

$y = \frac{x}{3}$

x	y
3	
6	
9	
12	

$x - 8 = y$

x	y
10	
11	
12	
13	

$y = 3x - 9$

x	y
3	
4	
5	
6	

Writing equations

Write an equation using the pattern in each table.

Equation: $y = x + 5$

x	y
1	6
2	7
3	8

$1 + 5 = 6$

$2 + 5 = 7$

$3 + 5 = 8$

Equation: ____________

x	y
9	5
10	6
11	7

Equation: ____________

x	y
5	15
6	18
7	21

Equation: ____________

x	y
2	1
4	2
6	3

Equation: ____________

x	y
8	15
9	16
10	17

Write an equation using the pattern in each table. Then fill in the missing values in each table.

Equation: ____________________

x	y
1	9
2	10
3	
	12

Equation: ____________________

x	y
1	6
2	12
	18
4	

Equation: ____________________

x	y
4	1
	2
12	3
16	

Equation: ____________________

x	y
5	3
6	
7	5
	6

Use the equation that models each real-world relationship to complete the table. Then plot the points from the table on the graph. Draw a line connecting the points to represent the equation on the coordinate plane.

Ian is selling raffle tickets for a fundraiser and has already sold 4 tickets. The equation that models the total number of tickets sold, y, after he sells x additional tickets is $y = x + 4$.

x	y
1	
2	
3	
4	

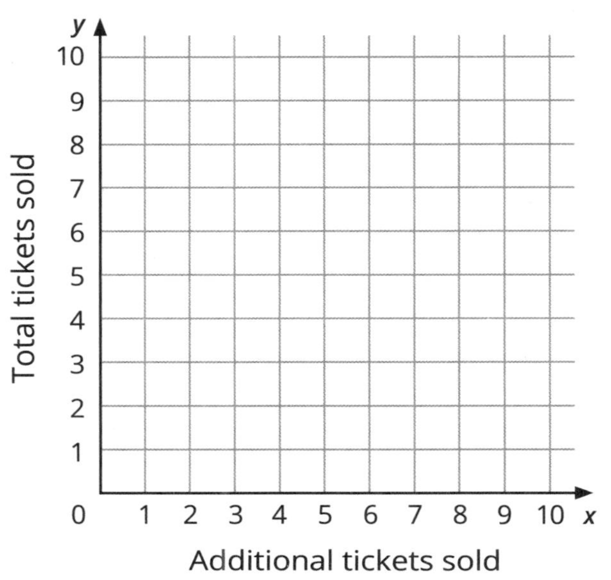

Ayana uses 12 beads for every key chain she makes. The equation that models the total number of beads she uses, y, for making x key chains is $y = 12x$.

x	y
2	
3	
4	
5	

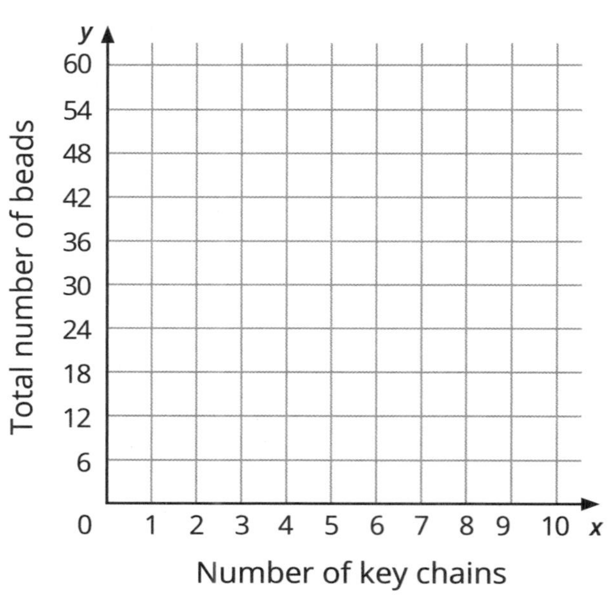

Keep going! Use the equation to complete the table and create a graph.

David has $100 saved in his bank account. The equation that models the amount of money saved in his account, y, after he spends x dollars is $y = 100 - x$.

x	y
10	
20	
30	
40	

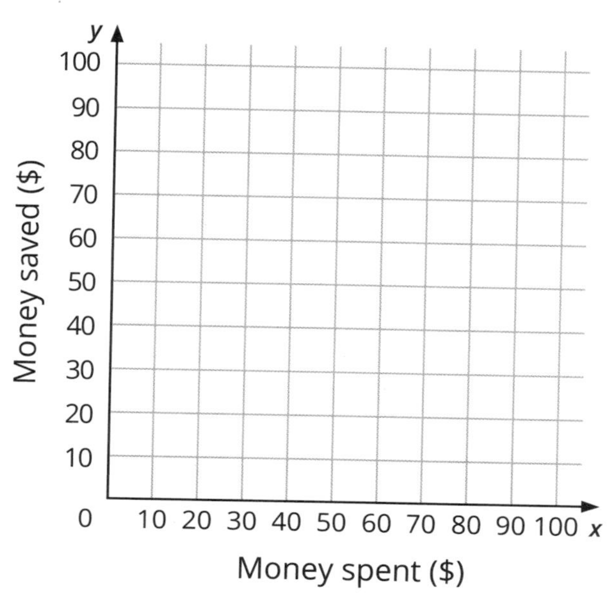

A train travels between two cities at an average speed of 50 miles per hour. The equation that models the total distance traveled, y, after x hours is $y = 50x$.

x	y
2	
4	
6	
8	

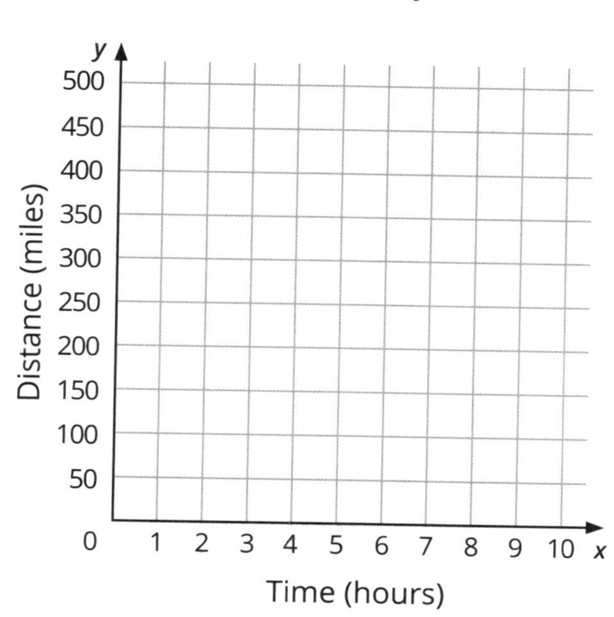

IXL.com skill ID EY5

Identifying statistical questions

Learn!

A **statistical question** is a question that can be answered by collecting data. The data is expected to vary. So, if you ask a statistical question, you would expect more than one answer.

"How many pets do the students in Mr. Powell's class have?" is an example of a statistical question. This question can be answered by collecting data from all of the students in Mr. Powell's class. The data will vary since different students would have different numbers of pets.

"How many pets does Mr. Powell have?" is not a statistical question. There is only one answer to the question, so you do not need to collect data to answer it.

Determine whether each question is a statistical question.

How many ounces are in a pound?	Yes	(No)
How old are the people who live in Hallie's neighborhood?	Yes	No
How many siblings does Brandon have?	Yes	No
Last March, how many days did it rain in Johnsville?	Yes	No
How much do headphones cost?	Yes	No
How much do pumpkins weigh?	Yes	No
How many hurricanes were there last year?	Yes	No

Learn!

You can summarize a data set using the mean, median, mode, and range. Look at the example.

Talia is training for a bike race. She keeps track of the number of miles she bikes each day. Here is her data set: 7, 8, 7, 9, 9, 7, 10, 7.

The **mean** is the average of the values in a data set. To find the mean, add all of the data values. Then, divide by the number of values in the set.	$\frac{7 + 8 + 7 + 9 + 9 + 7 + 10 + 7}{8} = \frac{64}{8} = 8$ The mean is 8.
The **median** is the middle number. To find the median, put the values in order from least to greatest and find the middle. If there are two values in the middle, find their mean.	~~7~~ ~~7~~ ~~7~~ 7 8 ~~9~~ ~~9~~ ~~10~~ $\frac{7 + 8}{2} = 7.5$ The median is 7.5.
The **mode** is the number that appears the most in a data set. To find the mode, it may help to order the numbers from least to greatest.	⑦⑦⑦⑦ 8 9 9 10 The mode is 7.
The **range** is the difference between the largest value and the smallest value in a data set. To find the range, subtract.	$10 - 7 = 3$ The range is 3.

Find the mean, median, mode, and range.

Coach Chase records the total number of runs his baseball team scores in each game.

3 2 7 1 4 2 4 0 4

Mean = ________ Median = ________ Mode = ________ Range = ________

Mean, median, mode, and range

Keep going! Find the mean, median, mode, and range.

Ms. Vega keeps track of the number of cupcakes each customer purchases at her bakery.

1 1 3 2 1 4 2 1 12

Mean = _________ Median = _________ Mode = _________ Range = _________

Kayden records the number of minutes he practices his trumpet each day.

30 30 30 20 30 20 15

Mean = _________ Median = _________ Mode = _________ Range = _________

Seth's Sandwiches keeps track of the number of delivery orders they take each day.

50 17 25 28 33 46 46

Mean = _________ Median = _________ Mode = _________ Range = _________

Molly records her bowling score for each game she plays.

90 93 97 92 90 96

Mean = _________ Median = _________ Mode = _________ Range = _________

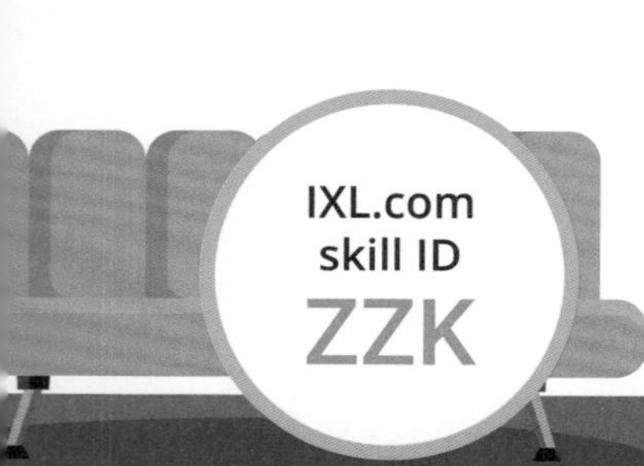

Use the frequency table to find the mean, median, mode, and range. Remember, a frequency table shows the number of times each value occurs in the data set.

Coach Blum records the shoe sizes of some players on his basketball team.

Shoe size	5	6	7	8
Frequency	1	2	3	4

Mean = ________ Median = ________ Mode = ________ Range = ________

Jada kept track of the level she reached every time she played *Escape Mania* this month.

Level	17	18	19	20
Frequency	4	2	2	1

Mean = ________ Median = ________ Mode = ________ Range = ________

Ms. Cass recorded her students' scores on a recent science quiz.

Score	60	70	80	90
Frequency	1	3	4	2

Mean = ________ Median = ________ Mode = ________ Range = ________

Mean absolute deviation

Learn!

The **mean absolute deviation (MAD)** is a number that describes how the data values vary from the mean. A larger MAD means the data is more spread out. Try it! Find the MAD of this data set: 7, 16, 14, 5, 13.

First, find the mean of the data set.

$$\textbf{Mean} = \frac{7 + 16 + 14 + 5 + 13}{5} = \frac{55}{5} = 11$$

Next, calculate the distance each data value is from the mean.

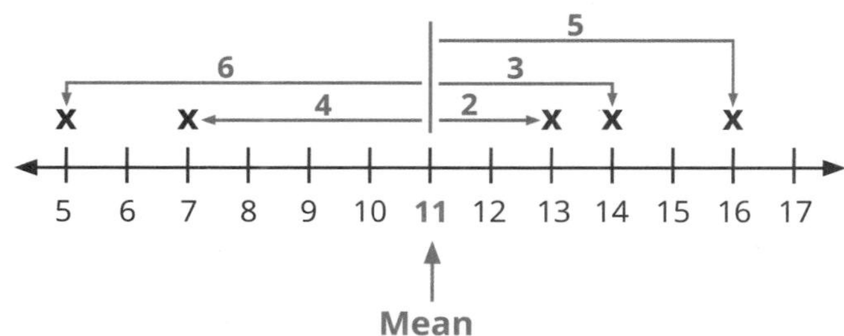

Last, find the mean of those distances.

$$\textbf{MAD} = \frac{6 + 4 + 2 + 3 + 5}{5} = \frac{20}{5} = 4$$

So, the MAD of the data set is 4.

Find the MAD of each data set.

10 15 30 45 50

MAD = ________

12 11 9 14 16 10

MAD = ________

Keep going! Find the MAD of each data set.

5 12 7 6 12 12

MAD = ________

58 42 70 50 75

MAD = ________

11 36 9 7 41 28

MAD = ________

26 32 25 34 18 40 35 38

MAD = ________

15 17 66 35 21 52 40 18

MAD = ________

Outliers

An outlier is a value that is much higher or lower than the other values in a data set. Identify the outlier in each data set.

Silas is shopping for a new phone case. He writes down the price of each case he likes.

\$25 \$25 \$15 \$65 \$30 \$25 \$20 \$25 \$20

Darnell records how many hours he volunteers each week.

16 11 15 12 15 0 13 12 18

The owner of Hill Street Salad keeps track of the number of salads sold each day.

112 115 189 175 193 295 168 141

Mrs. Jackson records how much money she spends on groceries for her family each week.

\$207 \$165 \$153 \$213 \$192 \$361 \$138 \$140

Javier keeps track of how many fish he catches each time he goes fishing.

4 14 1 2 2 4 3

Principal Peters tracks how many students are present each day at Orchard Ridge School.

352 229 347 337 349 332 342 339

An outlier can affect the mean of a data set. Answer each question.

The librarian at Golden Oak Library recorded the total number of books checked out each day.

204 195 183 197 174 168 83 183 179 164

What is the mean of the data set? ____________________

What is the mean of the data set *without the outlier*? ____________________

Without the outlier, did the mean increase or decrease? ____________________

The Culver City Cheetahs gave fans a discount on tickets if they brought in a canned food donation. The team's manager tracked the number of discounts they gave at each game.

143 117 151 156 310 115 128

What is the mean of the data set? ____________________

What is the mean of the data set *without the outlier*? ____________________

Without the outlier, did the mean increase or decrease? ____________________

Quartiles

Learn!

Quartiles divide a data set into four equal parts. When the data is written in order, the **median**, or Q_2, splits the data set into two equal parts. The median of the lower half and the median of the upper half split the data set into four equal parts. The median of the lower half is called the **lower quartile** or Q_1, and the median of the upper half is called the **upper quartile** or Q_3. Look at the example for this data set: 8, 9, 11, 14, 15, 18, 20, 22, 24.

Q_1 Q_2 Q_3

8 9 | 11 14 15 18 20 | 22 24

$\frac{9 + 11}{2} = 10$ $\frac{20 + 22}{2} = 21$

So, the lower quartile is 10, the median is 15, and the upper quartile is 21.

Find the lower quartile, median, and upper quartile of each data set.

7 4 12 10 8 6 13 4 9

Lower quartile = ____________

Median = ____________

Upper quartile = ____________

17 23 15 27 20 24

Lower quartile = ____________

Median = ____________

Upper quartile = ____________

41 49 40 50 47

Lower quartile = ____________

Median = ____________

Upper quartile = ____________

25 32 28 21 30 31 26

Lower quartile = ____________

Median = ____________

Upper quartile = ____________

Interquartile range

Learn!

The **interquartile range (IQR)** is the difference between the upper quartile and lower quartile. It shows how spread out the data values in the middle half of the data set are. A larger IQR means that the values are more spread out. Try it! Find the IQR of this data set: 17, 22, 15, 10, 20, 18.

First, write the data in order and split the data into quartiles.

Q_1 Q_2 Q_3

10 15 **17** ↓ **18** 20 **22**

17.5

Then, subtract the lower quartile from the upper quartile.

20 − 15 = 5

So, the IQR of the data set is 5.

Find the IQR of each data set.

15 18 10 20 12

IQR = ________

48 50 49 46 44 47

IQR = ________

34 42 19 36 47 25 29

IQR = ________

13 19 25 28 20 18 17 11

IQR = ________

12 37 15 28 14 22 29 19 20

IQR = ________

Dot plots

A dot plot is a type of graph that uses dots to represent data along a number line. Create a dot plot for each data set below.

Ms. Jacobs asked her class how many books each student read over spring break. The number of books read by each student is listed below. Use the list to create a dot plot. The first dot has been plotted for you.

Number of books read

0	2	1	1	1	4
3	2	2	0	0	1
0	3	4	1	0	1

Books read

0 1 2 3 4

Number of books read

Coach Lopez measured the height, in inches, of each player on the basketball team. He recorded the data and made the frequency table shown below. Use the frequency table to create a dot plot.

Height (inches)	Number of players
58	2
59	2
60	3
61	4
62	2
63	0
64	1

Height of players

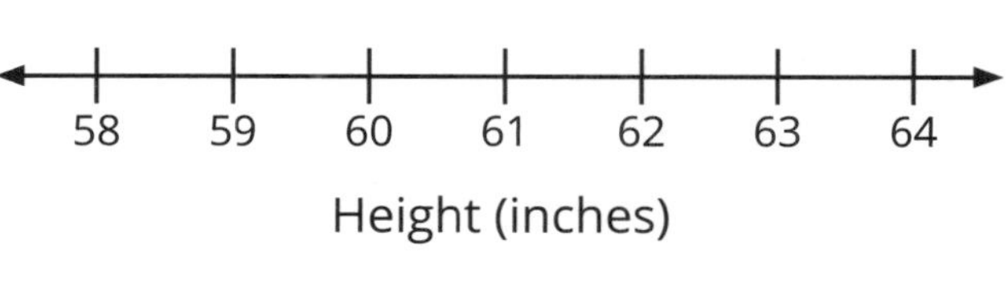

A **histogram** is a type of graph that uses bars to represent data. A histogram is similar to a bar graph, but it displays numerical data grouped into equal ranges, or **bins**. Create a histogram for each data set below.

Dr. Wu is a veterinarian at Clark City Conservation Center. Today, she examined and weighed each of the Humboldt penguins. The results are shown in the list below. Use the list to create a histogram. The first bar has been graphed for you.

Penguin weights (kilograms)

2 6 7 5 4 6
3 4 2 1 6 4
2 3

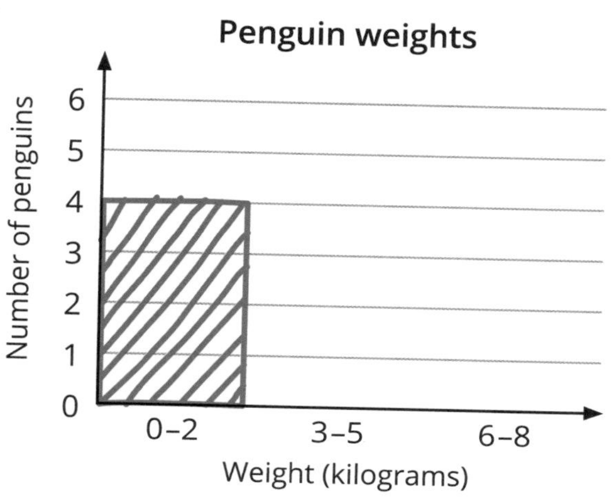

Sharon records how many hours she babysits each weekend. Her results are shown in the frequency table below. Use the frequency table to create a histogram.

Number of hours	Number of weekends
0	2
1	0
2	0
3	2
4	4
5	6
6	4
7	2

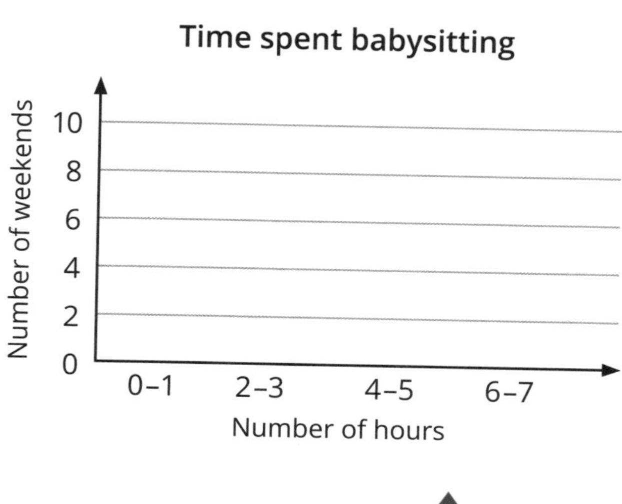

176 Box and whisker plots

Learn!

A **box and whisker plot**, or box plot, is a type of graph that displays the five-number summary of a data set along a number line. The five-number summary includes the **minimum**, **first quartile**, **median**, **third quartile**, and **maximum** of the data set.

Try it! Make a box plot for this data set: 7, 9, 11, 15, 6, 7, 15, 9, 12, 13.

First, order the data set from least to greatest. Then, find the median. For this example, the median is 10.

6 7 7 9 9 | 11 12 13 15 15

$$\frac{9 + 11}{2} = 10$$

Next, find the first and third quartiles. Here, the first quartile is 7, and the third quartile is 13.

6 7 (7) 9 9 | 11 12 (13) 15 15

Then, find the minimum and maximum. The minimum is 6, and the maximum is 15.

(6) 7 7 9 9 11 12 13 15 (15)

Finally, use the number line and the five-number summary to make your box plot.

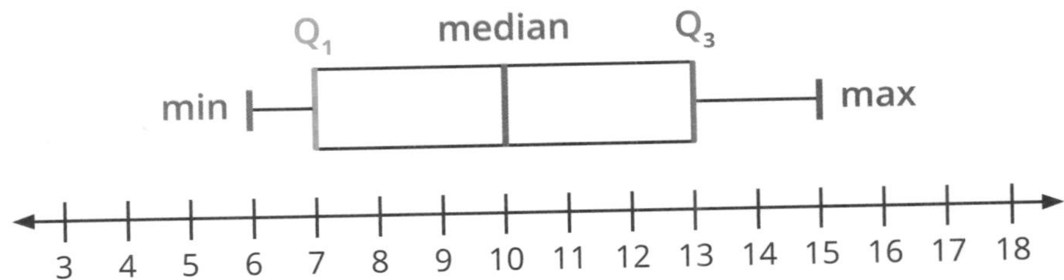

Find the five-number summary and make a box plot for the data set.

17 13 11 10 14 14 16 18 15 9

Minimum = ________

Q_1 = ________

Median = ________

Q_3 = ________

5 6 7 8 9 10 11 12 13 14 15 16 17 18 19 20

Maximum = ________

Keep going! Find the five-number summary and make a box plot for each data set.

Minimum = ________

Q_1 = ________

Median = ________

Q_3 = ________

Maximum = ________

33 28 31 34 36 34 29 33

Minimum = ________

Q_1 = ________

Median = ________

Q_3 = ________

Maximum = ________

12 18 23 26 27 15 16 26 13

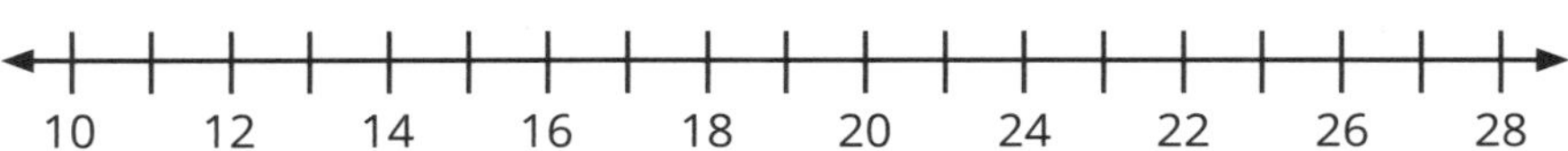

Minimum = ________

Q_1 = ________

Median = ________

Q_3 = ________

Maximum = ________

37 45 40 39 38 43 41 44 42 43 38

Shapes of distributions

Learn!

A graph shows the shape of a distribution. The distribution of values in a data set can be symmetric or skewed. Examples of the different shapes of distributions are shown below.

Symmetric distributions

Uniform: All bars are about the same height.

Symmetric: The left and right sides are mirror images of each other.

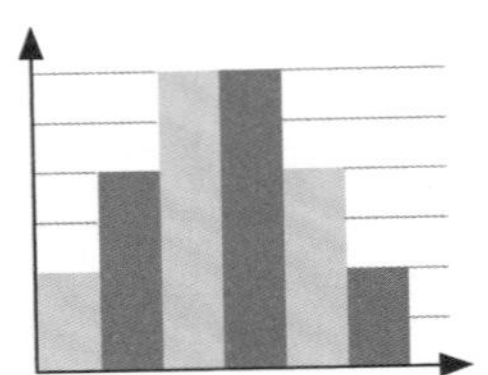

In symmetric distributions, both the mean and the median are appropriate to describe the center. Both the MAD and the IQR are appropriate to describe the variation.

Skewed distributions

Skewed left: Most of the data values are on the right. The tail is on the left.

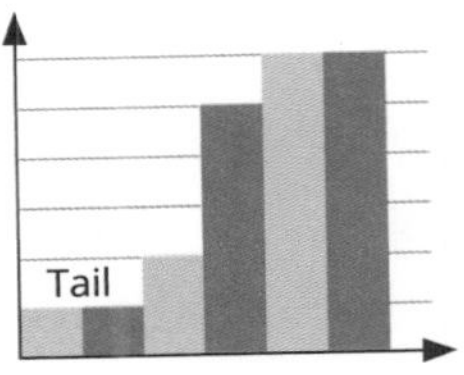

Skewed right: Most of the data values are on the left. The tail is on the right.

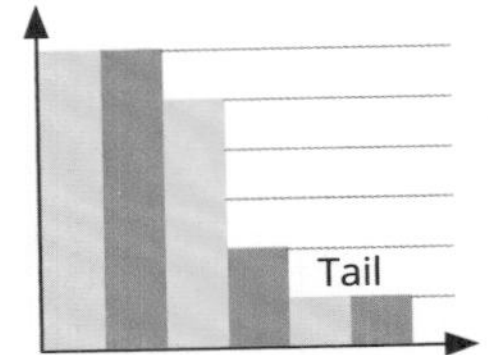

The mean and MAD can be strongly affected by a skewed distribution. So, it is more appropriate to use the median to describe the center and the IQR to describe the variation.

Choose the appropriate measures to describe each data set. There may be more than one correct answer.

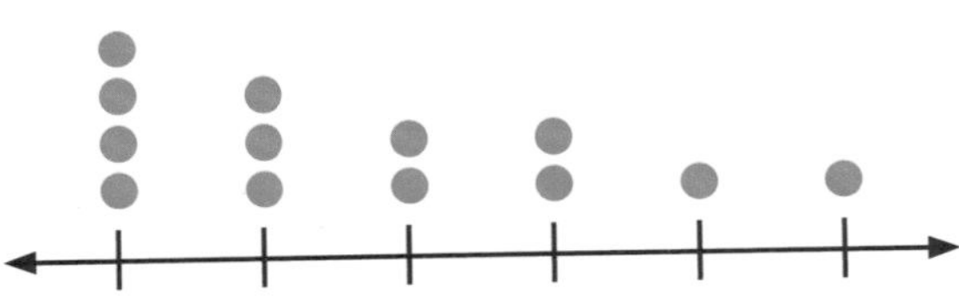

Shape: Symmetric Skewed

Measure of center: Mean Median

Measure of variability: MAD IQR

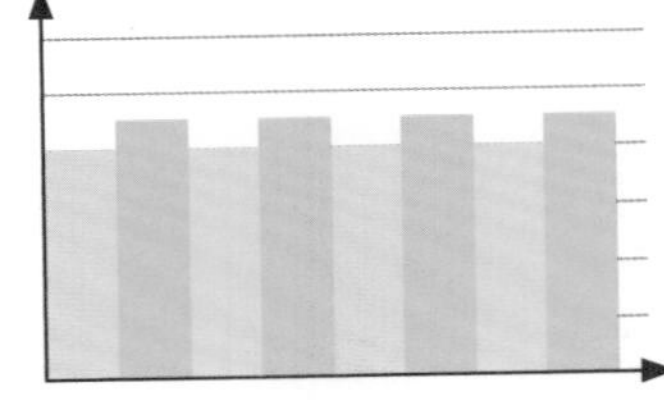

Shape: Symmetric Skewed

Measure of center: Mean Median

Measure of variability: MAD IQR

IXL.com skill ID **ES2**

Calculate the mean, median, mode, and range of the data set shown in each dot plot. Then describe the shape of the distribution.

The owner of Green Box Bakery asks customers to rate the new cinnamon-chili brownie on a scale of 1 to 10.

Mean = ________ Median = ________

Mode = ________ Range = ________

Shape: ____________________________

Ron uses the weather app on his phone to track the daily high temperature in Oak Valley.

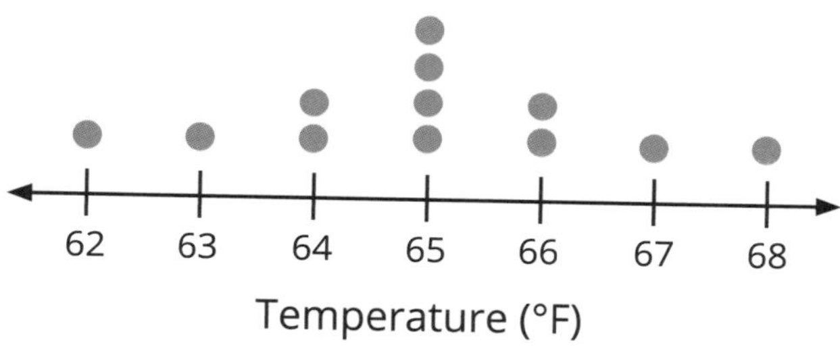

Mean = ________ Median = ________

Mode = ________ Range = ________

Shape: ____________________________

Brianna kept track of the total number of goals her soccer team scored in each game.

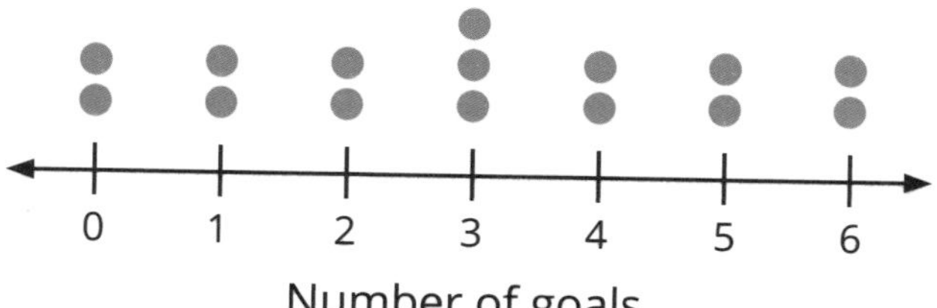

Mean = ________ Median = ________

Mode = ________ Range = ________

Shape: ____________________________

IXL.com skill ID RZL

Histograms

Describe the shape of each distribution. Then answer each question about the data set shown in the histogram.

Jaylen asks a group of his friends how many siblings they each have.

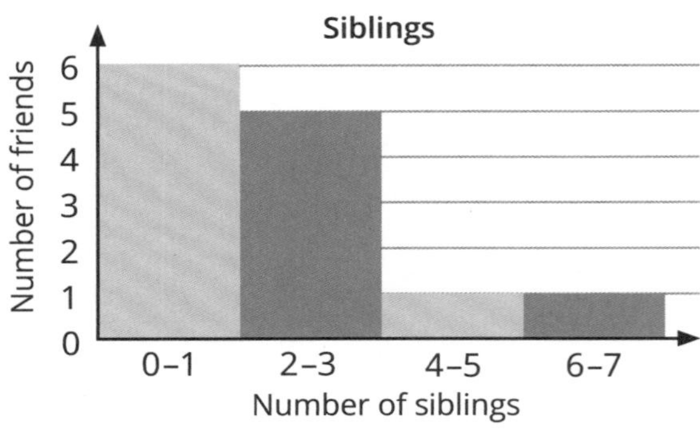

Shape: ______________________

How many friends did Jaylen ask?

____

Maura records the number of minutes she practices her viola each night.

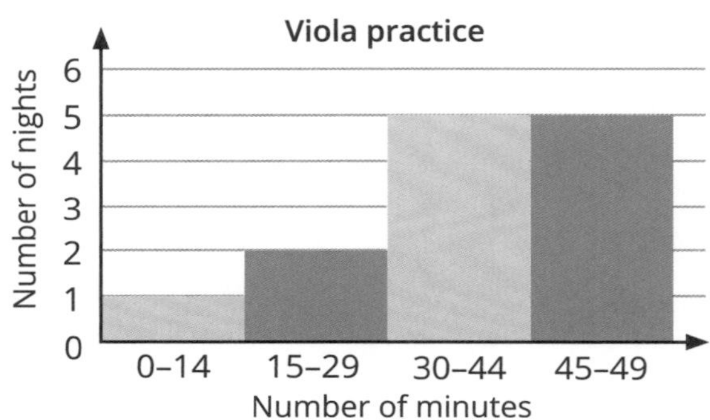

Shape: ______________________

Which interval contains the fewest data values? ______________________

Edward found out how many students are in each club at his school.

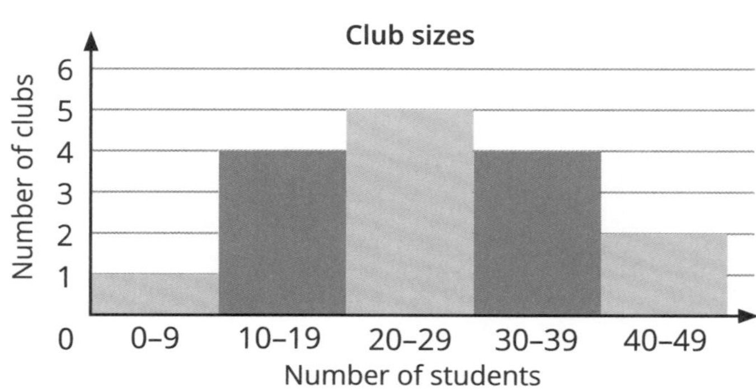

Shape: ______________________

Which interval contains the most data values? ______________________

How many clubs have fewer than 30 students? ______________________

IXL.com skill ID **CBF**

Calculate the measure of center and variation of the data set shown in each box and whisker plot. Then answer the question. Remember that each of the four sections of a box and whisker plot represents 25% of the data.

Judith surveyed some classmates to see how many times each person went to the beach during the summer.

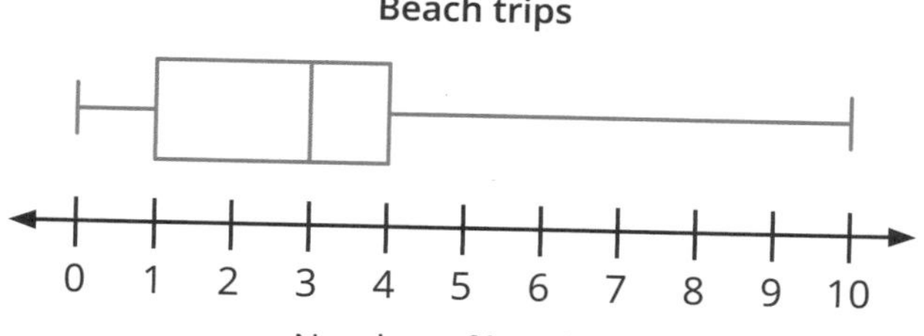

Median = __________ IQR = __________

What percent of those surveyed went to the beach 3 or more times?

____

Ms. Kathy records how many students attend the pottery class she teaches each week.

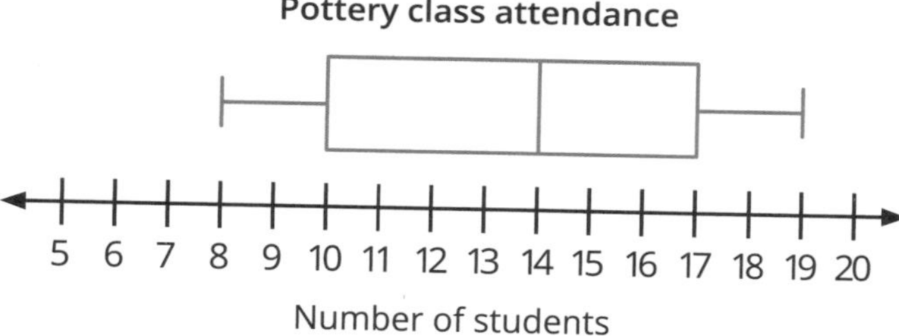

Median = __________ Range = __________

What percent of the classes had between 10 and 17 students? __________

The Oak City Nature Preserve surveys some houses in a neighborhood to see how many trees each one has on its property.

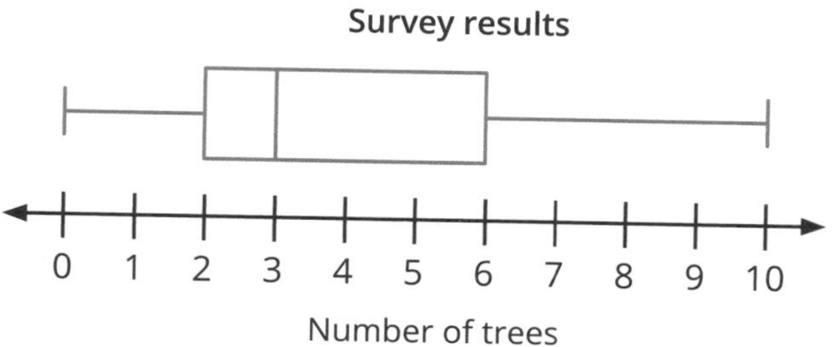

Median = __________ IQR = __________

What percent of the homes surveyed have more than 6 trees? __________

IXL.com skill ID E9F

Area of triangles

Learn!

To find the area of a triangle with base ***b*** and height ***h***, use the formula $A = \frac{1}{2}bh$.
Try it! Find the area of the triangle below.

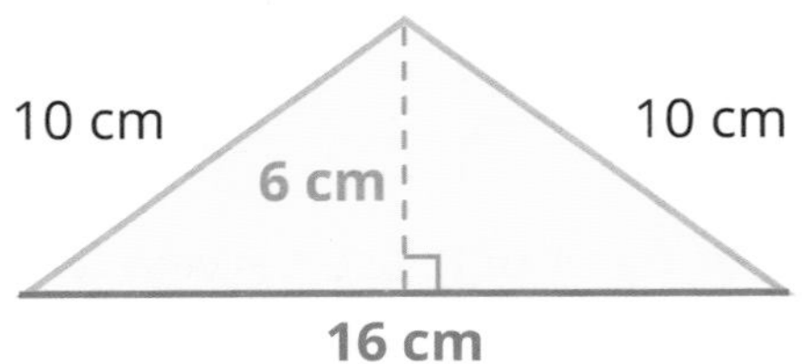

$A = \frac{1}{2} \cdot 16 \cdot 6$

$A = \frac{1}{2} \cdot 96$

$A = 48\ cm^2$

Find the area of each triangle.

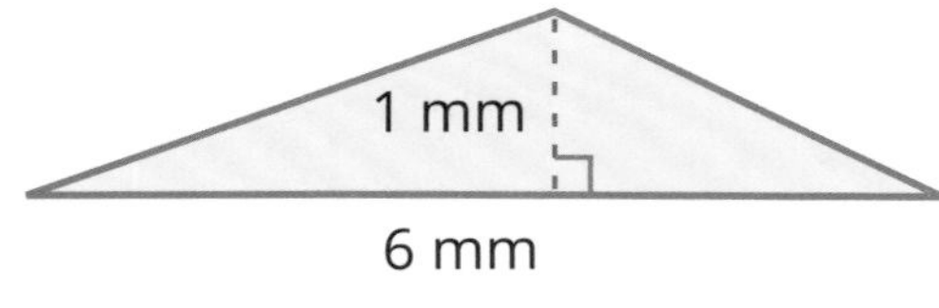

$A =$ ____________________

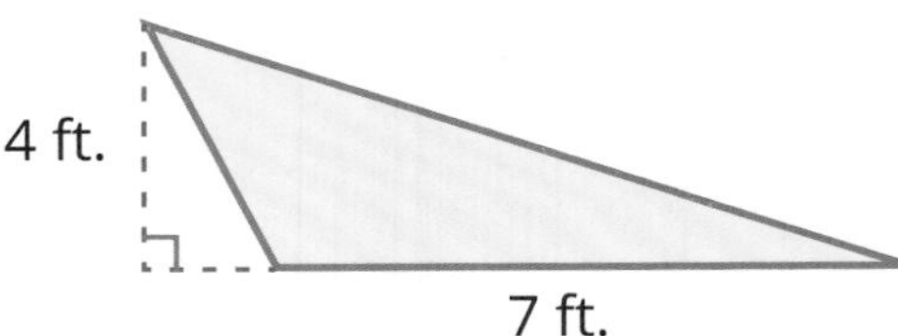

$A =$ ____________________

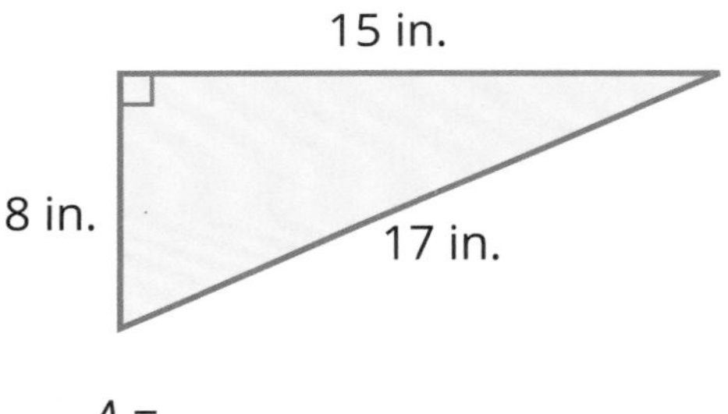

$A =$ ____________________

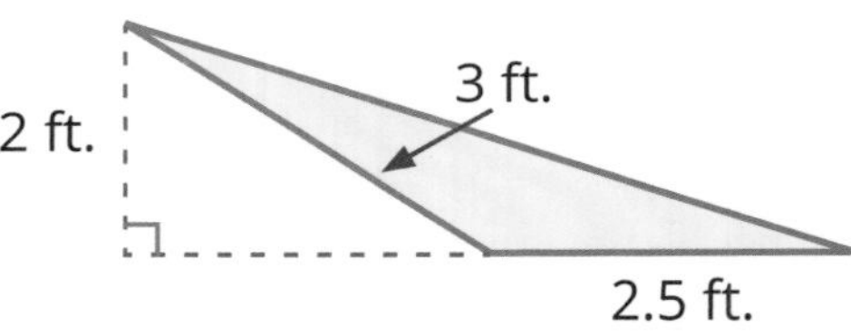

$A =$ ____________________

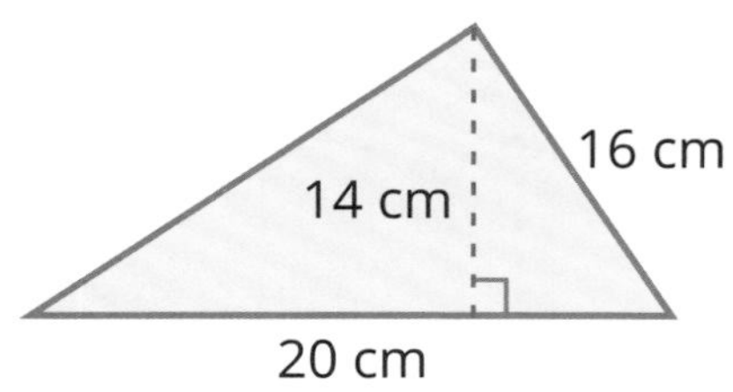

$A =$ ____________________

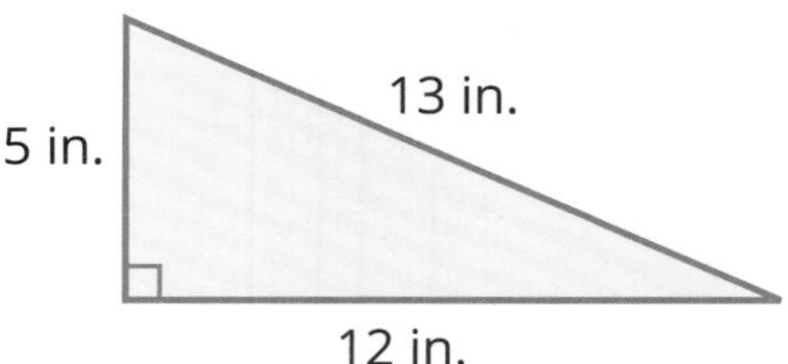

$A =$ ____________________

Use the given area to find the missing base or height of each triangle.

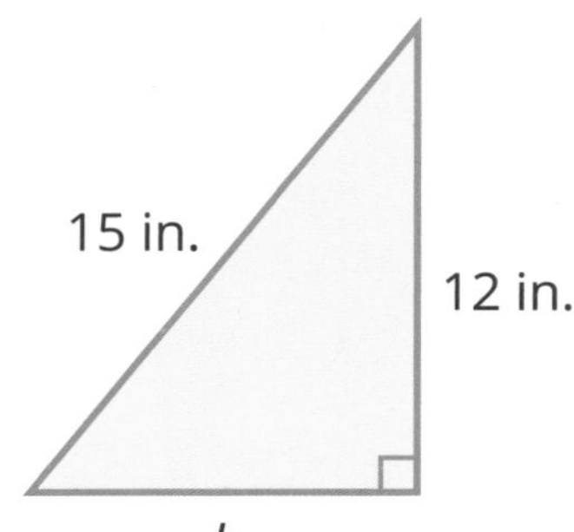

$A = 54$ in.^{2}

b = ____________

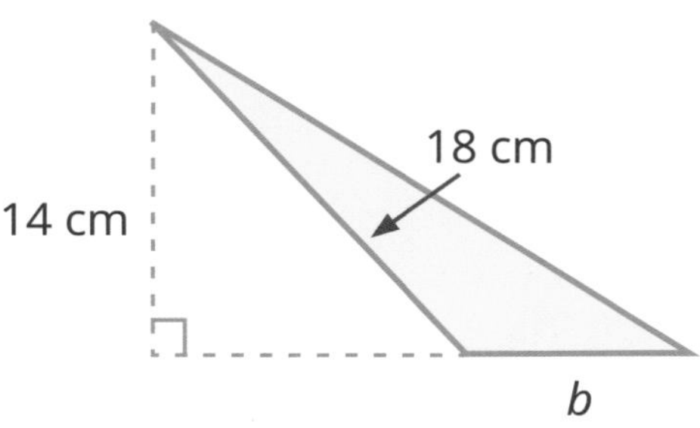

$A = 49$ cm^2

b = ____________

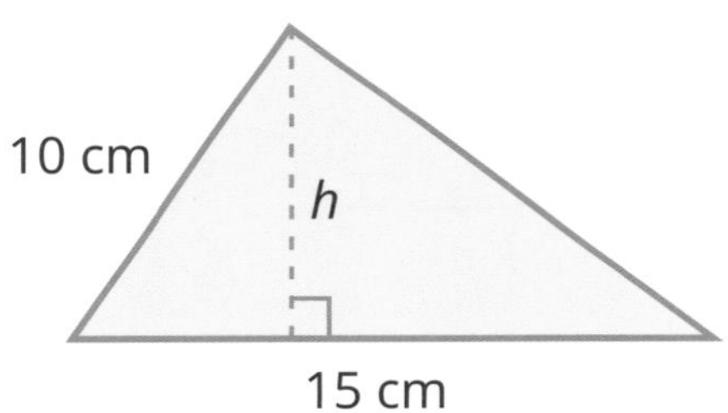

$A = 60$ cm^2

h = ____________

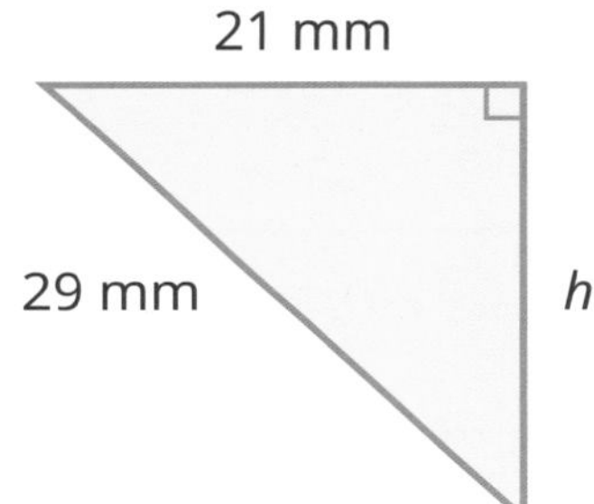

$A = 210$ mm^2

h = ____________

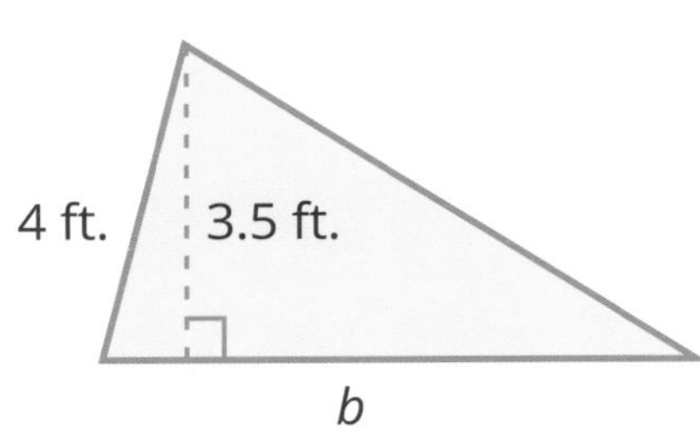

$A = 14$ ft.^{2}

b = ____________

184 Area of parallelograms

Learn!

To find the area of a parallelogram with base b and height h, use the formula $A = bh$.
Try it! Find the area of the parallelogram below.

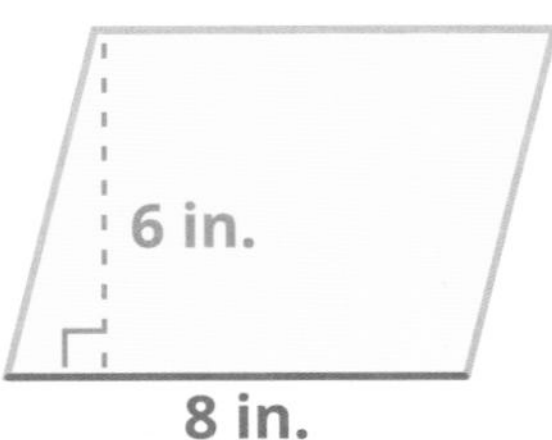

$A = 8 \cdot 6$

$A = 48 \text{ in.}^2$

Find the area of each parallelogram.

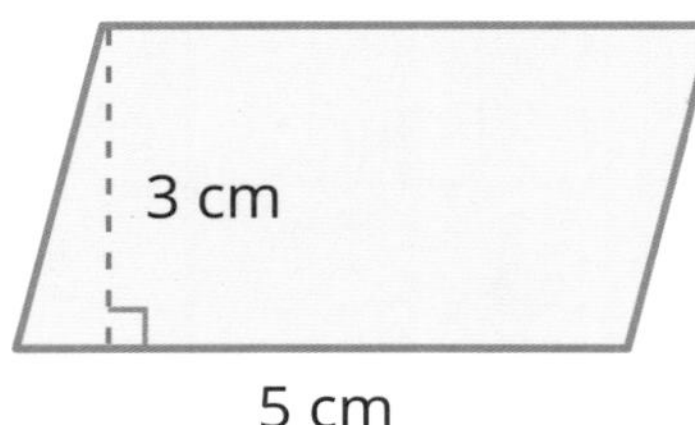

$A =$ ____________________

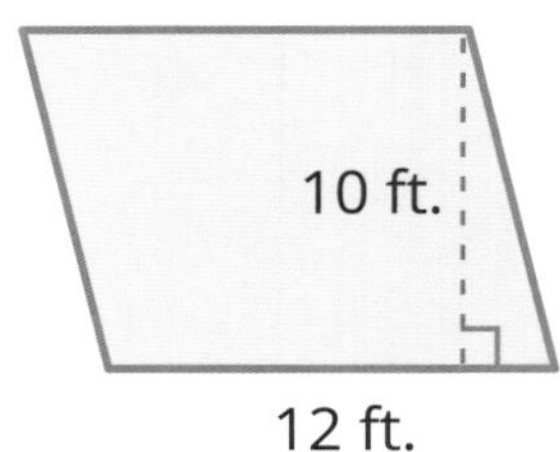

$A =$ ____________________

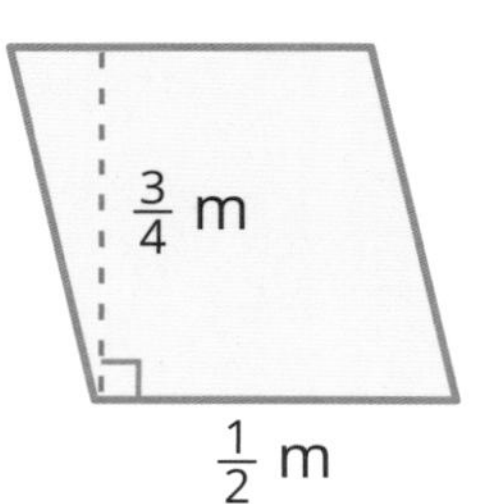

$A =$ ____________________

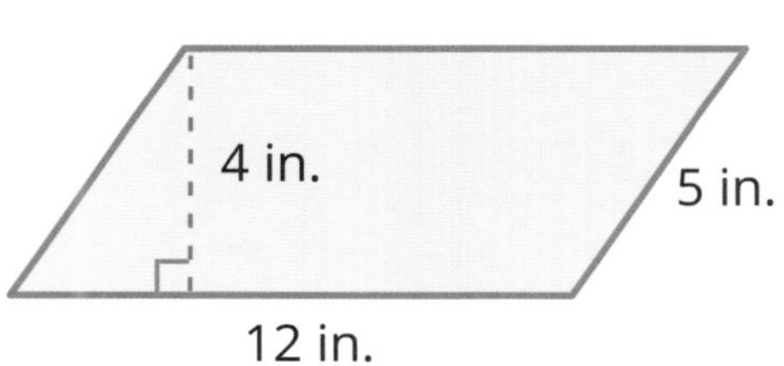

$A =$ ____________________

4.5 in.

3 in.

14 in.

$A =$ ____________________

Learn!

To find the area of a trapezoid with bases b_1 and b_2 and height h, use the formula $A = \frac{1}{2}(b_1 + b_2)h$. Try it! Find the area of the trapezoid below.

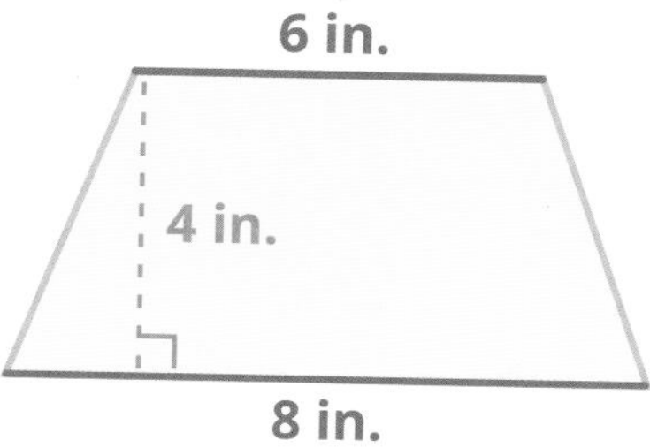

$A = \frac{1}{2}(8 + 6) \cdot 4$

$A = \frac{1}{2} \cdot 14 \cdot 4$

$A = 28 \text{ in.}^2$

Find the area of each trapezoid.

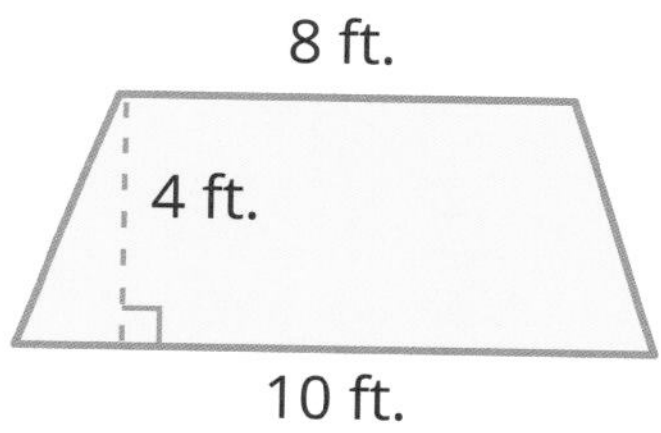

$A =$ ________________

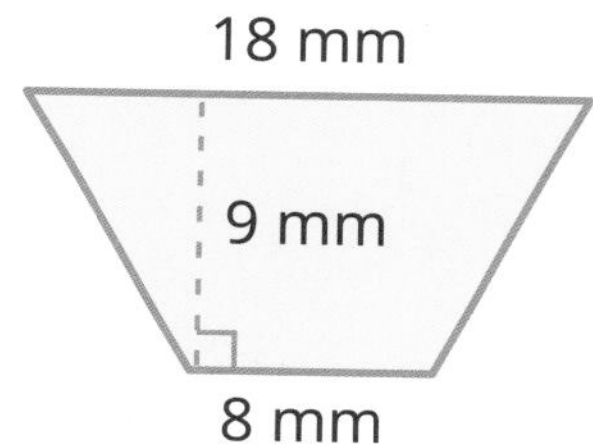

$A =$ ________________

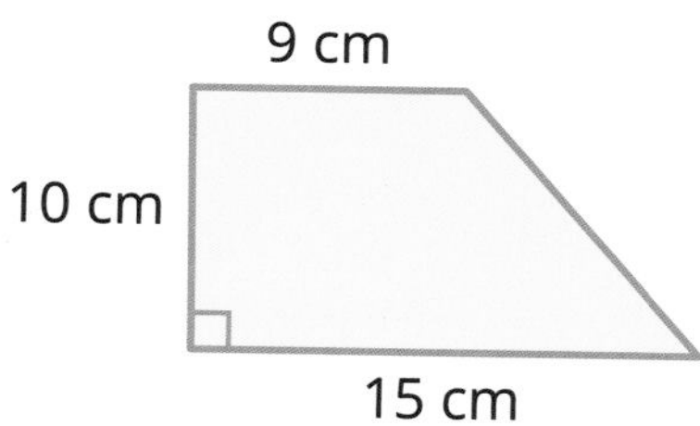

$A =$ ________________

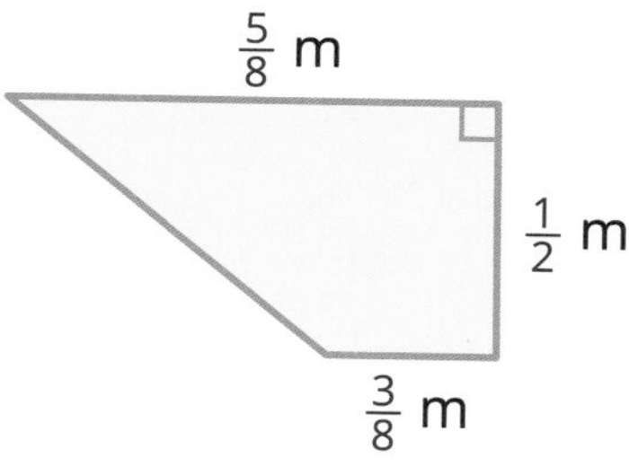

$A =$ ________________

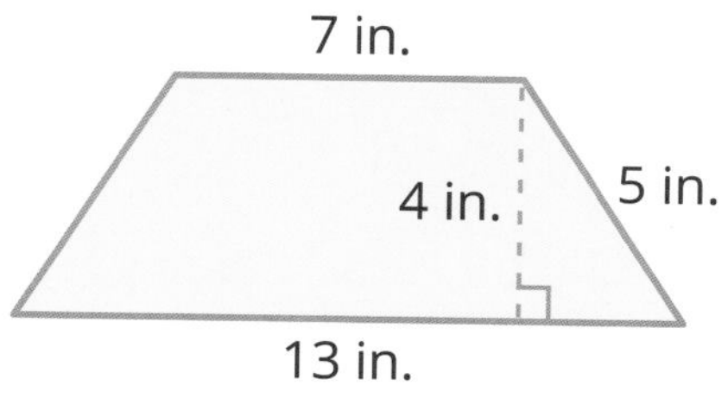

$A =$ ________________

Perimeter on the coordinate plane

You can draw polygons on the coordinate plane by plotting ordered pairs and drawing lines between them. Graph each shape on the coordinate plane. Then find its perimeter.

A(8, 6) *B*(3, 6) *C*(3, 1) *D*(8, 1)	*Q*(2, −2) *R*(2, −1) *S*(−4, −1) *T*(−4, −2)
Perimeter = ________ units	Perimeter = ________ units
W(−6, −4) *X*(−9, −4) *Y*(−9, 2) *Z*(−6, 2)	*J*(−4, 5) *K*(−8, 5) *L*(−8, 9) *M*(−4, 9)
Perimeter = ________ units	Perimeter = ________ units

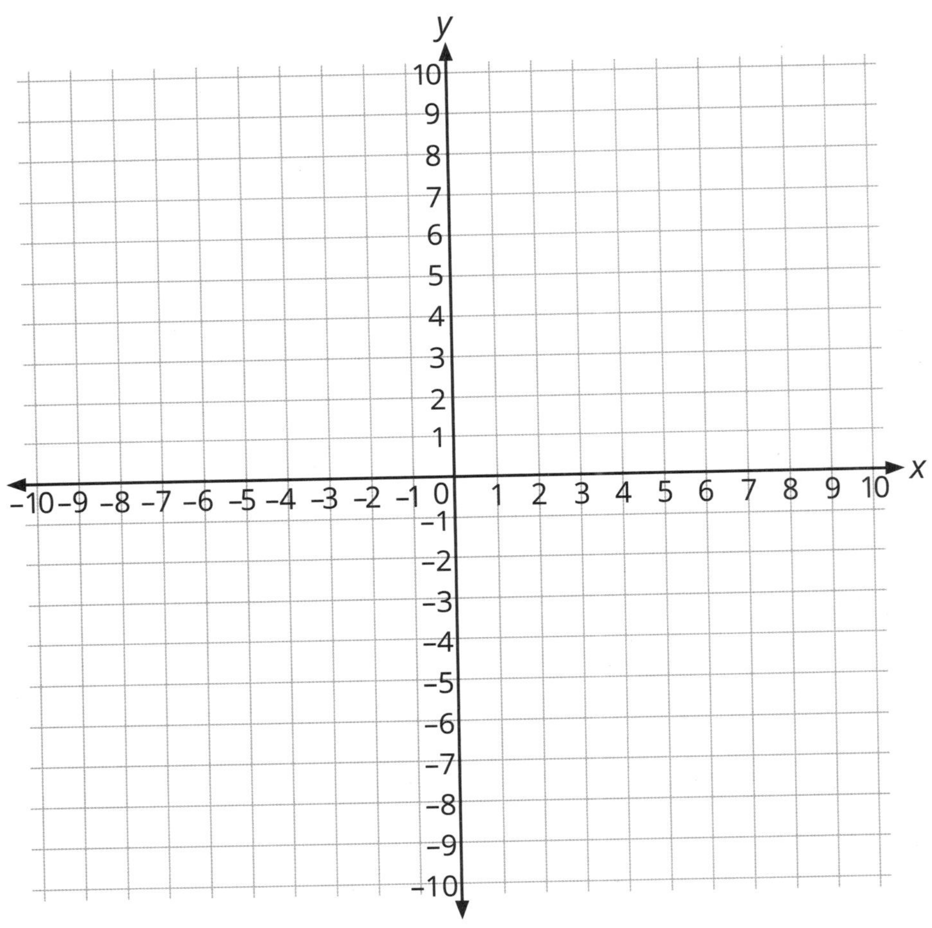

Area on the coordinate plane

Graph each shape on the coordinate plane. Then find its area.

$T(7, 3)$ $U(7, -2)$ $V(5, -2)$ $W(5, 3)$	$K(4, -4)$ $L(6, -4)$ $M(8, -7)$, $N(4, -7)$
Area = __________ square units	Area = __________ square units
$A(-8, -9)$ $B(-4, -9)$ $C(-6, -7)$	$P(-7, 4)$ $Q(-7, 9)$ $R(2, 4)$
Area = __________ square units	Area = __________ square units

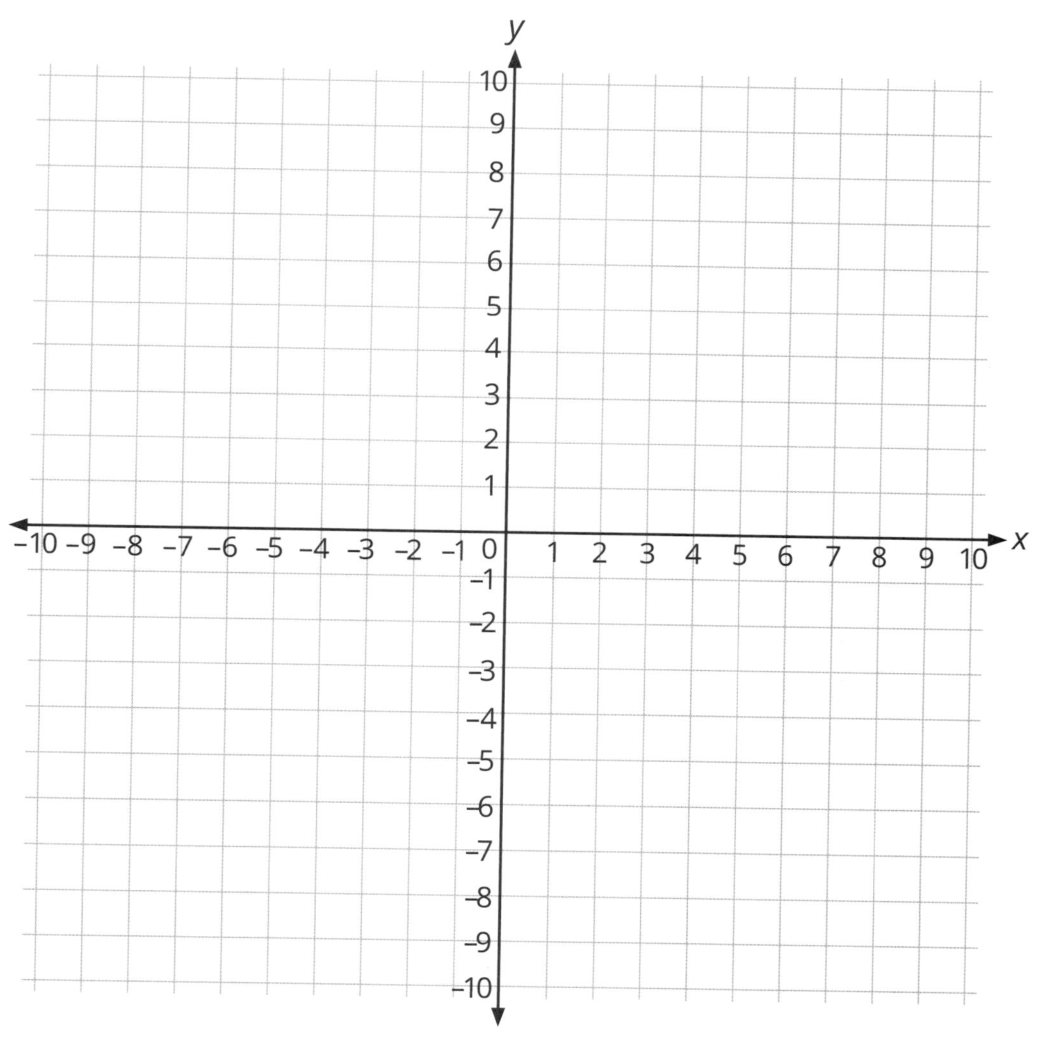

Exploration Zone

You have already found the areas of triangles and quadrilaterals. Now, use the grid to find the area of each figure below.

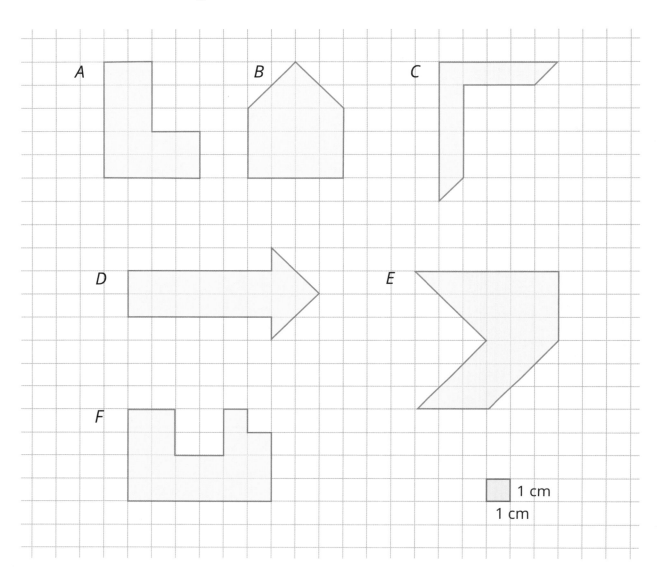

Area of figure *A* = ____________________

Area of figure *B* = ____________________

Area of figure *C* = ____________________

Area of figure *D* = ____________________

Area of figure *E* = ____________________

Area of figure *F* = ____________________

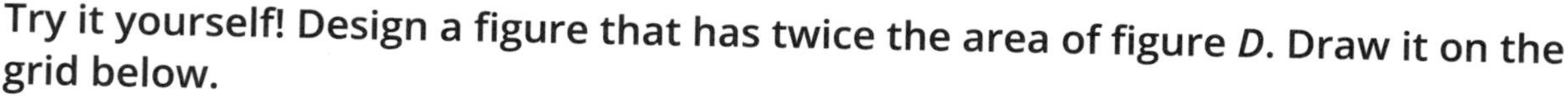

Try it yourself! Design a figure that has twice the area of figure *D*. Draw it on the grid below.

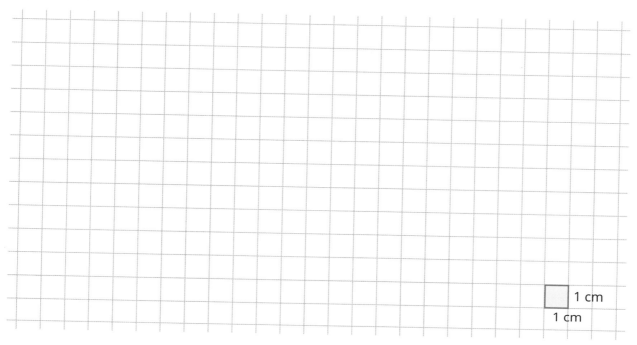

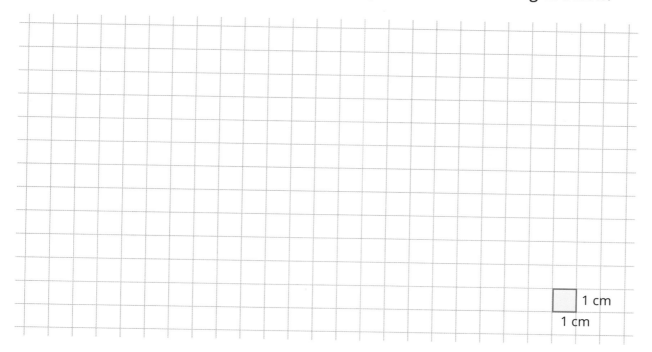

Now, design a figure that has half the area of figure *F*. Draw it on the grid below.

Area of compound figures

A **compound figure** is made up of basic shapes put together. To find the area of a compound figure, break the compound figure into basic shapes, such as rectangles or triangles. Then find the area of each basic shape and add the areas together.

Find the area of each compound figure.

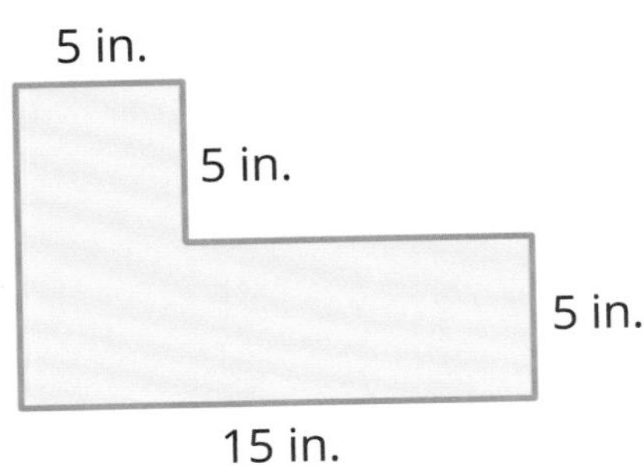

A = ____________

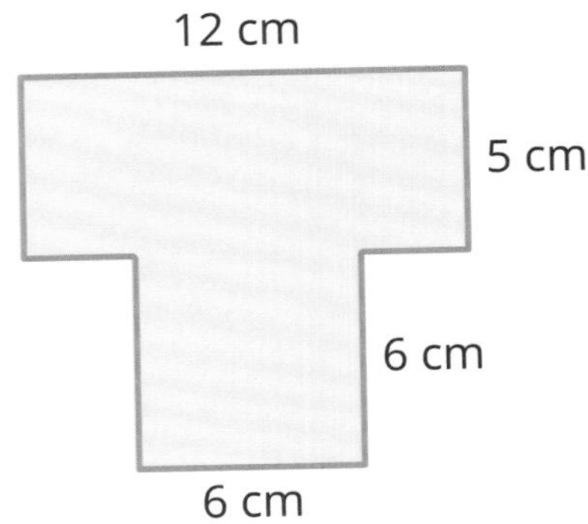

A = ____________

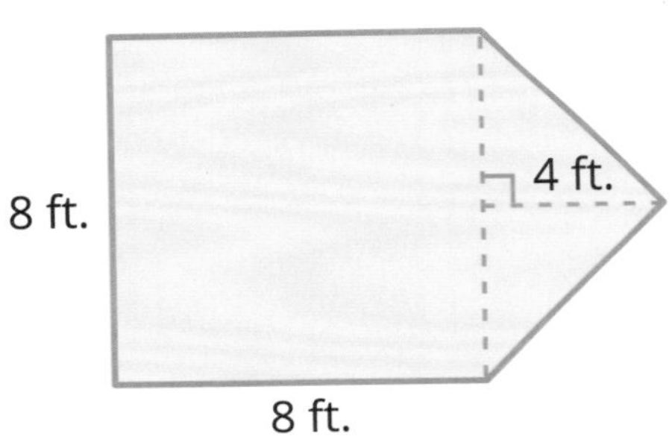

A = ____________

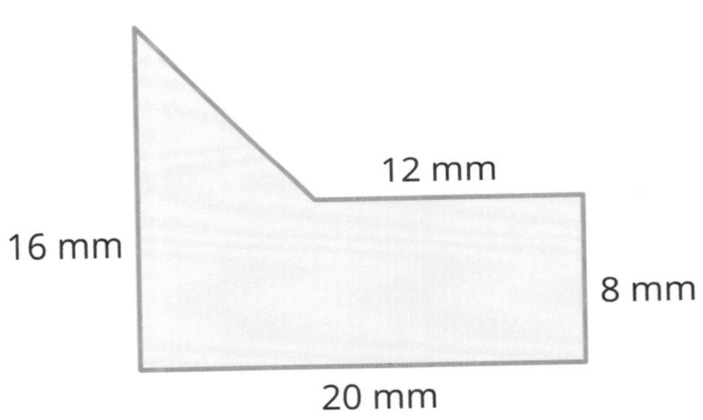

A = ____________

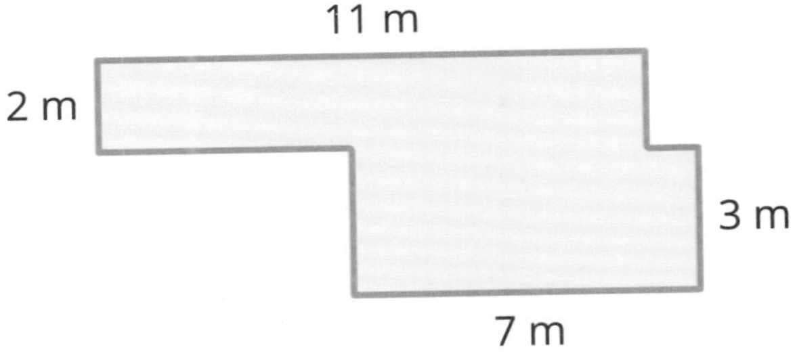

A = ____________

Keep going! Find the area of each compound figure.

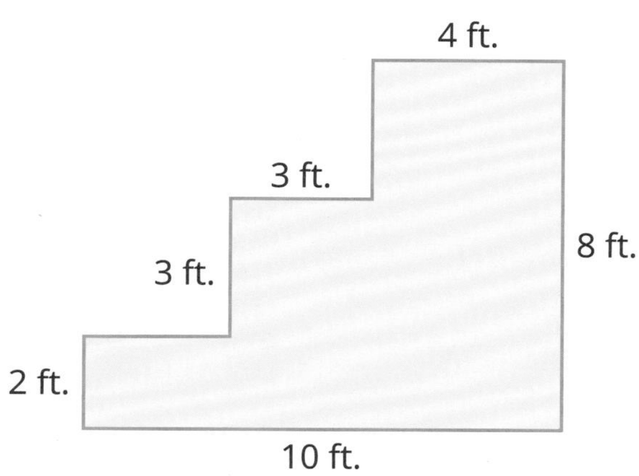

$A =$ ________________

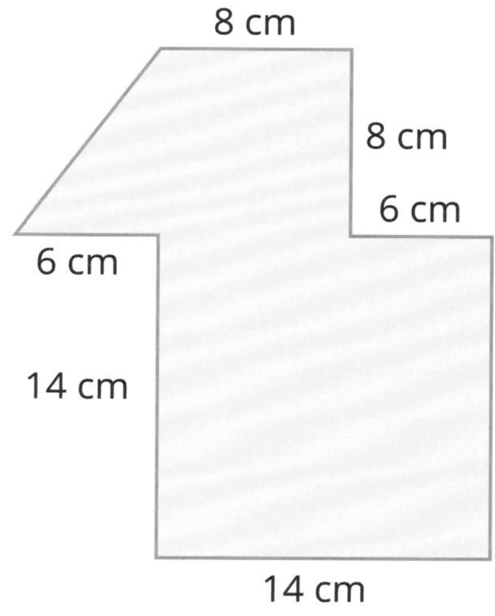

$A =$ ________________

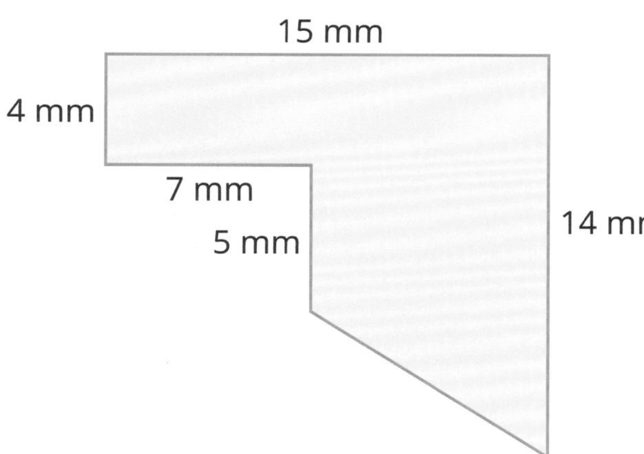

$A =$ ________________

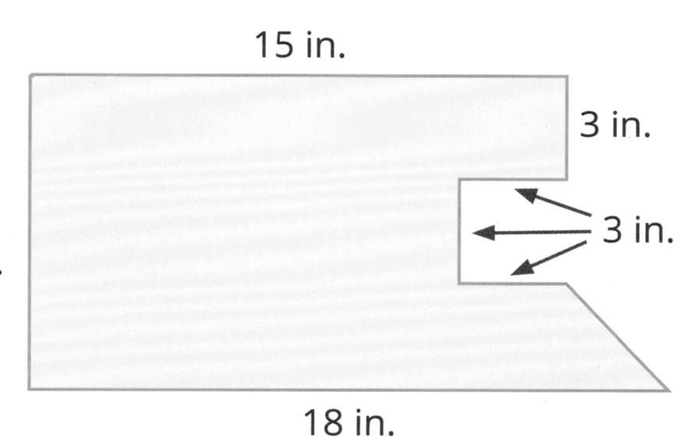

$A =$ ________________

Classifying solid figures

Learn!

A **polyhedron** is a three-dimensional figure. It is made of flat, polygon-shaped sides called **faces**. The line segment where two faces meet is called an **edge**. The point where three or more edges meet is called a **vertex**.

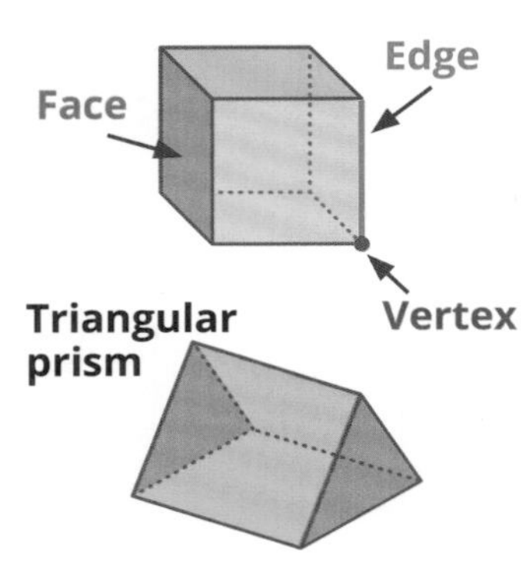

A **prism** is a polyhedron. A prism has two identical parallel faces called bases. All other faces of a prism are parallelograms. A prism is named by the shape of its base. Here, this prism is called a triangular prism because the base is a triangle.

A **pyramid** is also a polyhedron. A pyramid has one base, and all other faces of a pyramid are triangles that meet at a vertex. A pyramid is named by the shape of its base, too. Here, this pyramid is called a square pyramid because the base is a square.

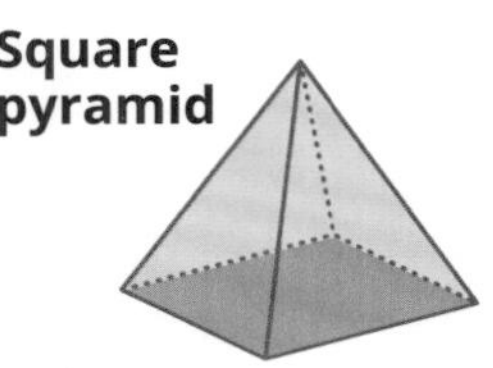

Classify each solid figure. Remember to use the shape of the base to help name each figure.

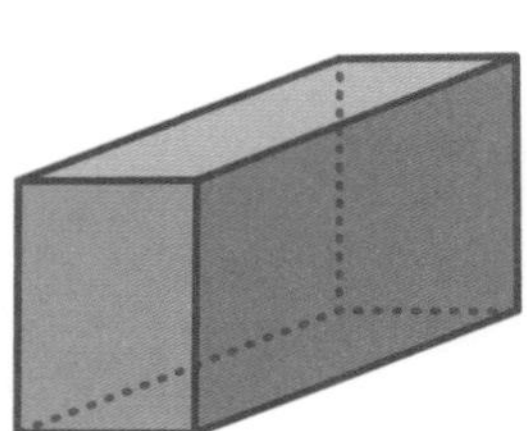

rectangular prism

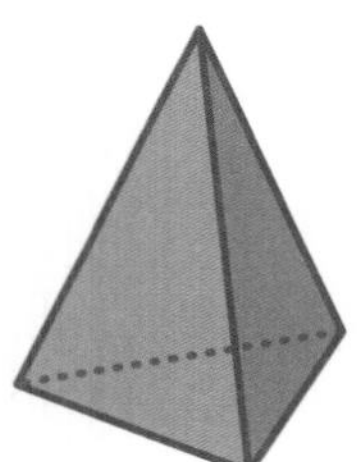

____

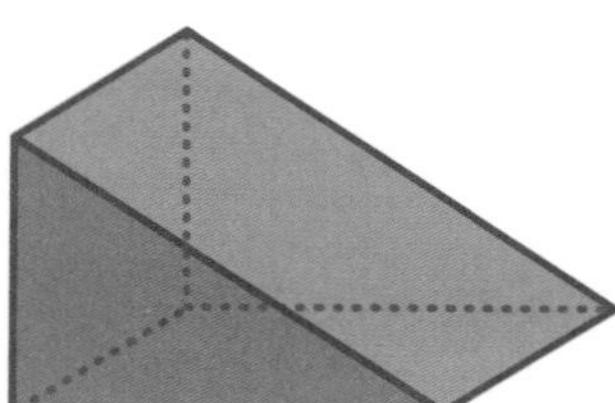

____

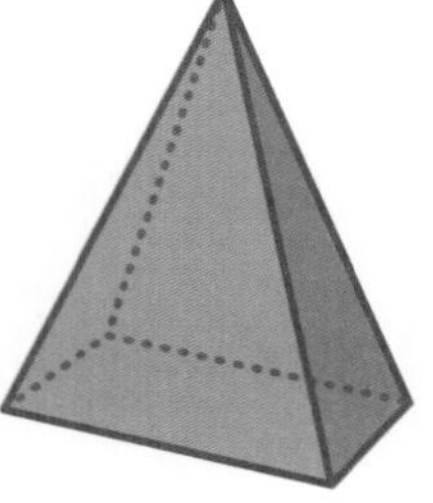

____

Learn!

A **net** is a two-dimensional pattern that can be folded to make a three-dimensional figure. Look at the example. This net can be folded to make a triangular pyramid.

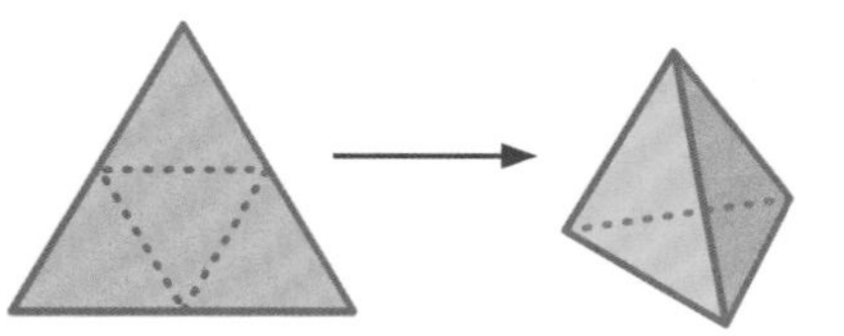

Draw a line matching the net to its 3D figure.

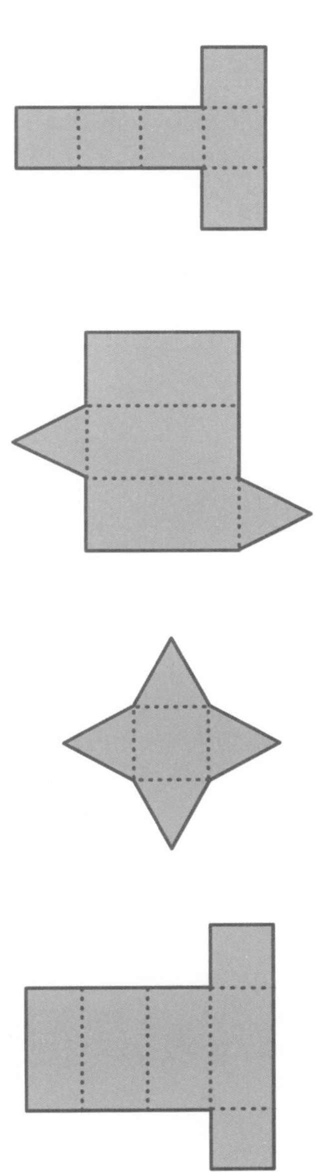

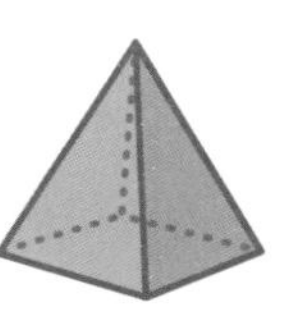

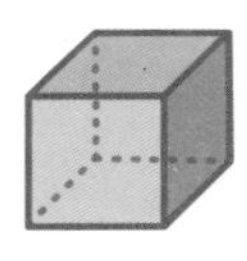

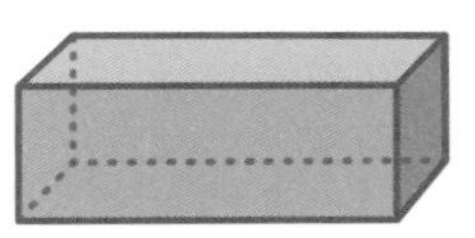

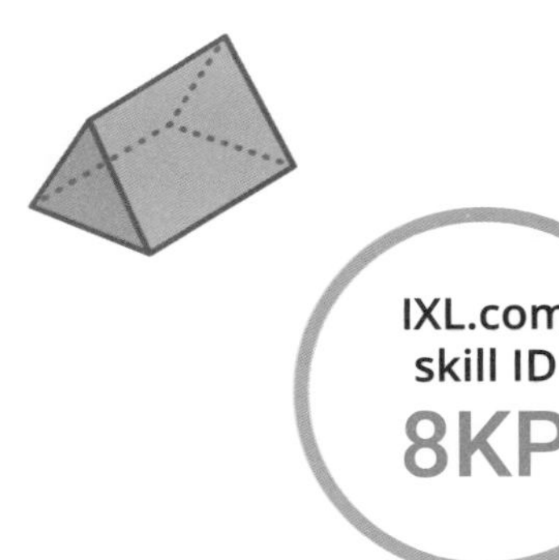

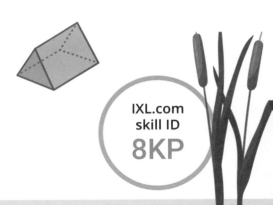

Learn!

Surface area is the sum of the areas of all the faces, or surfaces, of a three-dimensional figure. You can use a net to help you find surface area because it shows you all the faces at one time. Try it! Find the surface area of the rectangular prism below.

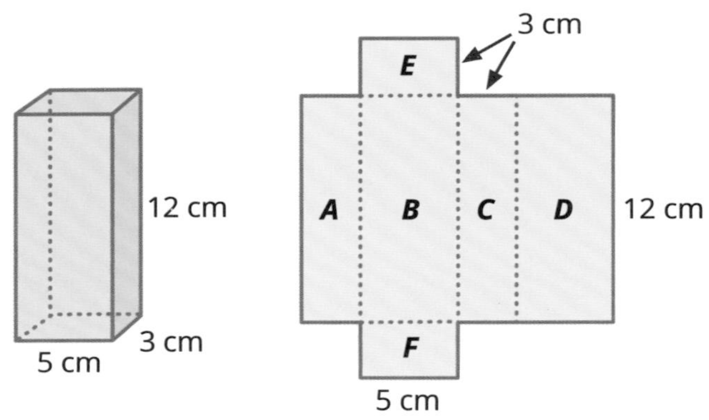

First, find the area of each face. Here, all the faces are rectangles.

***A*: 12 · 3 = 36 cm²** ***D*: 12 · 5 = 60 cm²**
***B*: 12 · 5 = 60 cm²** ***E*: 3 · 5 = 15 cm²**
***C*: 12 · 3 = 36 cm²** ***F*: 3 · 5 = 15 cm²**

Next, add all of the areas together.

36 + 60 + 36 + 60 + 15 + 15 = 222 cm²

So, the surface area of the rectangular prism is 222 square centimeters.

Find the surface area of each prism. Use the net to help.

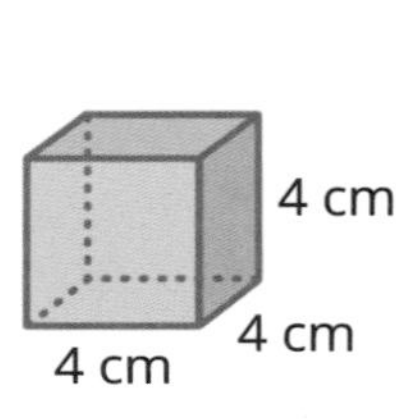

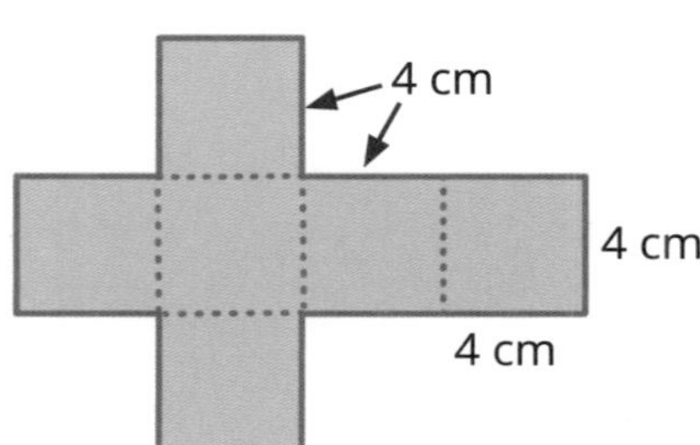

Surface area = ________________

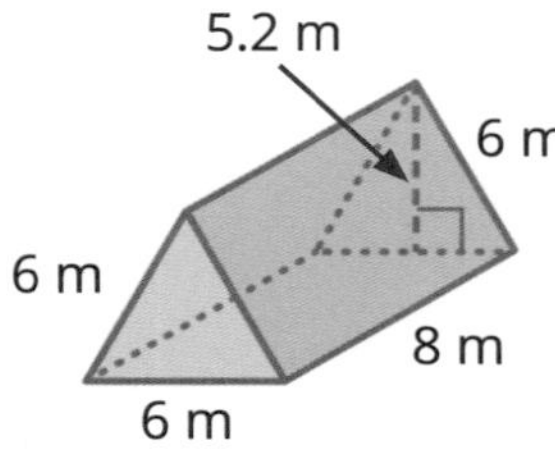

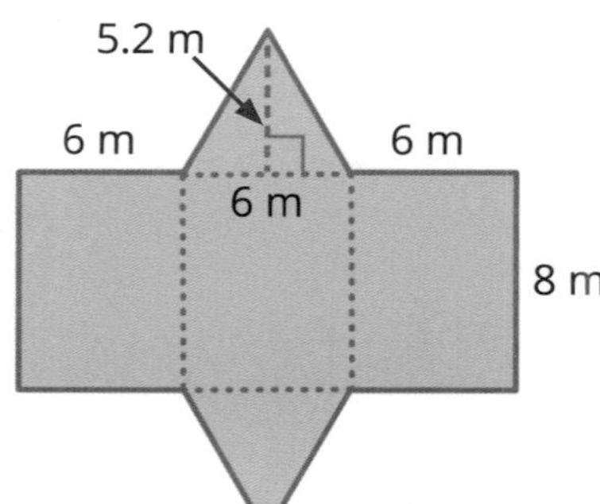

Surface area = ________________

Keep going! Find the surface area of each prism.

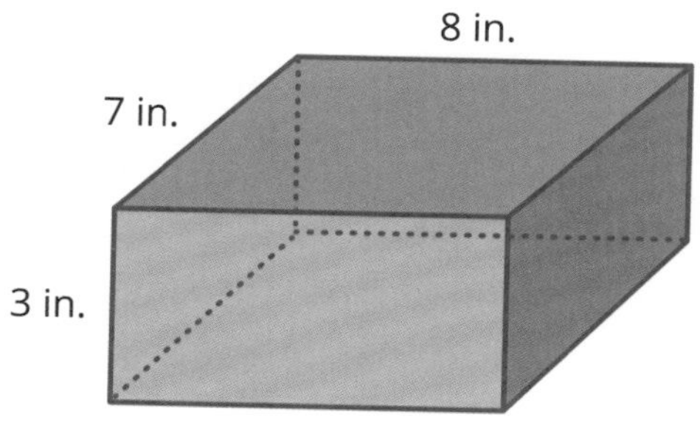

Surface area = ________________

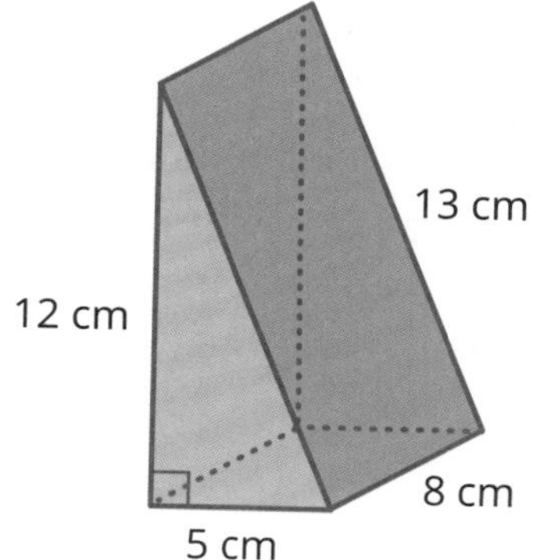

Surface area = ________________

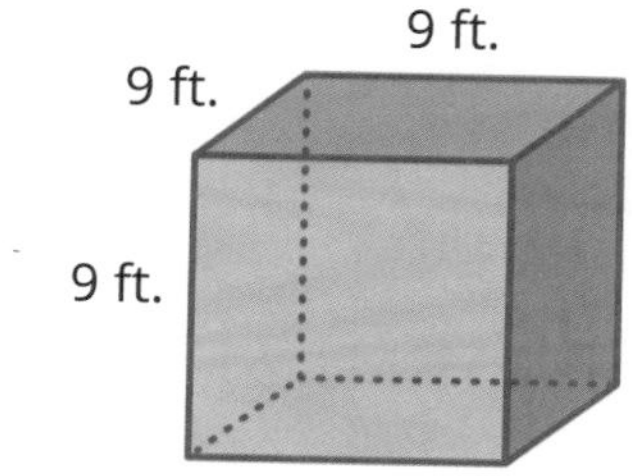

Surface area = ________________

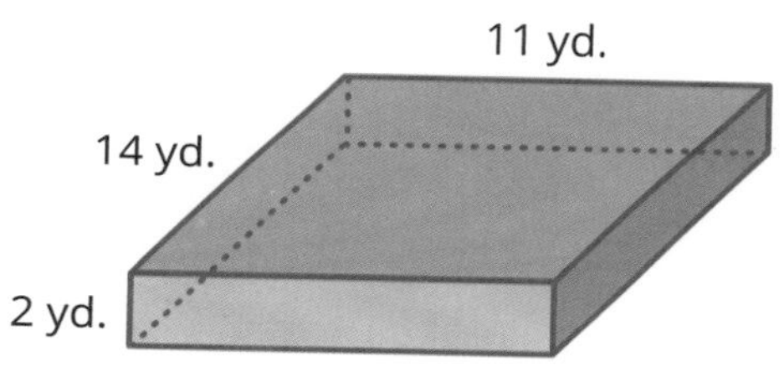

Surface area = ________________

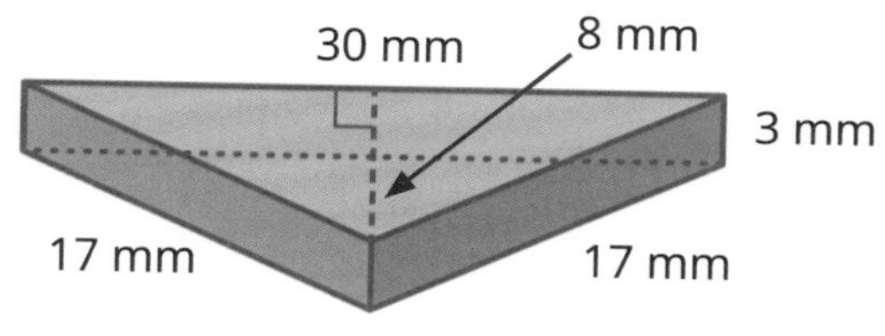

Surface area = ________________

Surface area of pyramids

Learn!

You can use a net to find the surface area of a pyramid, too. Find the area of each face. Then add the areas of all the faces together.

Try it! Find the area of the triangular pyramid below. The base of the pyramid, *B*, is an equilateral triangle, and faces *A*, *C*, and *D* are congruent triangles.

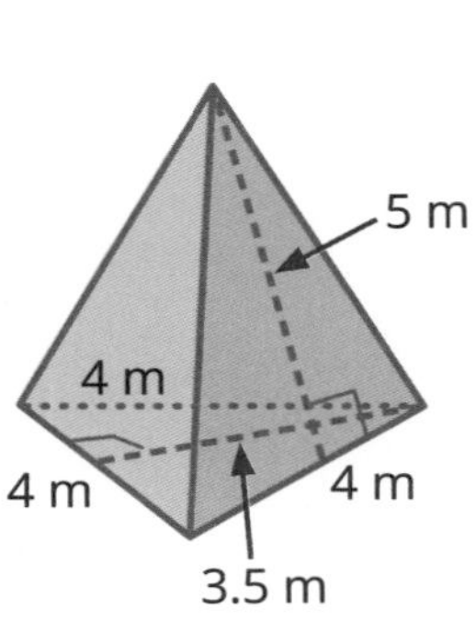

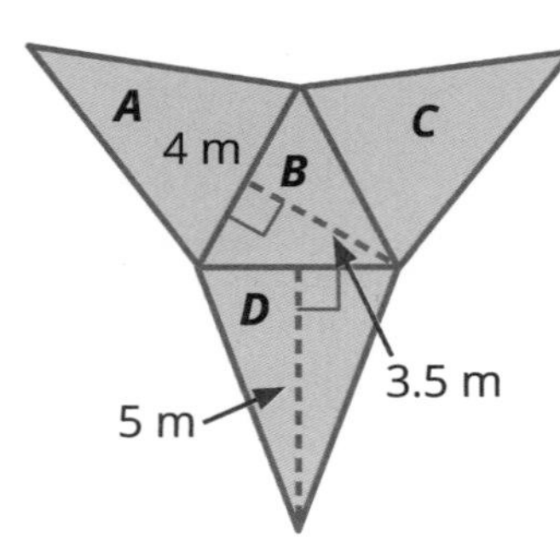

A: $\frac{1}{2} \cdot 4 \cdot 5 = 10 \text{ m}^2$

B: $\frac{1}{2} \cdot 4 \cdot 3.5 = 7 \text{ m}^2$

C: $\frac{1}{2} \cdot 4 \cdot 5 = 10 \text{ m}^2$

D: $\frac{1}{2} \cdot 4 \cdot 5 = 10 \text{ m}^2$

Surface area = 10 + 7 + 10 + 10 = 37 m²

So, the surface area of the triangular pyramid is 37 square meters.

Find the surface area of each pyramid. Use the net to help.

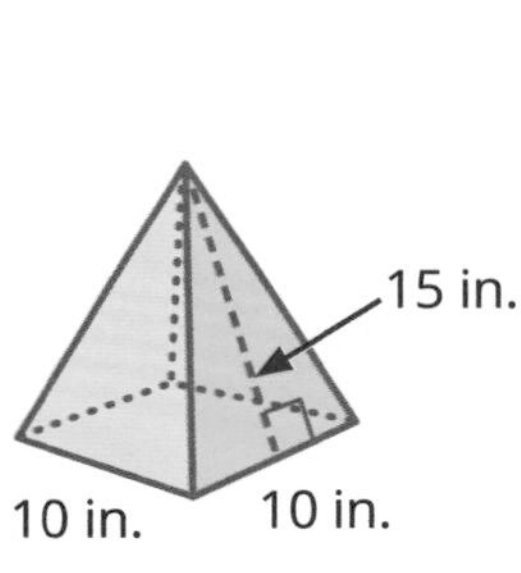

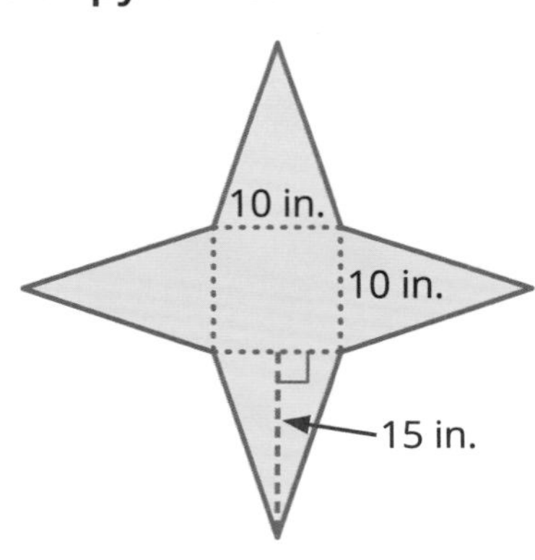

Surface area = ____________

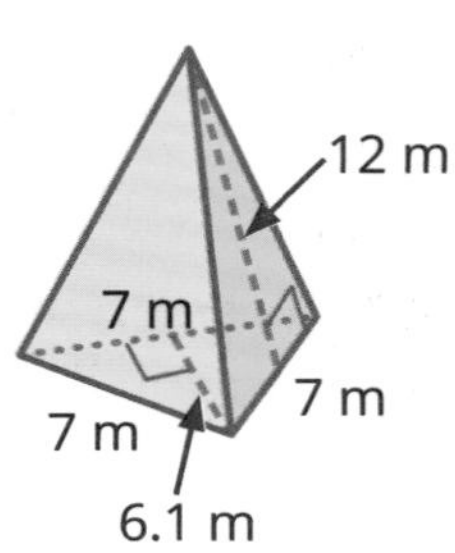

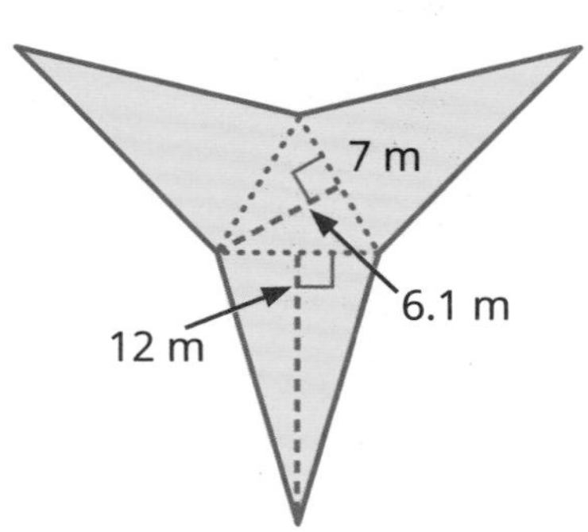

Surface area = ____________

Keep going! Find the surface area of each pyramid.

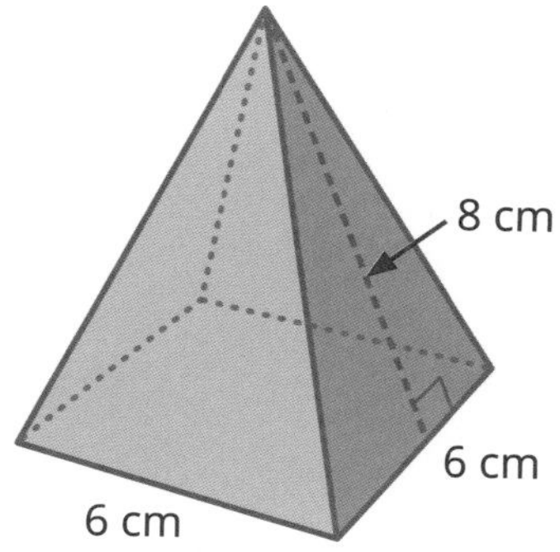

Surface area = ____________

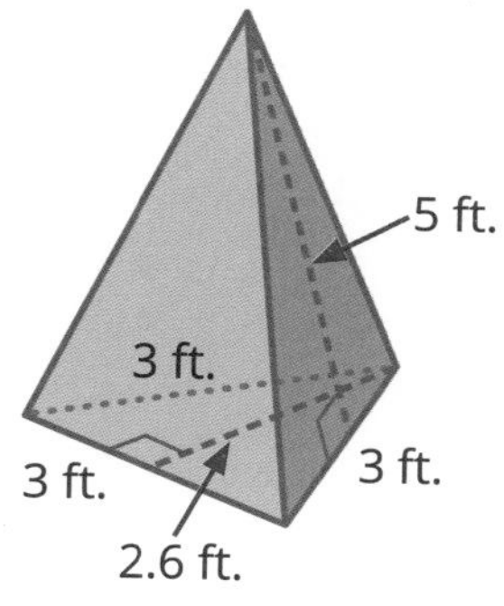

Surface area = ____________

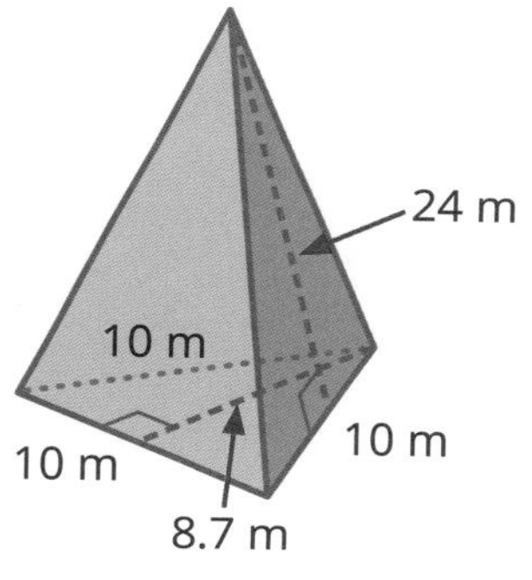

Surface area = ____________

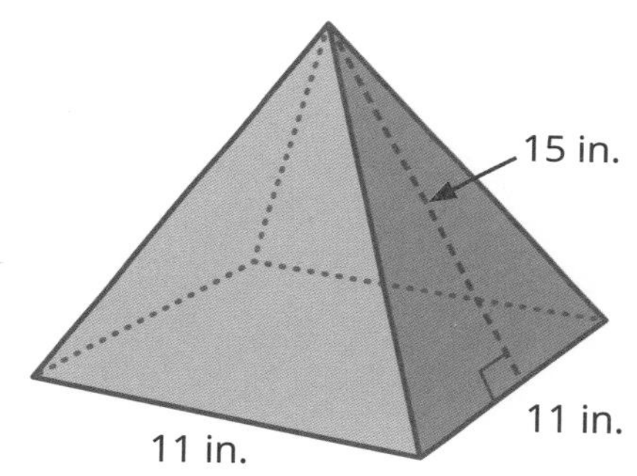

Surface area = ____________

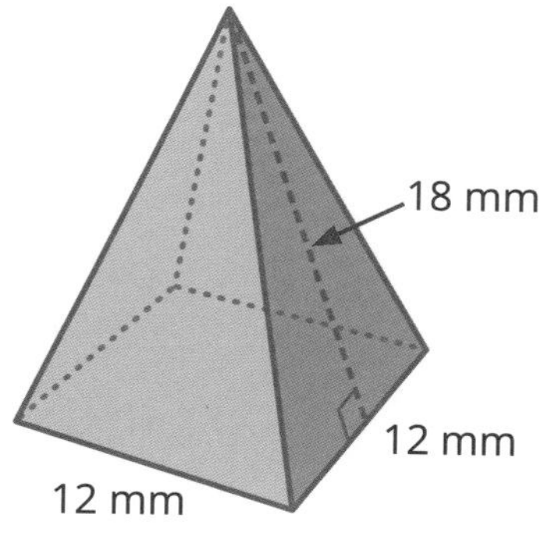

Surface area = ____________

Answer each question.

Paul built a wooden jewelry box for his sister, Rose. The box is shaped like a rectangular prism and is 8 inches long, 5 inches wide, and 4 inches high. Paul plans to stain the outside of the box, including the top and bottom of the box. What is the area that Paul will stain? ____________

Wendy is making props for the school play. She covers a square pyramid with foil to make it look like a piece of gold. The pyramid has a square base with 5-inch side lengths. The triangular faces of the pyramid all have a height of 7 inches. How much foil does Wendy need to cover the pyramid without any gaps or overlaps? ____________

Sebastian is decorating a plastic cube that has 6-inch side lengths for an art project. He wants to cover each side of the cube with construction paper. What is the total area that Sebastian will need to cover with construction paper if he does not want any gaps or overlaps? ____________

Kaia bought a bird feeder shaped like a triangular pyramid. The base of the feeder is an equilateral triangle with 15-centimeter side lengths and a height of 13 centimeters. The three other triangular faces of the feeder all have a height of 20 centimeters. Kaia plans to paint all sides of the bird feeder, including the bottom, with bright colors to attract birds. What is the area that Kaia will paint? ____________

Learn!

Volume is the amount of space an object takes up. It is measured in cubic units. To find the volume of a rectangular prism with length ℓ, width w, and height h, use the formula $\boldsymbol{V = \ell wh}$.

Find the volume of each rectangular prism.

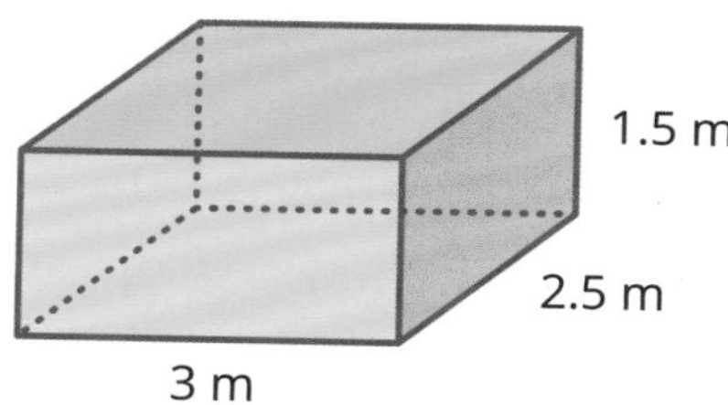

$V =$ ______________

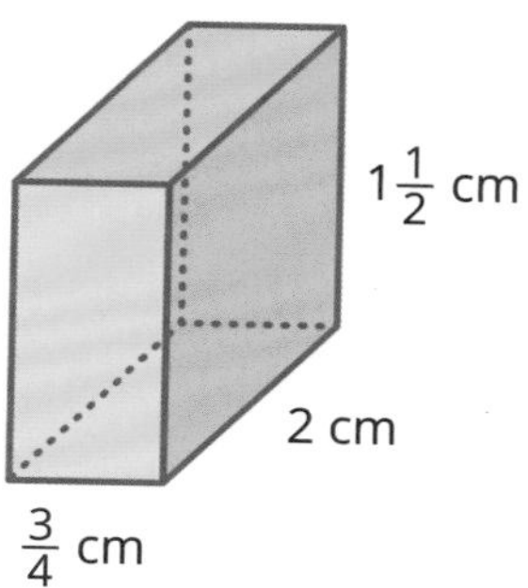

$V =$ ______________

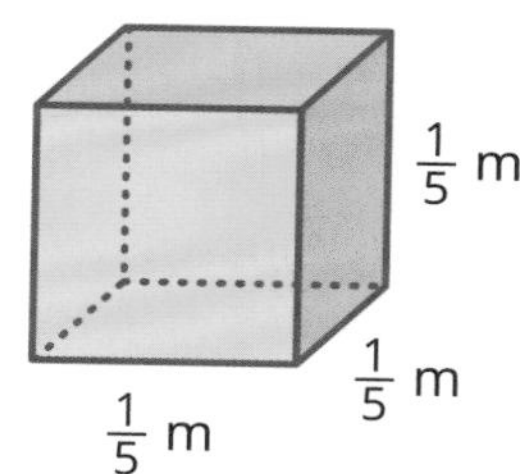

$V =$ ______________

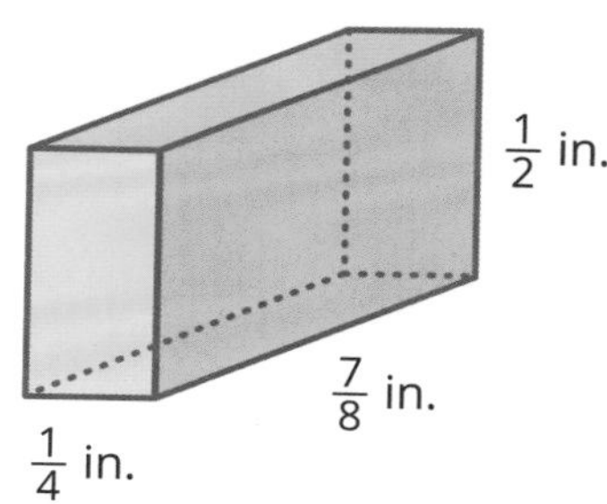

$V =$ ______________

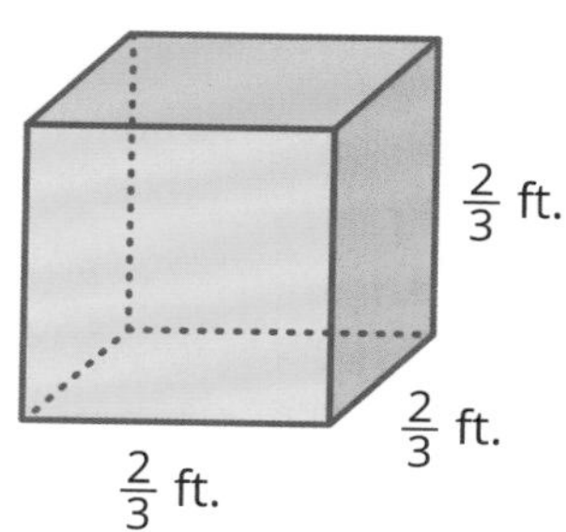

$V =$ ______________

Volume of rectangular prisms

Use the volume to find the missing dimension of each rectangular prism.

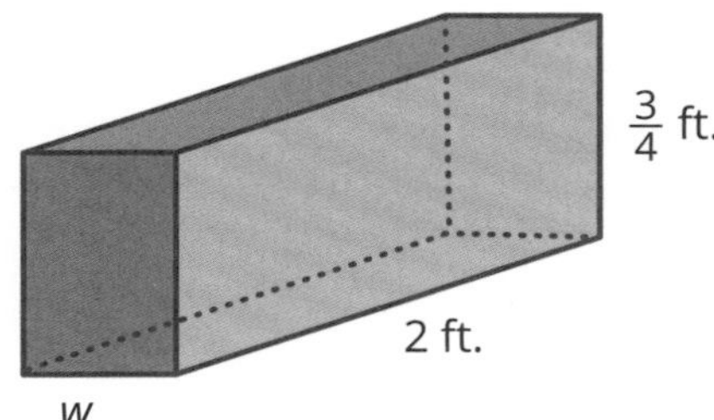

$V = \frac{3}{4}$ ft.^{3}

$w =$ ____________

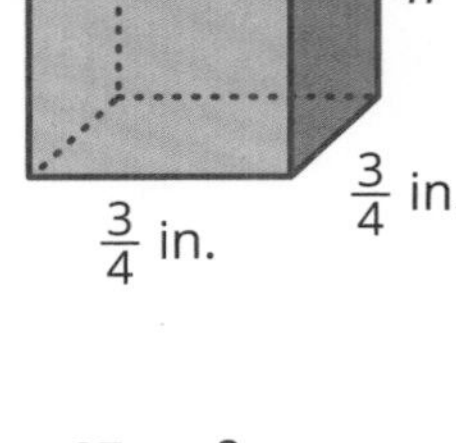

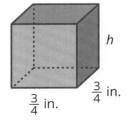

$V = \frac{27}{64}$ in.^{3}

$h =$ ____________

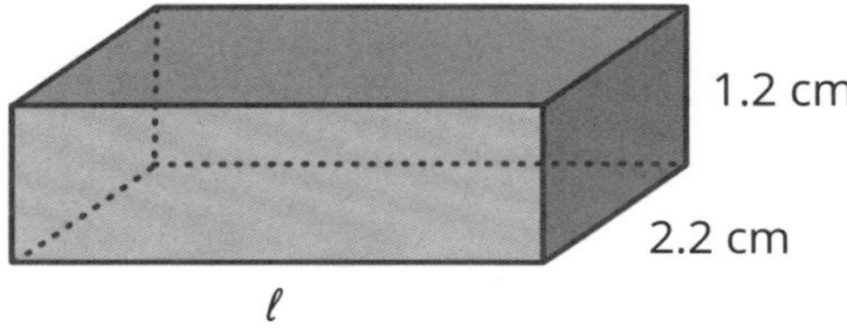

$V = 13.2$ cm^3

$\ell =$ ____________

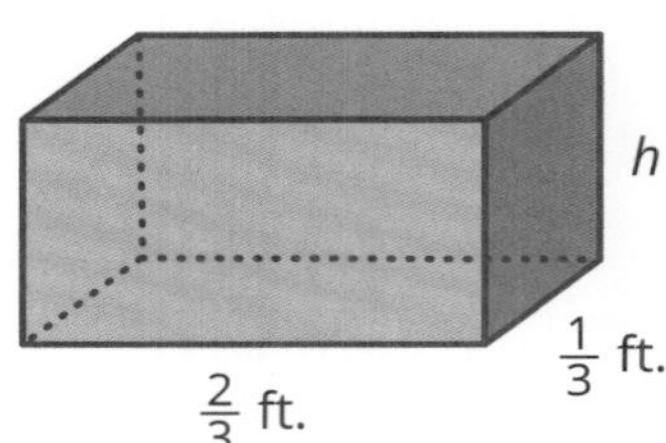

$V = \frac{2}{27}$ ft.^{3}

$h =$ ____________

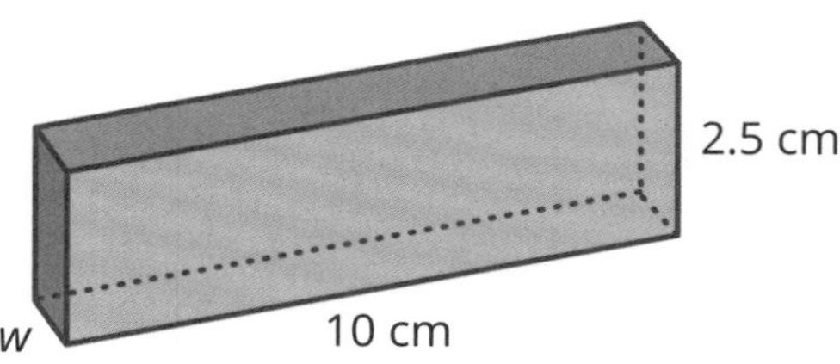

$V = 12.5$ cm^3

$w =$ ____________

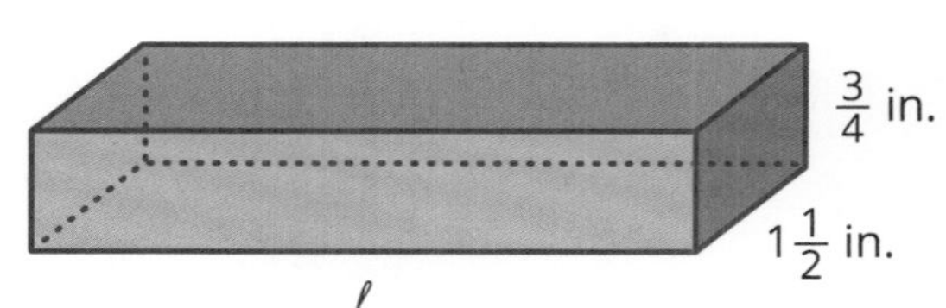

$V = 4\frac{1}{2}$ in.^{3}

$\ell =$ ____________

Answer each question.

The Patel family is spending the day at the park, so they packed their lunch in a picnic basket. The picnic basket is shaped like a rectangular prism and is $1\frac{1}{2}$ feet long, 1 foot wide, and $1\frac{1}{4}$ feet high. What is the volume of the picnic basket? ________________

Jerry built a wooden box shaped like a cube to store his coin collection. The cube measures $4\frac{1}{2}$ inches on each side. What is the volume of Jerry's box? ________________

Mitch has a carrier that he uses to take his cat, Whiskers, to the vet. The carrier is in the shape of a rectangular prism and measures $\frac{1}{2}$ of a meter long, $\frac{3}{10}$ of a meter wide, and $\frac{1}{5}$ of a meter high. What is the volume of the cat carrier? ________________

Evie keeps her angelfish in an aquarium shaped like a rectangular prism. The aquarium is 2 meters long, $\frac{2}{5}$ of a meter wide, and $\frac{1}{2}$ of a meter high. What is the volume of Evie's aquarium? ________________

Vivian is planting tulips in a flower box shaped like a rectangular prism. The flower box is $1\frac{1}{2}$ feet long, $\frac{3}{4}$ of a foot wide, and $\frac{1}{2}$ of a foot high. What is the volume of Vivian's flower box? ________________

IXL.com skill ID **BBM**

Time for review! Simplify each expression.

$8n - 3n + 11n =$ ____________

$6k + 3w + w - 4k =$ ____________

$7(a + 11) - 9 =$ ____________

$2(4r + 10) + 13 - 5r =$ ____________

$\frac{3}{8}c + \frac{2}{3} + \frac{1}{8}c - \frac{1}{4} =$ ____________

$11u + 5t + u - 3t =$ ____________

$\frac{1}{2}(8m + 12) - 2m + 3 =$ ____________

$1.8h + 3f + 2.1h - f =$ ____________

Solve each equation.

$9 + p = 17$

$p =$ ________

$6b = 30$

$b =$ ________

$a - 12 = 4$

$a =$ ________

$\frac{v}{9} = 3$

$v =$ ________

$0.7t = 8.4$

$t =$ ________

$z - \frac{1}{10} = \frac{4}{5}$

$z =$ ________

Nathan works as a lifeguard at Maple Hill Pool during the summer. He earns $25 for every hour that he works. The amount of money Nathan earns, *m*, depends on the number of hours he works, *h*.

Identify the independent and dependent variable.

Independent variable: ________ Dependent variable: ________

Use Nathan's hourly rate to complete the table and plot the points from the table on the graph. Then draw a line connecting the points.

h	*m*
2	
4	
6	
8	
10	

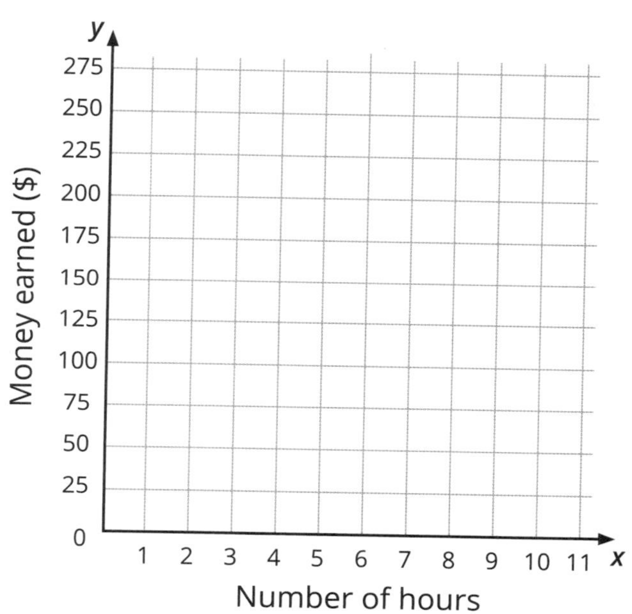

Answer each question.

Write an equation that represents the relationship between *h* and *m*. ____________

Nathan worked 15 hours last week. How much money did he earn? ____________

During the last week of the summer, Nathan earned $437.50. How many hours did he work that week? ____________

IXL.com skill ID **KZD**

Lucy is going to brunch at her aunt's house and wants to bring blueberry muffins. She creates a shopping list and goes to the grocery store to buy the ingredients she will need to make the muffins.

Answer each question.

Lucy needs to buy a bag of flour. A 5-pound bag of Green Dot Flour costs $2.75. There is also a 4-pound bag of Best Quality Flour that costs $2.40. Lucy wants to buy the bag of flour that is cheaper per pound.

How much does the 5-pound bag of Green Dot Flour cost per pound? $________ per pound

How much does the 4-pound bag of Best Quality Flour cost per pound? $________ per pound

Which bag should Lucy buy?

Green Dot Flour | Best Quality Flour

Eggs are the next item on Lucy's shopping list. Her family usually buys a carton of 18 eggs for $6.30. However, a carton of 12 eggs is on sale for $3.96. Lucy wants to buy the carton that is the better deal.

How much does the carton of 18 eggs cost per egg? $________ per egg

How much does the carton of 12 eggs cost per egg? $________ per egg

Which carton should Lucy buy?

Carton of 18 eggs | Carton of 12 eggs

Keep going! Answer each question.

The next ingredient Lucy needs to buy is buttermilk. Buttermilk is available in a $\frac{1}{2}$-gallon container for $3.84 or a 1-quart container for $2.50. Lucy wants to buy the size of buttermilk that is cheaper per quart.

How many quarts are in the $\frac{1}{2}$-gallon container? ______________

Which size of buttermilk should Lucy buy?

$\frac{1}{2}$-gallon	1-quart

The final ingredient on Lucy's list is blueberries. She needs $1\frac{1}{4}$ pints of blueberries. The blueberries are sold in packages that are $\frac{1}{4}$ of a pint.

How many packages does Lucy need to buy? ______________

If each package of blueberries costs $2.49, how much will Lucy pay for the blueberries? ______________

Fill in the table with the prices based on your answers to the questions on pages 204–205. Then find the total cost of Lucy's groceries.

Item	Price
Flour	
Eggs	
Buttermilk	
Blueberries	
Cost (without tax)	

Keep going! Answer each question.

Now that Lucy has all of her ingredients, she is ready to bake the blueberry muffins. Here is the list of ingredients for the recipe.

Blueberry muffins recipe

INGREDIENTS

$1\frac{1}{4}$ cups brown sugar	2 cups flour	$1\frac{1}{4}$ pints fresh blueberries
$\frac{3}{4}$ cup butter	$\frac{1}{2}$ teaspoon salt	$\frac{1}{2}$ cup buttermilk
2 large eggs	2 teaspoons baking powder	2 tablespoons white sugar

SUGAR

Lucy has 3 cups of brown sugar in her pantry. How many cups of brown sugar will Lucy have left after making the blueberry muffins? ____________

Lucy plans to replace $\frac{1}{3}$ of the butter with vegetable oil.

How many cups of vegetable oil will Lucy use? ____________

How many cups of butter will Lucy use? ____________

Lucy is using a $\frac{1}{4}$-cup measuring cup for the buttermilk. How many times will Lucy need to fill the measuring cup with buttermilk? ____________

Keep going! Answer each question.

The white sugar is sprinkled on top of the blueberry muffins. Lucy decides to mix $\frac{1}{2}$ of a teaspoon of cinnamon with the white sugar before sprinkling.

How many teaspoons of white sugar does the recipe say to use? ____________________

Lucy mixes the cinnamon and white sugar in a small bowl. What is the ratio of white sugar to cinnamon? ____________________

After 30 minutes of baking, the muffins are done! Lucy's recipe yielded 10 large blueberry muffins.

How many cups of blueberries did Lucy use? ____________________

About how many cups of blueberries does each muffin contain? ____________________

Lucy decides that the next time she bakes the blueberry muffins, she wants there to be about $\frac{1}{2}$ of a cup of blueberries in each muffin.

How many cups of blueberries will Lucy need to use? ____________________

How many pints of blueberries is this? ____________________

IXL.com skill ID ENK

Answer key

Rational numbers can be written in different ways. This answer key includes fractions and mixed numbers that are in simplest form. Keep in mind that there may be other equivalent answers that are also correct.

PAGE 4

$4^2 = 4 \times 4$

$2^5 = 2 \times 2 \times 2 \times 2 \times 2$

$9^3 = 9 \times 9 \times 9$

$12^4 = 12 \times 12 \times 12 \times 12$

$(0.6)^3 = 0.6 \times 0.6 \times 0.6$

$\left(\frac{1}{8}\right)^4 = \frac{1}{8} \times \frac{1}{8} \times \frac{1}{8} \times \frac{1}{8}$

$6 \times 6 = 6^2$

$5 \times 5 \times 5 \times 5 = 5^4$

$3 \times 3 \times 3 \times 3 \times 3 = 3^5$

$8 \times 8 \times 8 = 8^3$

$0.2 \times 0.2 \times 0.2 \times 0.2 = (0.2)^4$

$\frac{1}{4} \times \frac{1}{4} \times \frac{1}{4} = \left(\frac{1}{4}\right)^3$

PAGE 5

$8^2 = 8 \times 8 = 64$

$4^3 = 4 \times 4 \times 4 = 64$

$2^4 = 2 \times 2 \times 2 \times 2 = 16$

$12^1 = 12$

$10^4 = 10 \times 10 \times 10 \times 10 = 10{,}000$

$1^5 = 1 \times 1 \times 1 \times 1 \times 1 = 1$

$9^1 = 9$

$7^3 = 7 \times 7 \times 7 = 343$

$6^3 = 6 \times 6 \times 6 = 216$

$11^2 = 11 \times 11 = 121$

$3^5 = 3 \times 3 \times 3 \times 3 \times 3 = 243$

$5^3 = 5 \times 5 \times 5 = 125$

$2^5 = 2 \times 2 \times 2 \times 2 \times 2 = 32$

$8^3 = 8 \times 8 \times 8 = 512$

$12^2 = 12 \times 12 = 144$

PAGE 6

$24 = 2 \times 2 \times 2 \times 3$

$30 = 2 \times 3 \times 5$

$53 = 53$

$48 = 2 \times 2 \times 2 \times 2 \times 3$

PAGE 7

$27 = 3 \times 3 \times 3$

$41 = 41$

$77 = 7 \times 11$

$100 = 2 \times 2 \times 5 \times 5$

$84 = 2 \times 2 \times 3 \times 7$

$32 = 2 \times 2 \times 2 \times 2 \times 2$

$27 = 3^3$

$41 = 41$

$77 = 7 \times 11$

$100 = 2^2 \times 5^2$

$84 = 2^2 \times 3 \times 7$

$32 = 2^5$

PAGE 8

4	8
5	20
9	16

PAGE 9

2	4
3	1

PAGE 10

GCF: 4 $(4 \times 4) + (4 \times 5)$ $4(4 + 5)$	GCF: 3 $(3 \times 5) + (3 \times 3)$ $3(5 + 3)$
GCF: 10 $(10 \times 4) + (10 \times 3)$ $10(4 + 3)$	GCF: 14 $(14 \times 2) + (14 \times 3)$ $14(2 + 3)$
GCF: 5 $(5 \times 17) + (5 \times 4)$ $5(17 + 4)$	GCF: 12 $(12 \times 2) + (12 \times 3)$ $12(2 + 3)$

PAGE 11

12	45
30	40
60	55
72	

PAGE 12

30	84
198	350

PAGE 13

24 days

8 centerpieces

9 sandwiches

18 bags

48 inches

PAGE 14

18 R33	34	20 R5
12	6 R30	16
8	104 R8	124 R9
116	65 R3	96

PAGE 15

106	28	57 R44
67 R9	1,252	1,075 R4
1,239 R39	1,078 R91	208

PAGE 16

22	17	10 R54
14 R58	26 R67	7
13	139 R33	110

PAGE 17

1,629	736 R81	1,838 R168
1,687 R6	343	1,405

PAGE 18

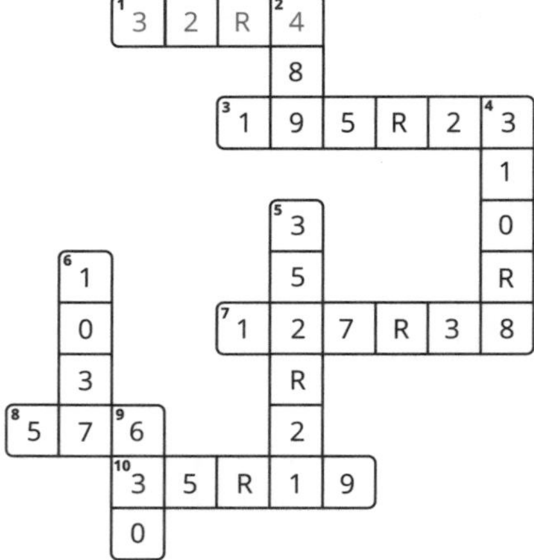

PAGE 19

27 pieces

4 games

250 cases

6 buses

8 levels

PAGE 20

58.7 + 63.25 = 121.95
94.83 − 13.22 = 81.61

388.67 − 212.09 = 176.58
245.95 + 36.25 = 282.2

78.6 + 94.53 = 173.13
987.4 − 65.31 = 922.09

67.936 − 8.25 = 59.686
406.81 − 93.005 = 313.805

641.71 + 225.6 = 867.31
6.747 + 18.59 = 25.337

890.5 − 46.307 = 844.193

PAGE 21

82.29	18.54
141.52	96.914
136.73	191.19
360.66	69.07
1.304	134.593
93.639	

PAGE 22

$14.98
1.5 kilograms
5.48 inches
19.05 ounces
3.8 milliliters
87.127 seconds

PAGE 23

14.1	21.8	7.24	96.4
× 1.3	× 3.4	× 8.1	× 0.26
18.33	74.12	58.644	25.064
62.8	35.2	2.46	76.93
× 0.15	× 6.4	× 0.25	× 7.8
9.42	225.28	0.615	600.054
5.19	75.42	16.23	80.96
× 1.3	× 0.89	× 4.7	× 0.72
6.747	67.1238	76.281	58.2912

PAGE 24

78.3	30.85	19.45	4.118
× 6.7	× 9.2	× 4.1	× 0.35
524.61	283.82	79.745	1.4413
29.08	6.352	2.67	3.849
× 3.4	× 5.6	× 0.18	× 0.85
98.872	35.5712	0.4806	3.27165

PAGE 25

6.7 ÷ 2 = 3.35
96.5 ÷ 5 = 19.3

64.96 ÷ 8 = 8.12
1.854 ÷ 9 = 0.206

0.946 ÷ 11 = 0.086
70.8 ÷ 15 = 4.72

296.1 ÷ 42 = 7.05
6.804 ÷ 72 = 0.0945

PAGE 26

460 ÷ 0.8 = 575
1.74 ÷ 0.3 = 5.8

42.7 ÷ 0.7 = 61
72 ÷ 0.04 = 1,800

PAGE 27

96.6 ÷ 0.6 = 161
86.38 ÷ 0.7 = 123.4

0.215 ÷ 0.02 = 10.75
120.18 ÷ 1.5 = 80.12

1,080 ÷ 0.24 = 4,500
319.95 ÷ 47.4 = 6.75

PAGE 28

61 < 61.5
55 > 52.5
32.8 < 37
15.6 = 15.6

PAGE 29

36 thousandths ÷ 6 thousandths = 6
10 hundredths ÷ 5 hundredths = 2
56 thousandths ÷ 7 thousandths = 8
18 tenths ÷ 3 tenths = 6

4	0.7
5	20
0.012	1.21

PAGE 30

9 movies
$78.75
2.25 pounds
$55

PAGE 31

45.72 − 6.04 = 39.68
56.48 ÷ 0.8 = 70.6

19.68 + 5.24 = 24.92
4.5 × 7.9 = 35.55

131.4 ÷ 2.5 = 52.56
32.71 − 11.8 = 20.91

7.81 × 0.53 = 4.1393
7.269 + 15.8 = 23.069

1.56 ÷ 0.16 = 9.75
87.6 − 3.125 = 84.475

PAGE 32

65.4 × 1.8 = 117.72
343.21 − 51.8 = 291.41

16.15 ÷ 1.9 = 8.5
12.5 + 8.972 = 21.472

19.5 − 7.63 = 11.87
7.32 × 0.95 = 6.954

82.6 ÷ 2.8 = 29.5
64.3 + 0.781 = 65.081

47.1 − 8.462 = 38.638
342.7 × 0.61 = 209.047

Answer key

PAGE 33

START

1.68 → ÷ 0.2 → 8.4

8.4 → − 2.65 → 5.75

5.75 → × 6.4 → 36.8

36.8 → + 12.9 → 49.7

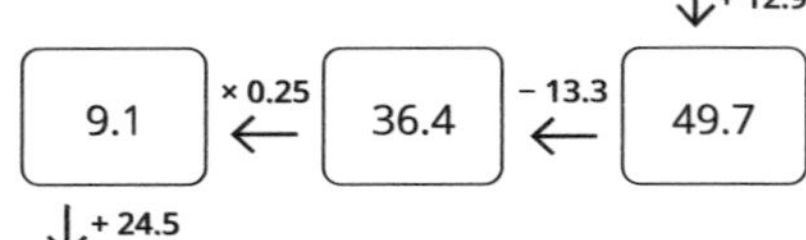

49.7 → − 13.3 → 36.4

36.4 → × 0.25 → 9.1

9.1 → + 24.5 → 33.6

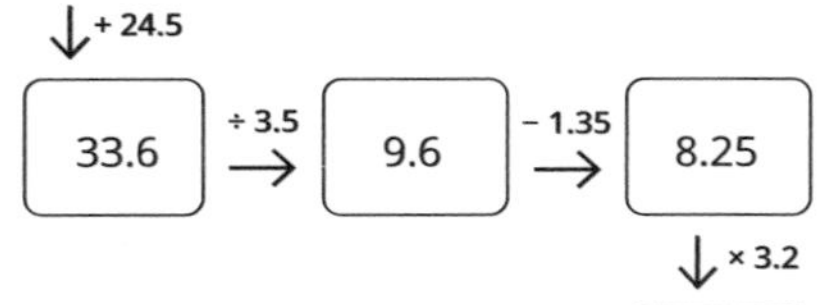

33.6 → ÷ 3.5 → 9.6

9.6 → − 1.35 → 8.25

8.25 → × 3.2 → 26.4

FINISH

PAGE 34

6 tickets

$7.40

$3.44

$3.51

$5.51

PAGE 35

$3\frac{1}{2} \times \frac{2}{3} = 2\frac{1}{3}$

$\frac{10}{11} \times \frac{3}{8} = \frac{30}{88}$

$\frac{5}{12} \times \frac{3}{5} = \frac{1}{4}$

$5\frac{1}{3} \times \frac{1}{8} = \frac{2}{3}$

$3\frac{3}{4} \times \frac{2}{5} = 1\frac{1}{2}$

$\frac{3}{10} \times 2\frac{1}{6} = \frac{13}{20}$

$\frac{1}{5} \times 9 = 1\frac{4}{5}$

$\frac{3}{5} \times 2\frac{3}{4} = 1\frac{13}{20}$

$\frac{5}{6} \times \frac{2}{3} = \frac{5}{9}$

$\frac{7}{9} \times 1\frac{3}{5} = 1\frac{11}{45}$

$\frac{5}{12} \times \frac{4}{15} = \frac{1}{9}$

PAGE 36

$2\frac{1}{3} \times 5\frac{1}{2} = 12\frac{5}{6}$

$1\frac{3}{5} \times 3\frac{3}{4} = 6$

$2\frac{1}{4} \times 4\frac{1}{5} = 9\frac{9}{20}$

$3\frac{1}{8} \times 2\frac{1}{2} = 7\frac{13}{16}$

$1\frac{4}{5} \times 3\frac{2}{3} = 6\frac{3}{5}$

$1\frac{1}{4} \times 2\frac{2}{3} = 3\frac{1}{3}$

$1\frac{2}{5} \times 6\frac{2}{3} = 9\frac{1}{3}$

$2\frac{5}{6} \times 7\frac{1}{2} = 21\frac{1}{4}$

PAGE 37

$3\frac{1}{3} \times 2 \times \frac{1}{2} = 3\frac{1}{3}$

$\frac{2}{3} \times 3 \times 1\frac{1}{4} = 2\frac{1}{2}$

$\frac{1}{2} \times 2\frac{2}{3} \times \frac{1}{6} = \frac{2}{9}$

$4\frac{1}{3} \times \frac{3}{5} \times \frac{2}{3} = 1\frac{11}{15}$

$\frac{3}{4} \times \frac{2}{5} \times 3\frac{1}{2} = 1\frac{1}{20}$

$1\frac{2}{3} \times 2\frac{1}{2} \times \frac{4}{5} = 3\frac{1}{3}$

PAGE 38

$\left(\frac{2}{3}\right)^4 = \frac{16}{81}$

$\left(\frac{1}{2}\right)^5 = \frac{1}{32}$

$\left(\frac{7}{8}\right)^1 = \frac{7}{8}$

$\left(\frac{2}{5}\right)^2 = \frac{4}{25}$

$\left(\frac{3}{7}\right)^3 = \frac{27}{343}$

$\left(\frac{9}{10}\right)^2 = \frac{81}{100}$

$\left(\frac{3}{5}\right)^3 = \frac{27}{125}$

$\left(\frac{5}{6}\right)^2 = \frac{25}{36}$

$\left(\frac{1}{3}\right)^5 = \frac{1}{243}$

$\left(\frac{3}{4}\right)^4 = \frac{81}{256}$

PAGE 39

$\frac{3}{8}$ of a cup

$1\frac{1}{2}$ yards

$3\frac{3}{4}$ feet

8 miles

6 games

PAGE 40

$5 \div \frac{1}{2} = 10$

$3 \div \frac{3}{4} = 4$

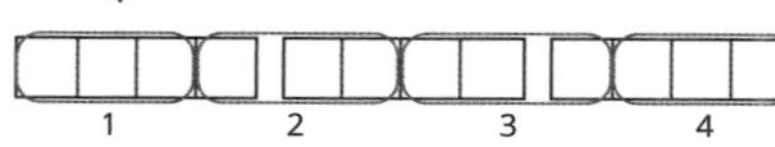

$1 \div \frac{3}{5} = 1\frac{2}{3}$

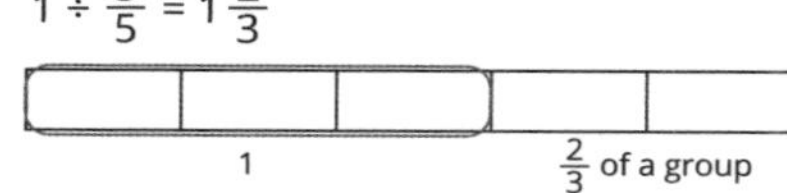

PAGE 40, *continued*

$3 \div \frac{2}{3} = 4\frac{1}{2}$

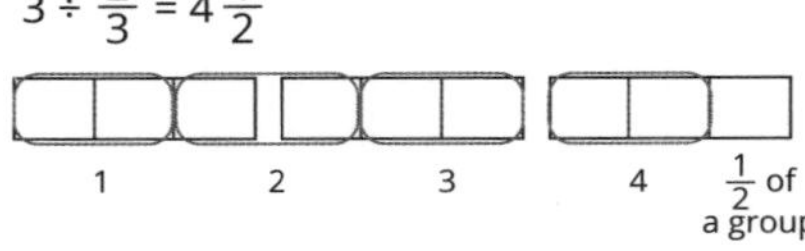

PAGE 41

$\frac{1}{4} \div 3 = \frac{1}{12}$

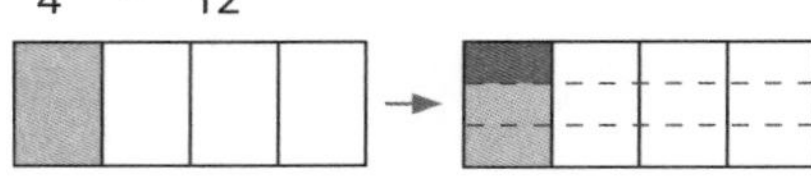

$\frac{4}{5} \div 2 = \frac{2}{5}$

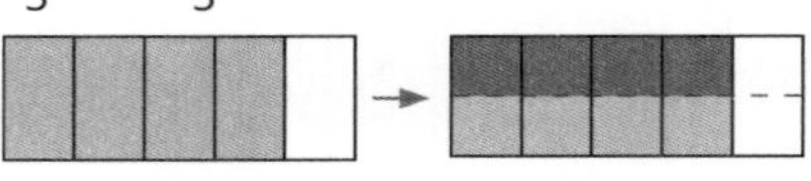

$\frac{2}{3} \div 4 = \frac{1}{6}$

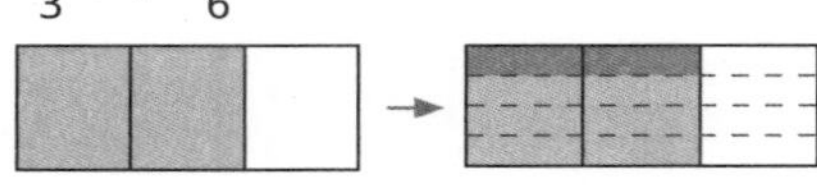

$\frac{2}{5} \div 6 = \frac{1}{15}$

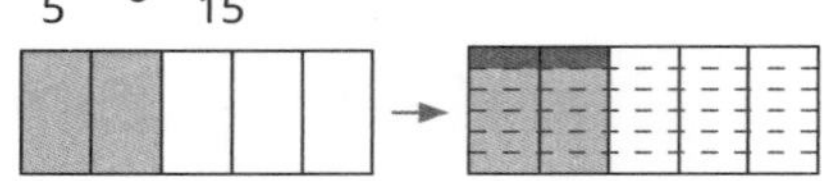

PAGE 42

$\frac{1}{2} \div \frac{1}{6} = 3$

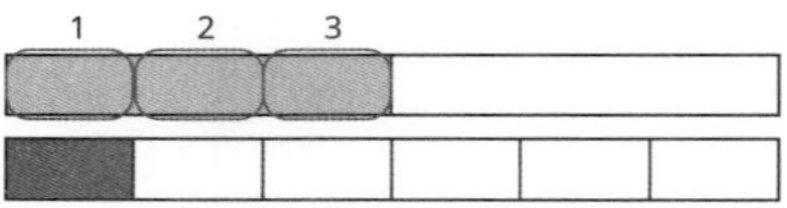

$\frac{3}{4} \div \frac{1}{2} = 1\frac{1}{2}$

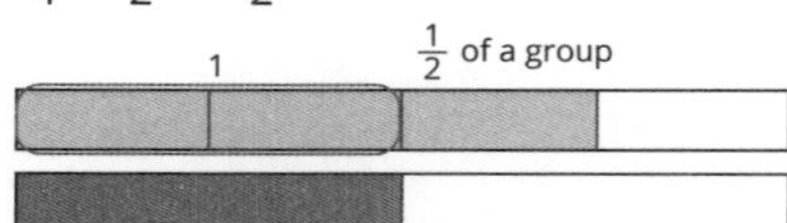

$\frac{7}{8} \div \frac{1}{4} = 3\frac{1}{2}$

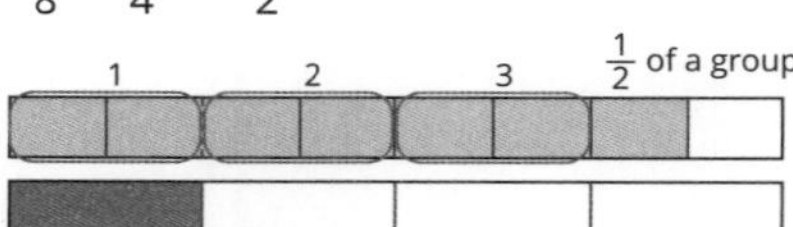

$\frac{9}{10} \div \frac{2}{5} = 2\frac{1}{4}$

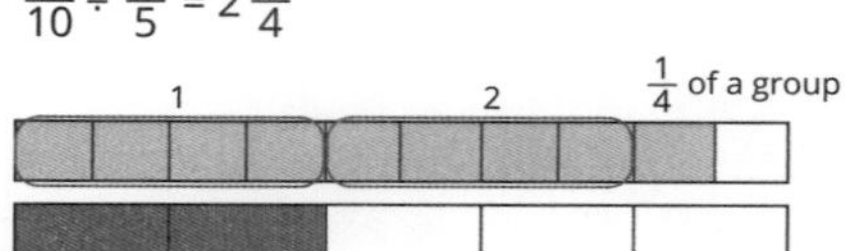

PAGE 43

$5 \div \frac{3}{4} = 6\frac{2}{3}$ $8 \div \frac{1}{6} = 48$ $3 \div \frac{4}{7} = 5\frac{1}{4}$

$\frac{1}{4} \div 6 = \frac{1}{24}$ $\frac{3}{8} \div 3 = \frac{1}{8}$ $\frac{5}{6} \div 4 = \frac{5}{24}$

$\frac{1}{3} \div \frac{7}{8} = \frac{8}{21}$ $\frac{4}{7} \div \frac{2}{5} = 1\frac{3}{7}$

PAGE 44

$\frac{1}{9} \div \frac{4}{5} = \frac{5}{36}$ $8 \div \frac{3}{5} = 13\frac{1}{3}$

$\frac{5}{6} \div \frac{3}{4} = 1\frac{1}{9}$ $\frac{3}{10} \div \frac{1}{12} = 3\frac{3}{5}$

$\frac{4}{7} \div \frac{3}{11} = 2\frac{2}{21}$ $\frac{5}{9} \div 4 = \frac{5}{36}$

$\frac{5}{8} \div \frac{1}{10} = 6\frac{1}{4}$ $\frac{2}{3} \div \frac{7}{12} = 1\frac{1}{7}$

$\frac{8}{9} \div \frac{5}{6} = 1\frac{1}{15}$ $\frac{2}{5} \div \frac{7}{8} = \frac{16}{35}$

$\frac{2}{7} \div \frac{6}{11} = \frac{11}{21}$ $6 \div \frac{3}{7} = 14$

$\frac{3}{8} \div \frac{7}{10} = \frac{15}{28}$

PAGE 45

$\frac{3}{4} \div \frac{5}{12} = 1\frac{4}{5}$ $\frac{2}{3} \div \frac{11}{12} = \frac{8}{11}$

$\frac{3}{5} \div \frac{1}{10} = 6$ $6 \div \frac{2}{7} = 21$

$\frac{3}{8} \div \frac{3}{7} = \frac{7}{8}$ $\frac{1}{9} \div \frac{3}{10} = \frac{10}{27}$

$\frac{7}{12} \div 2 = \frac{7}{24}$ $\frac{5}{8} \div \frac{3}{4} = \frac{5}{6}$

$\frac{3}{7} \div \frac{9}{10} = \frac{10}{21}$ $\frac{5}{12} \div \frac{5}{8} = \frac{2}{3}$

$\frac{2}{5} \div \frac{7}{10} = \frac{4}{7}$ $\frac{5}{6} \div 15 = \frac{1}{18}$

PAGE 46

$2\frac{4}{5} \div 4 = \frac{7}{10}$ $6 \div 1\frac{2}{3} = 3\frac{3}{5}$

$3 \div 8\frac{1}{2} = \frac{6}{17}$ $5\frac{1}{4} \div 3 = 1\frac{3}{4}$

$\frac{2}{5} \div 2\frac{3}{10} = \frac{4}{23}$ $3\frac{1}{3} \div \frac{5}{6} = 4$

$4\frac{3}{5} \div \frac{3}{10} = 15\frac{1}{3}$ $\frac{5}{6} \div 1\frac{3}{8} = \frac{20}{33}$

PAGE 47

$\frac{2}{3} \div 5\frac{1}{2} = \frac{4}{33}$ $4\frac{4}{5} \div \frac{3}{4} = 6\frac{2}{5}$

$2\frac{2}{9} \div \frac{3}{5} = 3\frac{19}{27}$ $8\frac{1}{3} \div 1\frac{1}{6} = 7\frac{1}{7}$

$\frac{11}{12} \div 2\frac{3}{4} = \frac{1}{3}$ $2\frac{2}{9} \div 4\frac{2}{3} = \frac{10}{21}$

$3\frac{1}{5} \div 1\frac{1}{3} = 2\frac{2}{5}$ $2\frac{3}{5} \div 1\frac{9}{10} = 1\frac{7}{19}$

$3\frac{7}{8} \div 5\frac{1}{6} = \frac{3}{4}$

PAGE 48

$\frac{5}{11} \div \frac{4}{5} = \frac{25}{44}$ $12 \div 3\frac{3}{7} = 3\frac{1}{2}$

$3\frac{1}{3} \div 4\frac{1}{8} = \frac{80}{99}$ $2\frac{4}{5} \div 6\frac{2}{3} = \frac{21}{50}$

$5\frac{5}{8} \div 1\frac{1}{6} = 4\frac{23}{28}$ $3\frac{1}{5} \div \frac{4}{15} = 12$

$7\frac{1}{3} \div 2\frac{2}{5} = 3\frac{1}{18}$ $10 \div \frac{8}{9} = 11\frac{1}{4}$

PAGE 49

$\frac{4}{5} \div 2\frac{1}{2} = \frac{8}{25}$ $3\frac{6}{7} \div 9 = \frac{3}{7}$

$12 \div 2\frac{1}{4} = 5\frac{1}{3}$ $2\frac{1}{3} \div 2\frac{5}{8} = \frac{8}{9}$

$5\frac{1}{3} \div \frac{7}{12} = 9\frac{1}{7}$ $3\frac{3}{5} \div 1\frac{7}{9} = 2\frac{1}{40}$

PAGE 50

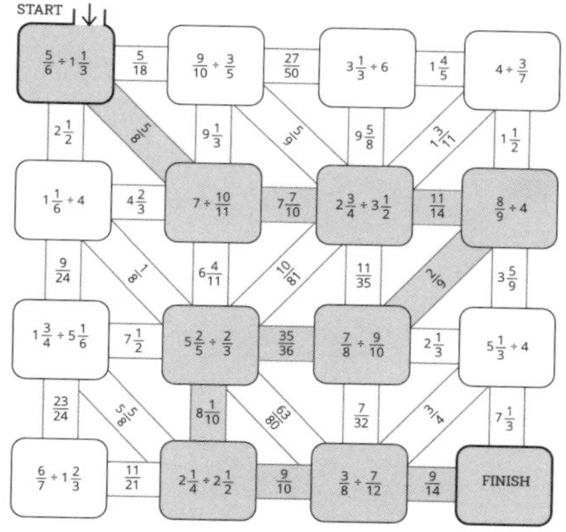

PAGE 51

$\frac{1}{8}$ of a cup

4 servings

10 days

6 bibs

$\frac{5}{8}$ of an inch

6 days

PAGE 52

The opposite of –2 is 2.

The opposite of 8 is –8.

The opposite of –10 is 10.

The opposite of 15 is –15.

The opposite of –12 is 12.

The opposite of 20 is –20.

The opposite of –50 is 50.

PAGE 53

–7

80

50

–32

14

–45

–2

PAGE 54

$-4 < 4$

$-2 > -6$

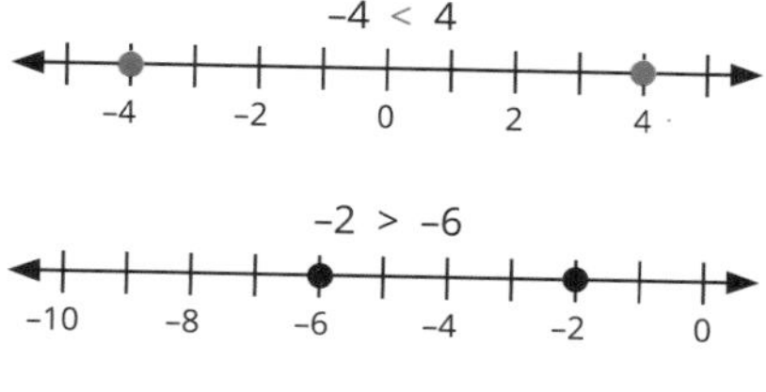

$7 > 3$

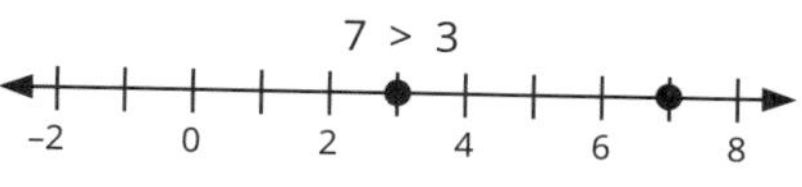

$-5 < 2$

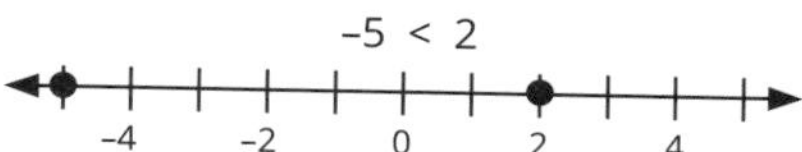

PAGE 54, *continued*

10 < -5

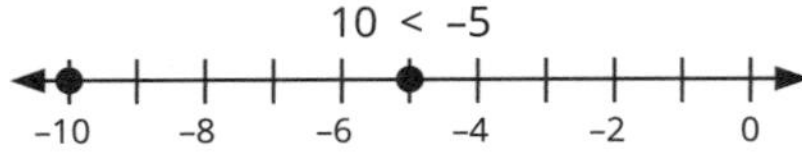

-35 > -40

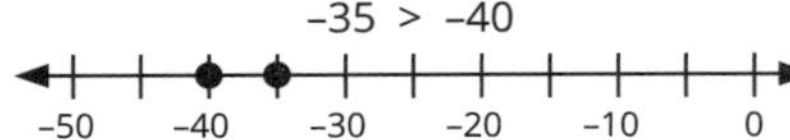

15 < 40

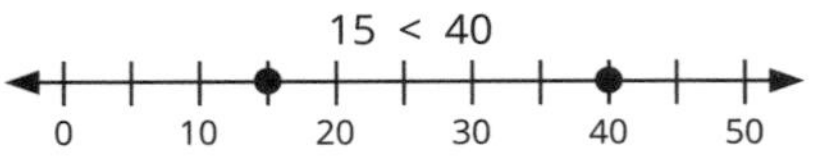

-25 < -20

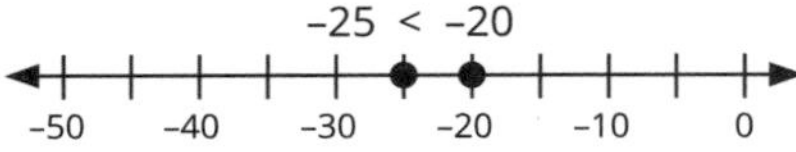

-90 < -50

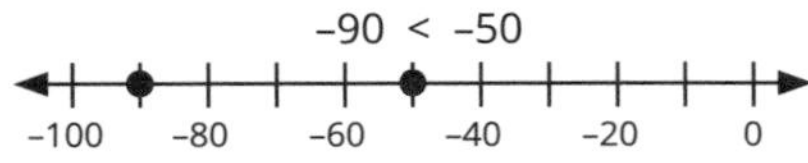

10 > -30

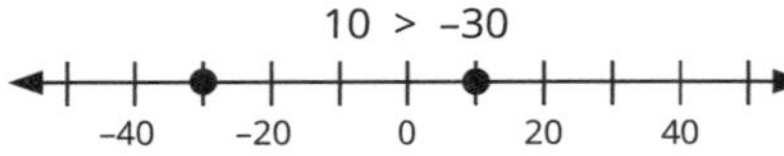

PAGE 55

-34 < 33	10 > -15	-25 > -28
70 > -60	-46 < -40	76 > 57
-33 < 29	-99 < 9	-75 < -68
-6 > -60	-83 < -28	-54 < -46
-10 > -100	-89 > -93	-25 < -22

PAGE 56

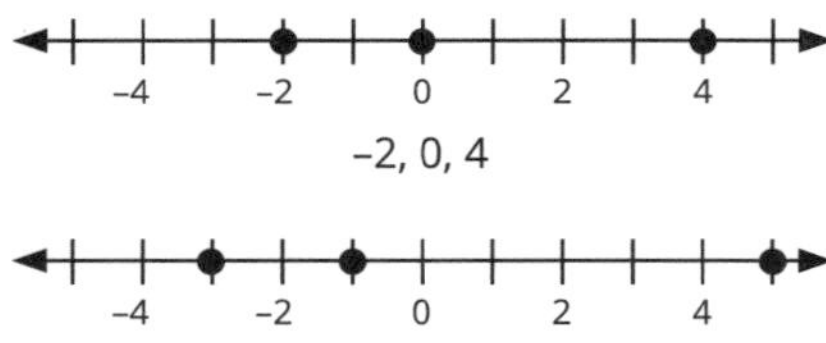

-2, 0, 4

-3, -1, 5

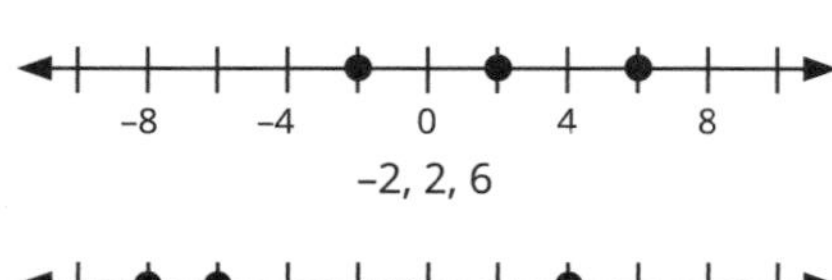

-2, 2, 6

-20, -15, 10

PAGE 56, *continued*

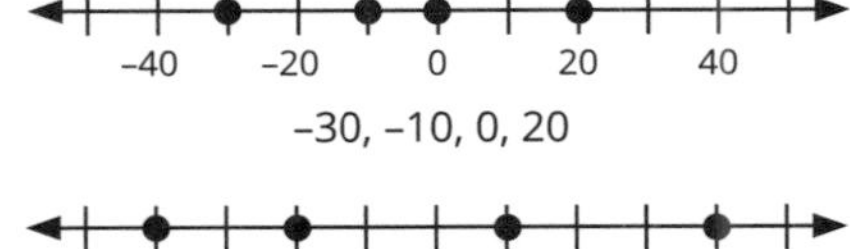

-30, -10, 0, 20

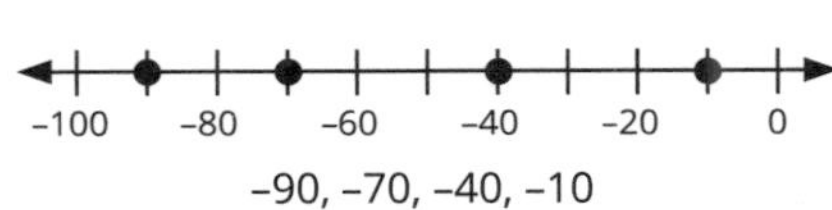

-90, -70, -40, -10

PAGE 57

-13, 8, 17

-28, -20, 25

-58, -53, 0, 56

-92, -80, 12, 47

-80, -55, -40, -25

-60, -32, 17, 60, 74

-86, -41, -29, 14, 92

-97, -72, -64, -33, -16

PAGE 58

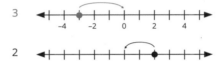

3
2

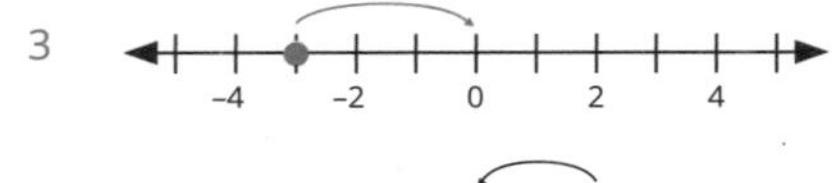

1

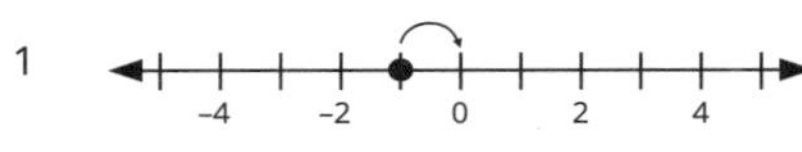

6

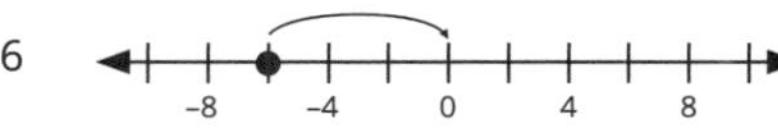

8

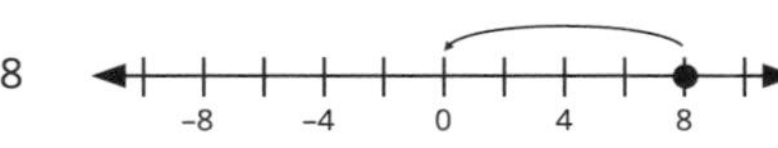

25

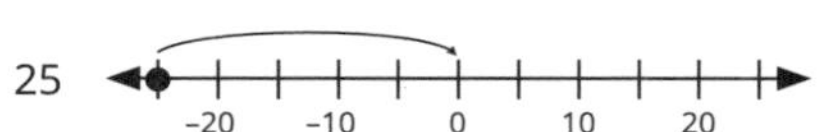

PAGE 59

6	9	12
18	22	65
29	43	52
30	84	77

-36	-88	-73
-51	-63	-98

PAGE 60

|10| = |-10|

-25 < |20|

|98| = |-98|

PAGE 60, *continued*

|-41| > 14

|16| < |-62|

|6| > -6

|-34| = |34|

|25| < |28|

|37| < |77|

-76 < |18|

53 = |53|

|40| = |-40|

5 < |50|

|-11| > -11

|46| > |-42|

PAGE 61

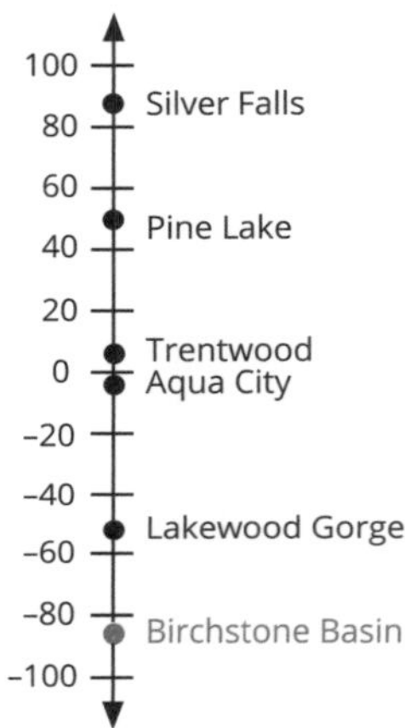

Birchstone Basin

-85 meters

Silver Falls

87 meters

Aqua City

Birchstone Basin

Birchstone Basin, Lakewood Gorge, Aqua City

PAGE 62

Sunday

Friday

Sunday, Saturday, Monday, Friday

Mole

Groundhog

Chipmunk

PAGE 63

0.6

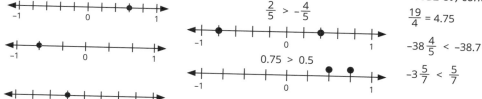

$-\frac{2}{3}$

−1.25

7

$-3\frac{1}{2}$

$\frac{6}{2}$

2.07

$-\frac{7}{4}$

PAGE 64

$-\frac{5}{9}$

−11

$\frac{20}{3}$

19.75

$-70\frac{5}{8}$

−90.3

$\frac{4}{11}$

$7\frac{9}{10}$

0.2

$-\frac{3}{7}$

68.4

$-\frac{11}{12}$

$-54\frac{1}{2}$

46.38

$-99\frac{1}{9}$

PAGE 65

$2\frac{1}{2}$	$\frac{7}{12}$	4.55
50.4	4.6	$\frac{4}{9}$
0.08	$3\frac{7}{8}$	10.9
$7\frac{7}{10}$	$\frac{1}{6}$	$2\frac{3}{5}$
$-49\frac{2}{7}$	−0.82	$-6\frac{1}{2}$
−61.4	$-\frac{3}{4}$	−5.01

PAGE 66

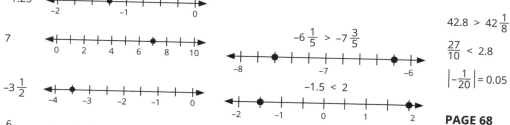

$\frac{2}{5} > -\frac{4}{5}$

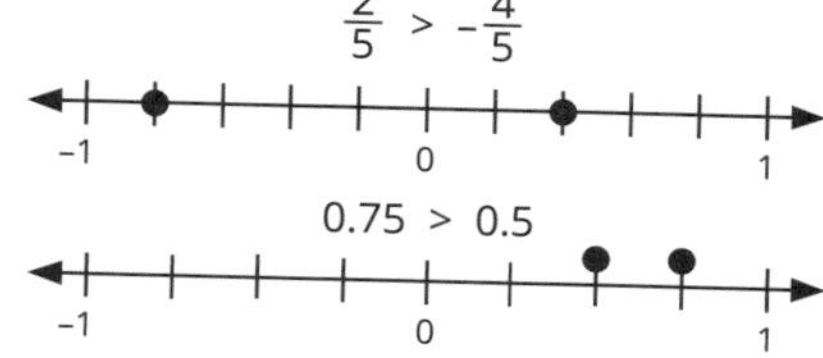

0.75 > 0.5

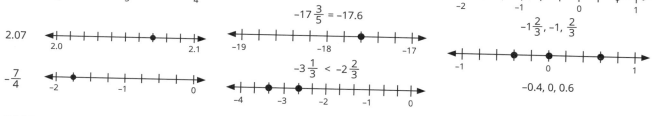

$-6\frac{1}{5} > -7\frac{3}{5}$

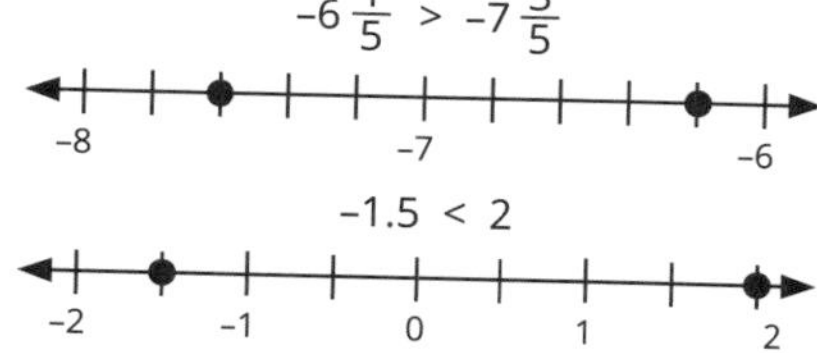

−1.5 < 2

$-17\frac{3}{5} = -17.6$

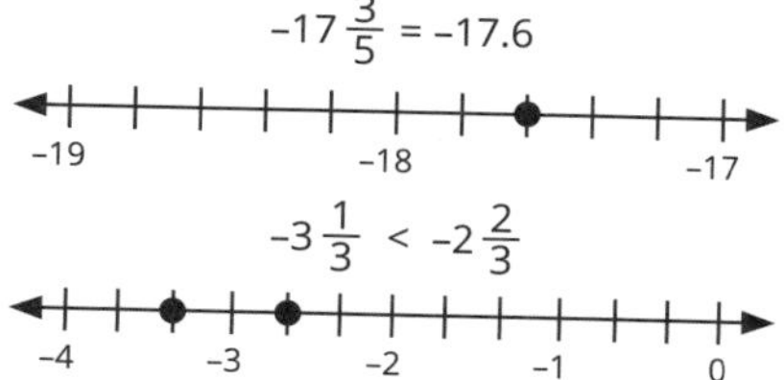

$-3\frac{1}{3} < -2\frac{2}{3}$

$-9\frac{3}{10} > -9.7$

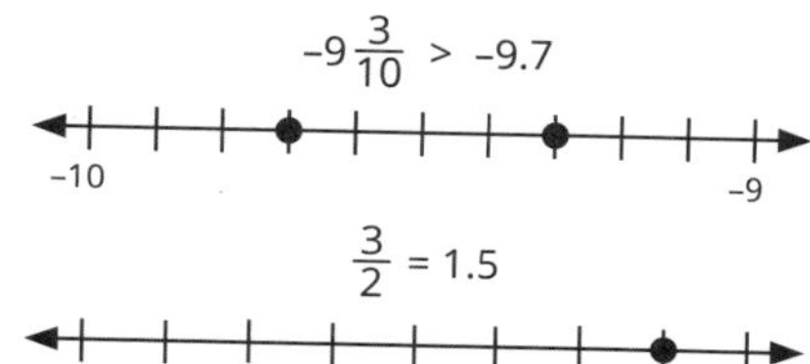

$\frac{3}{2} = 1.5$

PAGE 67

$-\frac{2}{3} < \frac{1}{3}$

$|-5| > -5$

−25.1 < −2.63

$\frac{14}{5} > -\frac{16}{5}$

$3\frac{5}{8} > -4\frac{7}{8}$

$8.07 < |-8.7|$

−40.1 < −40.09

$-13\frac{3}{4} < |-13.75|$

$15.23 > -15\frac{2}{3}$

PAGE 67, *continued*

$\frac{19}{4} = 4.75$

$-38\frac{4}{5} < -38.7$

$-3\frac{5}{7} < \frac{5}{7}$

$42.8 > 42\frac{1}{8}$

$\frac{27}{10} < 2.8$

$\left|-\frac{1}{20}\right| = 0.05$

PAGE 68

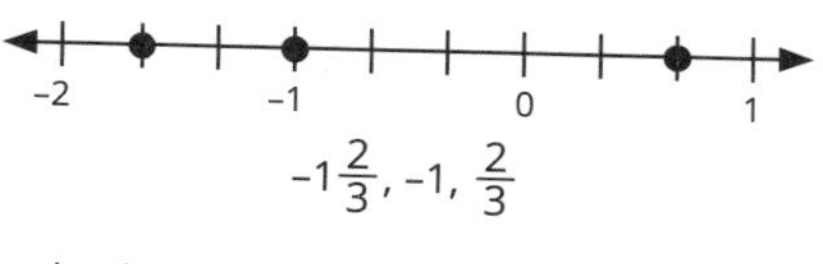

$-1\frac{2}{3}, -1, \frac{2}{3}$

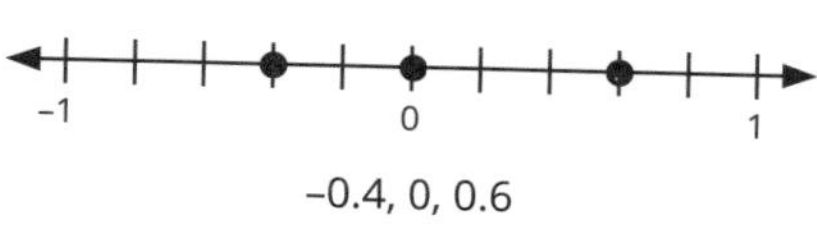

−0.4, 0, 0.6

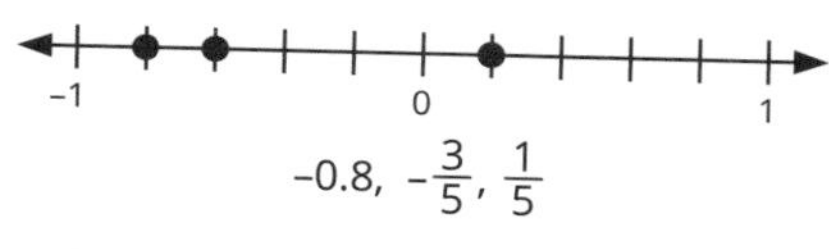

$-0.8, -\frac{3}{5}, \frac{1}{5}$

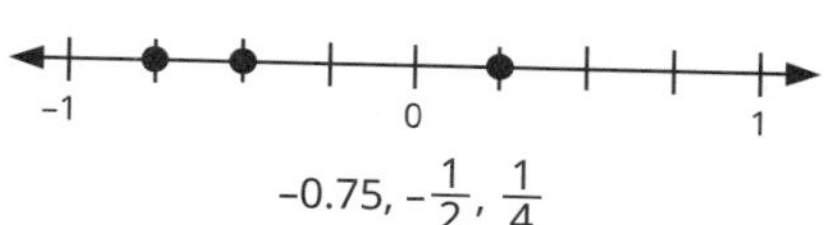

$-0.75, -\frac{1}{2}, \frac{1}{4}$

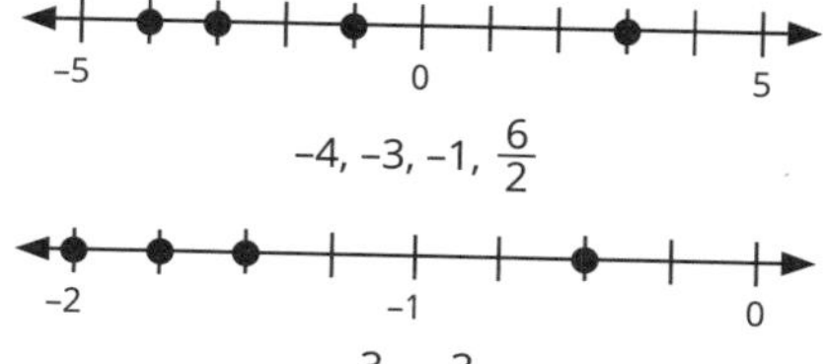

$-4, -3, -1, \frac{6}{2}$

$-2, -1\frac{3}{4}, -\frac{3}{2}, -0.5$

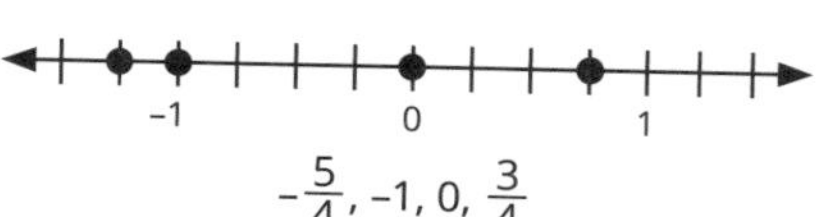

$-\frac{5}{4}, -1, 0, \frac{3}{4}$

PAGE 69

$-8, \frac{15}{2}, \left|-8\frac{1}{2}\right|$

−30.3, −30, 30.5

$-2\frac{1}{4}, 0, 0.14, 2.4$

$-10\frac{3}{4}, -10\frac{1}{4}, -10, |-10.5|$

Answer key

PAGE 69, *continued*

$-16, \left|16\frac{2}{5}\right|, 16.5, \left|-16\frac{7}{10}\right|$

$-44\frac{1}{5}, -4.5, 4\frac{4}{5}, 44.5, 45$

$-3, -1, \left|-1\frac{3}{4}\right|, 2.25, \frac{7}{3}$

$-5\frac{7}{8}, -5.75, -5.6, -5\frac{1}{2}, -5.1$

PAGE 70

↓ START

-10.5	$-\frac{22}{2}$	$-7\frac{4}{5}$	-6.8	$-5\frac{2}{9}$
$-9\frac{7}{8}$	$-\frac{23}{3}$	-6.45	$-4\frac{4}{5}$	-6
$-\frac{11}{1}$	-7.9	$-8\frac{5}{6}$	-2.05	$-\frac{9}{4}$
$-2\frac{2}{5}$	1	$\frac{8}{9}$	$\left|-\frac{1}{12}\right|$	0
$\frac{13}{4}$	$\|-4.5\|$	$-4\frac{1}{8}$	-0.05	$\frac{5}{3}$
$\left|-1\frac{1}{6}\right|$	$5\frac{3}{4}$	6.1	$\frac{17}{2}$	$\|-10\|$

↓ FINISH

PAGE 71

Lavender Sage

Orange Blossom

Orange Blossom, Fresh Rose, Smooth Vanilla, Honey Oatmeal, Bright Berry, Lavender Sage

Bright Berry and Lavender Sage

PAGE 73

always true

sometimes true

never true

sometimes true

always true

always true

never true

always true

PAGE 74

A (5, 2)	*E* (–2, –5)
B (–4, –2)	*F* (–2, 3)
C (4, –3)	*G* (3, 4)
D (0, 1)	*H* (–3, 0)

PAGE 75

P(–3, 3.5)	*T*(1.5, 0)
Q(4.5, –2)	*U*(2.5, 2.5)
R(–4.5, –1)	*V*(0, –3.5)
S(1, 4.5)	*W*(–2.5, –2.5)

PAGE 76

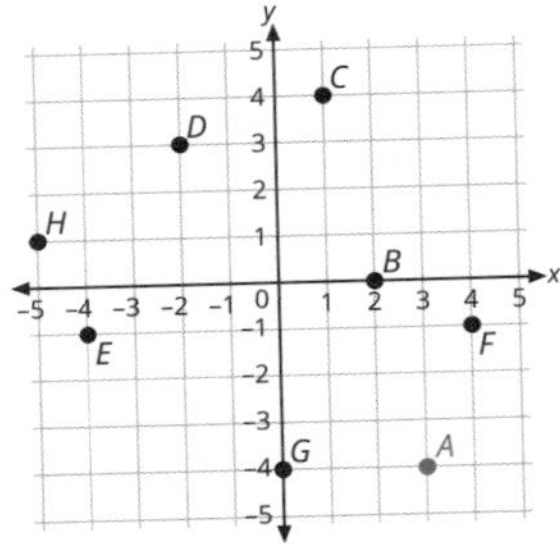

PAGE 77

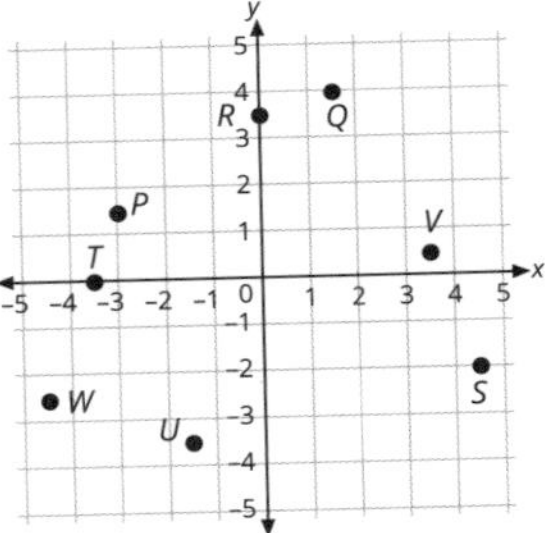

PAGE 78

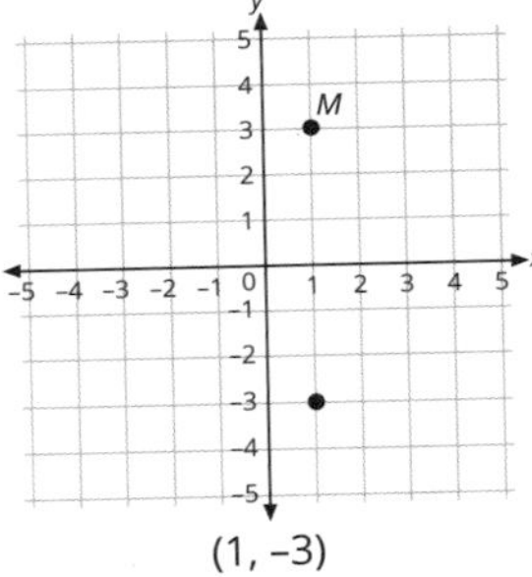

(1, –3)

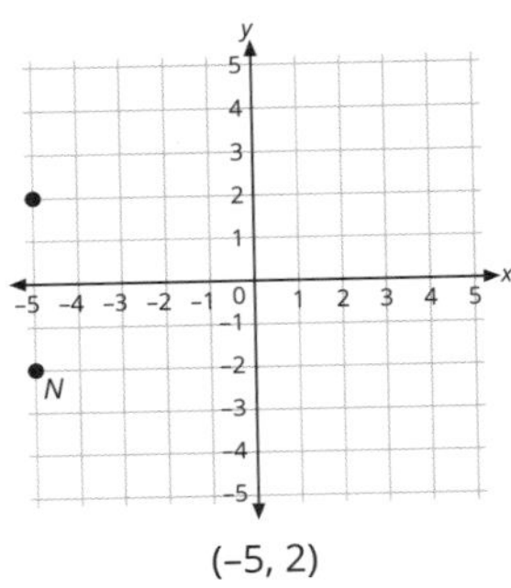

(–5, 2)

PAGE 79

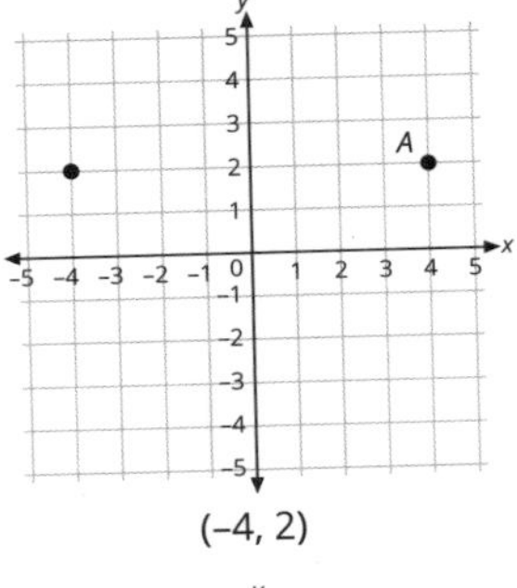

(–4, 2)

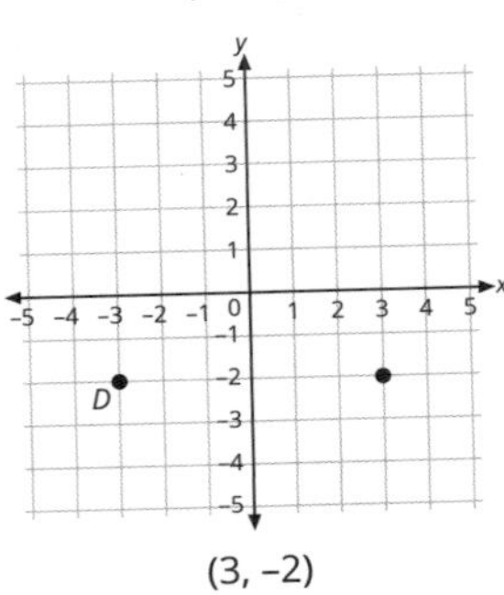

(3, –2)

Answers may vary. One possible answer is shown below.

If the point (3, 5) were reflected over the *x*-axis and then the *y*-axis, its new coordinates would be (–3, –5). The coordinates of (–1, 4) would be (1, –4) if it were reflected in the same way.

PAGE 80

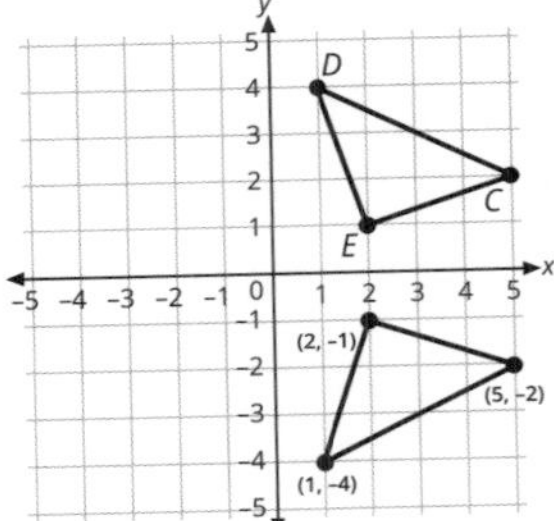

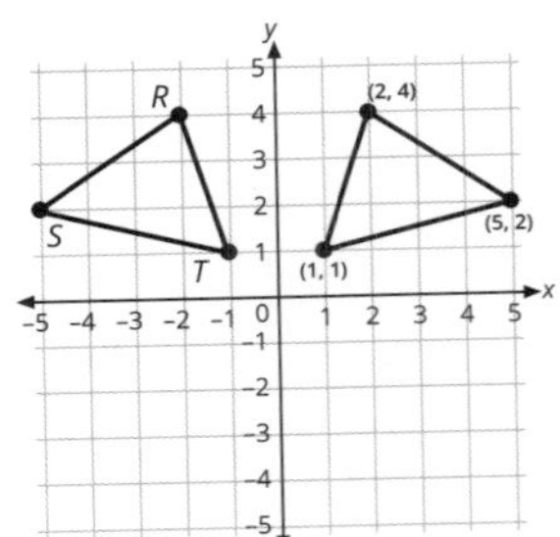

PAGE 80, *continued*

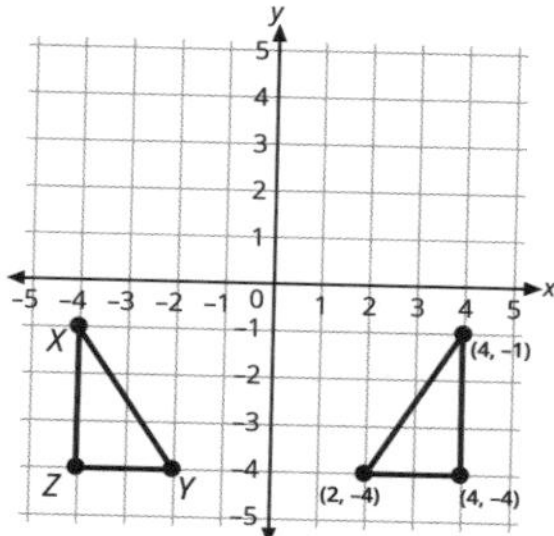

PAGE 81

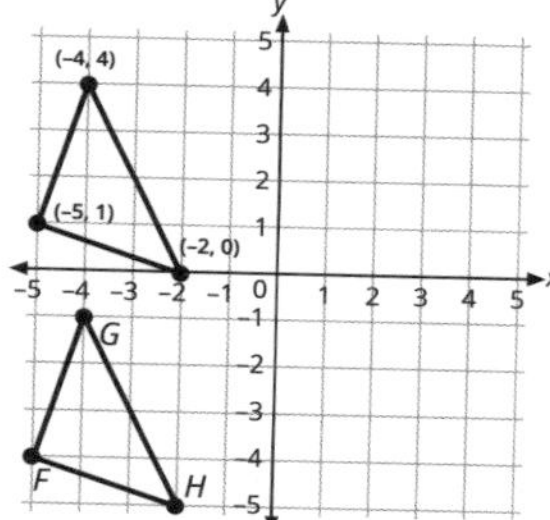

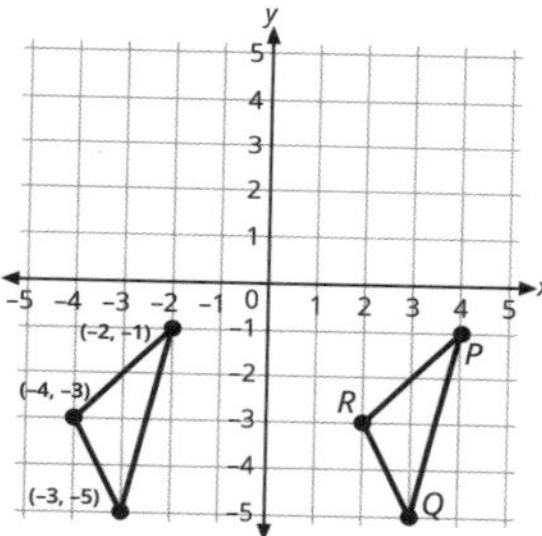

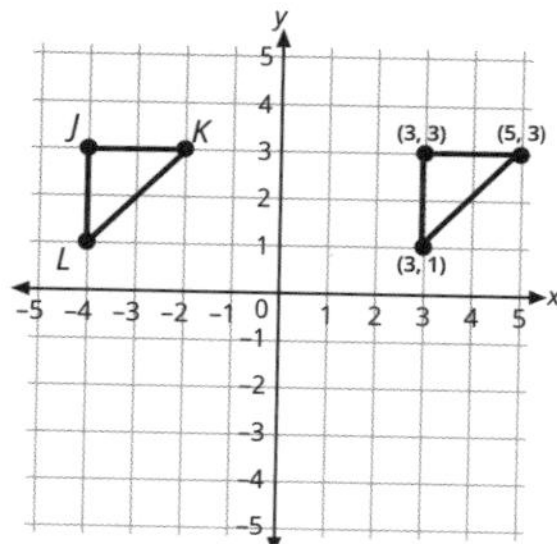

PAGE 82

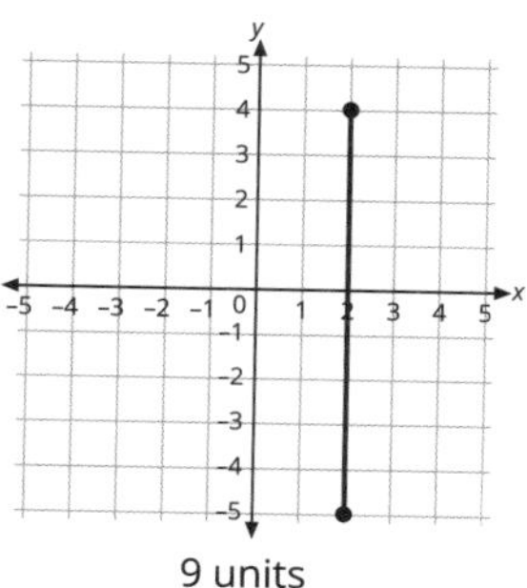

9 units

PAGE 82, *continued*

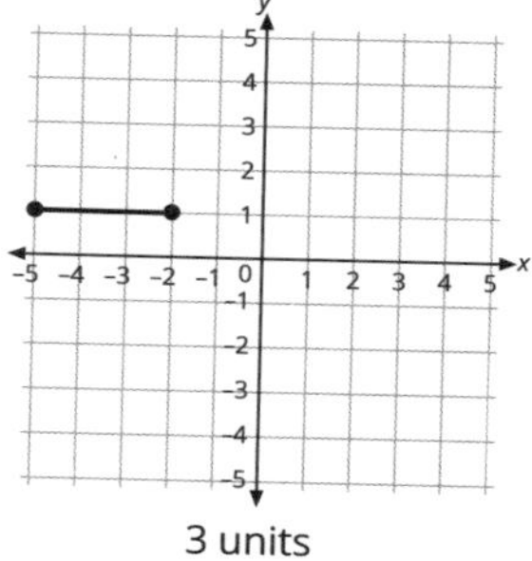

3 units

PAGE 83

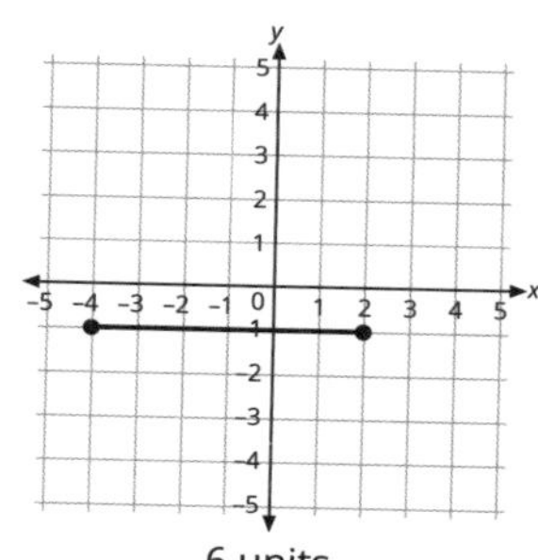

6 units

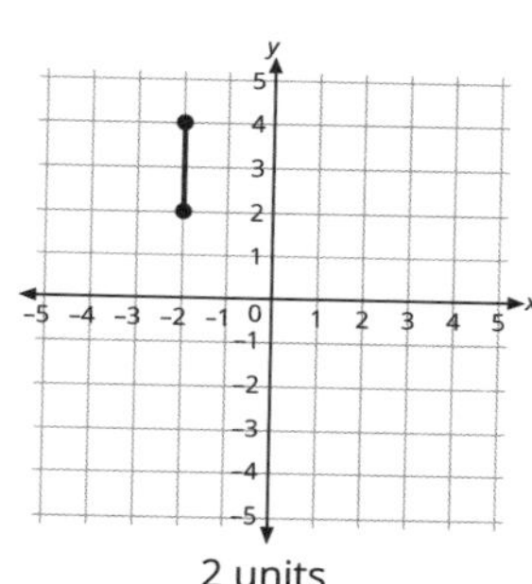

2 units

4 units
2 units
8 units
6.75 units
$1\frac{1}{2}$ units

PAGE 84

(–4, –5)
Roller coaster
Gift shop
2 units
(1, 3)
Roller coaster or Ferris wheel
9 units
Arcade

PAGE 85

(–4, –3.5)
Town hall
6 units
Public library
Public pool
(–4, 4)
Grocery store
5 units

PAGE 86

4:3   3:5
2:7   5:2
9:1

PAGE 87

5:7
2:25
11:19
17:28
8:23
25:14

PAGE 88

3:5 12:9 15:25
10:7 20:14 4:1
24:18 4:3 12:9
3:8 9:24 15:6
2:9 3:10 6:27
9:15 18:30 3:5
8:2 16:4 4:1 48:3
2:10 1:9 5:45 3:27

PAGE 89

Ratios may vary. Some possible ratios are shown below.

2:5 = 4:10   6:1 = 12:2   7:3 = 14:6
18:12 = 3:2   8:14 =4:7   2:8 = 1:4

18:20 = 9:10   42:14 = 6:2   32:48 = 4:6
30:12 = 10:4   4:20 = 8:40   50:40 = 10:8
4:9 = 44:99   75:50 = 3:2   45:18 = 5:2
60:84 = 5:7   18:27 = 54:81   12:36 = 6:18

Answer key

PAGE 90

No

Yes

Yes

No

Yes

No

PAGE 91

1	2	3	4	5
7	14	21	28	35

7	8	9	10	11
77	88	99	110	121

3	6	9	12	15
12	24	36	48	60

5	10	15	20	25
1	2	3	4	5

2	4	6	8	10
10	20	30	40	50

4	8	12	16	20
12	24	36	48	60

3	4	5	6	7
36	48	60	72	84

6	18	30	42	54
1	3	5	7	9

12	14	16	18	20
6	7	8	9	10

PAGE 92

T-shirts	1	2	3	4
Cost	$15	$30	$45	$60

Tacos	2	4	6	8
Cost	$7	$14	$21	$28

Minutes	15	30	45	45
Miles	2	4	6	8

Lemons	4	8	12	16
Quarts	1	2	3	4

Tulips	3	9	18	27
Daffodils	5	15	30	45

Balls of yarn	5	10	15	20
Hats	4	18	12	16

PAGE 93

Hours	1	2	3	4
Miles	2	4	6	8

Wraps	2	6	10	14
Cost ($)	5	15	25	35

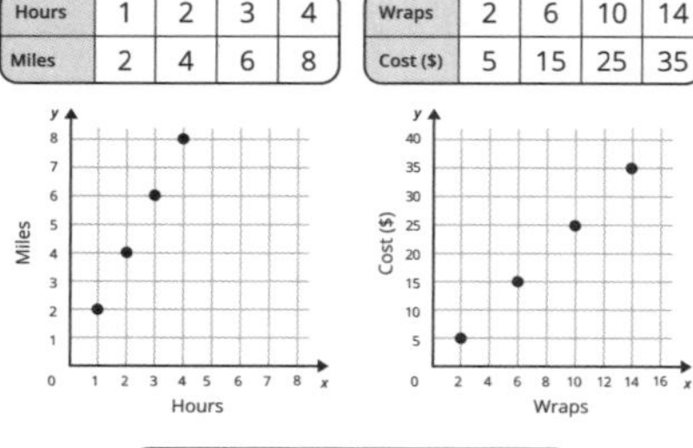

Cups of sour cream	2	4	6	8
Cups of yogurt	3	6	9	12

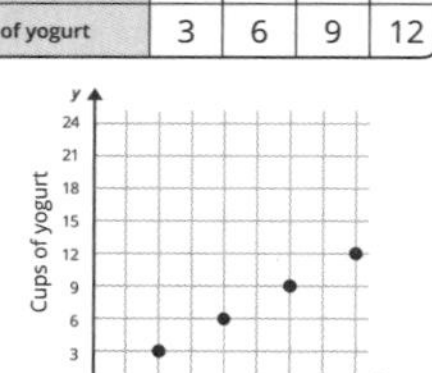

PAGE 94

Original	AB	BC	CD	DE	EF	FA
	2	3	1	1	1	2
Scaled copy	PQ	QR	RS	ST	TU	UP
	8	12	4	4	4	8

PAGE 95

Original	CD	DE	EF	FG	GH	HC
	9	6	3	3	6	3
Scaled copy	UV	VW	WX	XY	YZ	ZU
	3	2	1	1	2	1

Answers will vary. One possible answer is shown below.

The ratios of each side length in the original figure to its corresponding side in the scaled figure are equivalent. In the first table, the ratios are all equivalent to 1:4. In the second table, the ratios are all equivalent to 3:1.

PAGE 96

45 miles per hour

12 mailboxes per row

18 pencils per pack

8 apples per bag

15 books per shelf

7.25 fluid ounces per glass

6.5 meters per second

11 pages per day

PAGE 97

$5.25 per box

$2.75 per pound

$3.40 per square foot

$2.19 per jar

$2.24 per box

12-pack of markers for $2.28

$47.30 for 11 gallons of gas

$3.75 for a 3-pack of socks

$11.25 for 3 boxes of cat treats

PAGE 98

3 points per question

$24 per game

$0.98 per foot

1.5 tablespoons per cup

$1.19 per cup

PAGE 99

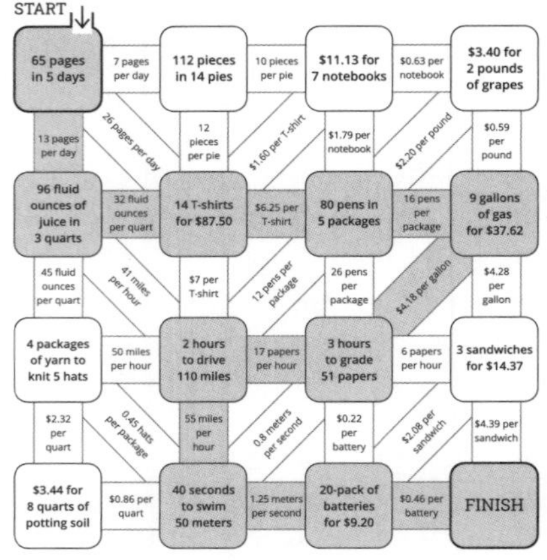

PAGE 100

Bongo

Emir

Ariana

kiwi-strawberry

PAGE 101

Miles	12	3	15
Hours	4	1	5

15 miles

Money	$67.50	$22.50	$45
Hours	3	1	2

$45

Jumping jacks	110	55	165
Hours	2	1	3

165 jumping jacks

Cost	$59.65	$11.93	$155.09
Signs	5	1	13

$155.09

PAGE 102

5 ft. = 60 in.

4 yd. = 12 ft.

1.5 gal. = 6 qt.

0.25 ton = 8,000 oz.

48 pt. = 6 gal.

32 oz. = 2 lb.

3 c. = 48 tbsp.

24 tsp. = 8 tbsp.

3 pt. = 48 fl. oz.

1,320 ft. = 0.25 mi.

PAGE 103

2 ft. < 30 in.

4 c. > 24 fl. oz.

2.5 tons = 5,000 lb.

9 yd. < 30 ft.

3.5 gal. > 7 qt.

30 tbsp. < 3 c.

3.5 yd. > 120 in.

16 pt. > 0.5 gal.

2 tbsp. = 6 tsp.

3 lb. < 50 oz.

72 in. = 6 ft.

4.5 lb. > 64 oz.

2,640 yd. = 1.5 mi.

4 pt. = 8 c.

3,200 oz. < 1 ton

PAGE 104

100 cm = 1,000 mm
2,400 mL = 2.4 L

0.5 m = 50 cm
380 g = 380,000 mg

3.2 L = 3,200 mL
3,500 mm = 350 cm

1,250 g = 1.25 kg
450,000 mg = 0.45 kg

200 m = 0.2 km
0.75 m = 750 mm

PAGE 105

650 m < 6.5 km
2.8 kg > 280 g

200 m > 0.02 km
40 L > 4,000 mL

245 g < 2.4 kg
7,999 mg > 0.8 g

95 m = 9,500 cm
415 g < 40.5 kg

13.4 cm < 13,500 mm
1,250 g = 1.25 kg

0.25 km = 250 m
85,000 mm > 8.45 m

8,200 cm < 8.2 km
0.83 km = 83,000 cm

0.46 kg > 45,000 mg

PAGE 106

2 L ≈ 0.5 gal.
5 ft. ≈ 1.5 m
9 L ≈ 9.5 qt.
4 m ≈ 13.1 ft.
12 gal. ≈ 45.5 L

8 qt. ≈ 7.6 L
10 in. = 25.4 cm
40 cm ≈ 15.6 in.
6 lb. ≈ 2.7 kg
65 g ≈ 2.6 oz.
32 oz. ≈ 907.2 g

PAGE 107

15°C = 59°F
25°C = 77°F

32°F = 0°C

PAGE 108

43%	$\frac{43}{100}$	0.43
70%	$\frac{7}{10}$	0.7
6%	$\frac{3}{50}$	0.06
125%	$\frac{5}{4}$ or $1\frac{1}{4}$	1.25

PAGE 109

Fraction	Decimal	Percent
$\frac{23}{100}$	0.23	23%
$\frac{57}{100}$	0.57	57%
$\frac{79}{100}$	0.79	79%
$\frac{9}{10}$	0.9	90%
$\frac{2}{5}$	0.4	40%
$\frac{3}{4}$	0.75	75%
$\frac{1}{100}$	0.01	1%
$\frac{1}{8}$	0.125	12.5%
$1\frac{7}{100}$	1.07	107%
$\frac{3}{1,000}$	0.003	0.3%
$\frac{6}{5}$ or $1\frac{1}{5}$	1.2	120%

PAGE 110

Malik
Candace
Prime Pizza
Gina
Lions

PAGE 111

20%	60%	34%
30%	25%	32.5%
145%	64%	120%
87.5%	5%	

PAGE 112

35	5	1
12	44	38
63	150.5	15
	52	0.16

PAGE 113

30	64	40
50	85	120
80	20	200
400	60	

PAGE 114

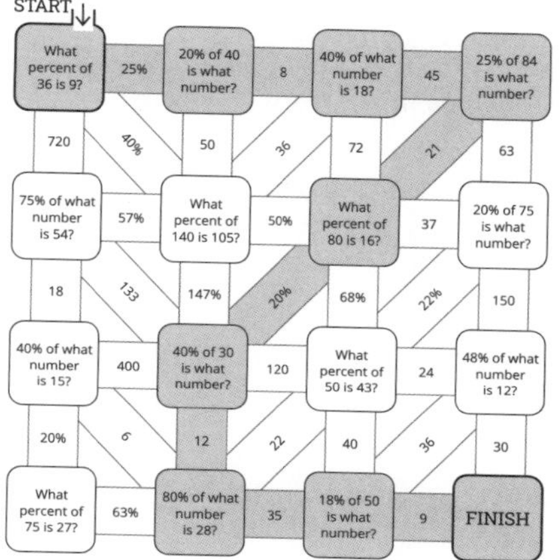
START
What percent of 36 is 9?
25%
20% of 40 is what number?
8
40% of what number is 18?
45
25% of 84 is what number?
720
40%
50
36
72
21
63
75% of what number is 54?
57%
What percent of 140 is 105?
50%
What percent of 80 is 16?
37
20% of 75 is what number?
18
133
147%
20%
68%
22%
150
40% of what number is 15?
400
40% of 30 is what number?
120
What percent of 50 is 43?
24
48% of what number is 12?
20%
6
12
22
40
36
30
What percent of 75 is 27?
63%
80% of what number is 28?
35
18% of 50 is what number?
9
FINISH

PAGE 115

10%
2 students
50 penguins
$14
40 levels
80%

PAGE 116

7	2
26	38
18	25

PAGE 117

20	67
9	23
24	35
19	

Answer key

PAGE 118

$5 + 2 \cdot 3^2$

$5 + 2 \cdot 9$

$5 + 18$

23

Explanations may vary. One possible explanation is shown below.

Farid added 5 + 2 before he multiplied 2 × 9.

$40 - (8 + 7) + 4^2$

$40 - 15 + 4^2$

$40 - 15 + 16$

$25 + 16$

41

Explanations may vary. One possible explanation is shown below.

Madelyn evaluated the exponent incorrectly. She multiplied 4 × 2 instead of multiplying 4 × 4.

PAGE 119

6.5 29
8 2
7.7 5.9
1.2

PAGE 120

9 $2\frac{1}{2}$

$\frac{5}{9}$ $\frac{5}{12}$

$\frac{3}{4}$ $\frac{2}{5}$

$1\frac{1}{4}$

PAGE 121

$6^2 \div (3 \cdot 4) + 7 = 10$

$50 - 2^3 \cdot (5 - 2) = 26$

$3^2 \cdot (11 - 8) + 16 = 43$

$(2^4 + 8) \div 2 \cdot 4 = 48$

$4 + (8 - 6) \cdot 4^2 = 36$

$6^2 \div (2 + 4) \cdot 4 = 24$

$3 + 5^2 - (8 + 6) \div 2 = 21$

$8 + 2^3 \cdot (3^2 - 5) + 10 = 50$

PAGE 122

3 2.5

d and f a and b

5 0.3

9 3

t and u $\frac{2}{3}$

12 h and k

PAGE 123

Expressions may vary. Some possible expressions are shown below.

$5w$ $\frac{8}{h}$ $b - 10$

$k - 17$ $6 + r$ $12q$

$\frac{d}{20}$ $c - \frac{7}{8}$ $14u$

$3\frac{1}{6} + n$ $\frac{t}{6.3}$

PAGE 124

Expressions may vary. Some possible expressions are shown below.

$3(j - 4)$ $4 + \frac{c}{2}$

$\frac{h}{10 + u}$ $16 - \frac{v}{7}$

$pz + 15$ $(d - 1.5) \cdot 6$

$\frac{4}{5}(m + 18)$ $\frac{x}{n} + 0.9$

$\frac{t}{4} - \frac{7}{10}$ $2(3\frac{2}{3} + k)$

PAGE 125

Expressions may vary. Some possible expressions are shown below.

$\frac{t}{3}$

$s + 3$

$n - 5$

$\frac{d - 3}{4}$

$5a + 2c$

PAGE 126

6 14
21 5
10 3

PAGE 127

13 21
80 36
8 1
29 13

PAGE 128

$\frac{7}{8}$ 7 450

9 12 5

26.75 2.6 4

PAGE 129

120 minutes
4 cups
12 inches
12.5 meters per second
$92.50

PAGE 130

Commutative property
Identity property

Associative property
Commutative property

$= k + 11 + 5$ $= 4w + (6 + 5)$
$= k + 16$ $= 4w + 11$

$= 7b + 9 + 8$
$= 7b + 17$

PAGE 131

Commutative property
Zero property

Associative property
Identity property

$= 6 \cdot 4 \cdot n$ $= (10 \cdot 7) \cdot m$
$= 24n$ $= 70m$

$= 3k$

PAGE 132

$= 7(c) + 7(2)$
$= 7c + 14$

$= 3(5) - 3(n) - 3(t)$
$= 15 - 3n - 3t$

$28 + 4k$
$10g - 30$
$8y + 10$

$9w + 54$
$3 - 2b$
$12a - 3b + 2$
$20f + 6 - 50t$

PAGE 133

$15 + n$
$9 + k$
$17 + 16v$
$26 + 13f - 13s$
$2p + 13.4$
$9d + 6a + 15$
$2 + 12b + 4w$

$4w - 20$
$8.5c$
$48a$
$36x - 3 + 4y$
$3q - 4z + 2d$
$0.3y + 0.7f + 1$

PAGE 134

$13h$
$4j$
$12k + 4$
$6t + 7r$
$7d + 5 + 2f$

$2q$
w
$17c$
$8u + 7v$
$13p + 8n + 7$

PAGE 135

$16t^2$
$5j^3$
$2b^2 + 9c$
$8u + 4u^3$
$3.4y + 2.9z^2$

$7a^3$
$18u^2$
$4w^3 + 16v$
$9d^2 + 14d$
$\frac{3}{4}q^2 - \frac{1}{5} + r^3$

PAGE 136

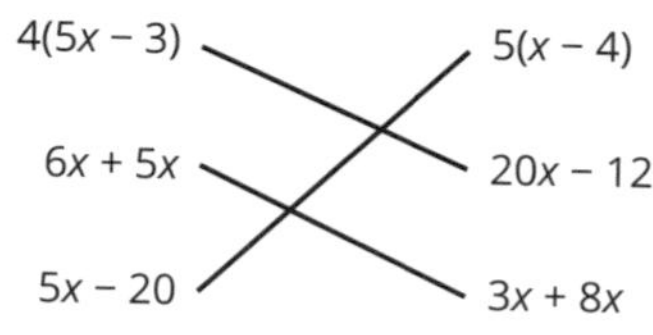

16x + 3x − 5x —— 2(7x)

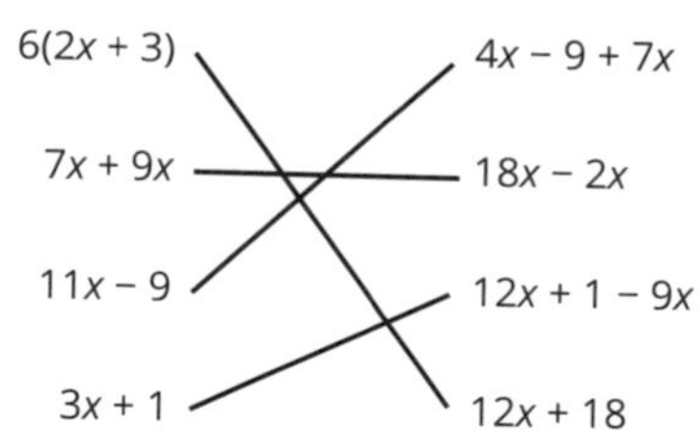

PAGE 137

$7n - 35$
$9 + 10b$
$2t - 6$
$10z - 50y$
$22d + 30$
$26k + 11w$
$6 + 7u$

$4a + 5$
$15c + 10$
$6g + 9$
$7k + 11m$
$35p - 3$
$24h + 5$

PAGE 138

Equations may vary. Some possible equations are shown below.

$17 + n = 32$	$\frac{63}{k} = 7$
$h - 11 = 14$	$40 = 8b$
$x + 28 = 51$	$58 = \frac{p}{3}$
$b - 81 = 14$	$f + 61 = 80$
$\frac{r}{8} = 5.6$	$2v = \frac{7}{8}$
$\frac{1}{2} + m = \frac{9}{10}$	$8 = c - 2.2$

PAGE 139

$n = 25$	$s = 15$	$g = 3$
$b = 15$	$f = 41$	$u = 42$
$q = 7$	$h = \frac{4}{5}$	$c = 18$
$d = 63$	$j = 4.5$	$p = 18.4$

PAGE 140

$b = 17$	$h = 2$	$r = 16$
$m = 12$	$c = 23$	$z = 39$
	$d = 52$	$g = 23$

PAGE 141

$d = 4$	$h = 53$	$p = 43$
$k = 15.3$	$a = \frac{4}{5}$	$m = 27$
$r = \frac{1}{6}$	$u = 16.3$	$g = \frac{2}{3}$
$c = 19.8$	$f = 25.8$	$t = \frac{7}{10}$
$s = 17\frac{4}{7}$	$w = 9\frac{3}{8}$	

PAGE 142

$b = 16$	$u = 6$	$z = 10$
$k = 45$	$h = 3$	$a = 32$
	$w = 16$	$x = 9$

PAGE 143

$y = 5$	$a = 39$	$c = 4.8$
$h = 28$	$u = 4$	$b = 15$
$m = 7$	$r = \frac{3}{5}$	$w = 8.5$
$k = \frac{2}{5}$	$z = 1.6$	$p = 17$
$t = 2\frac{2}{5}$	$x = 28.14$	

PAGE 144

$c = 7$	$k = 8$	$u = 30$
$r = 51$	$t = 70$	$m = 14$
$n = 3$	$x = 37$	$p = 7.4$
$h = \frac{1}{2}$	$g = 6.3$	$y = 20$
	$z = 493$	$j = 59$

PAGE 145

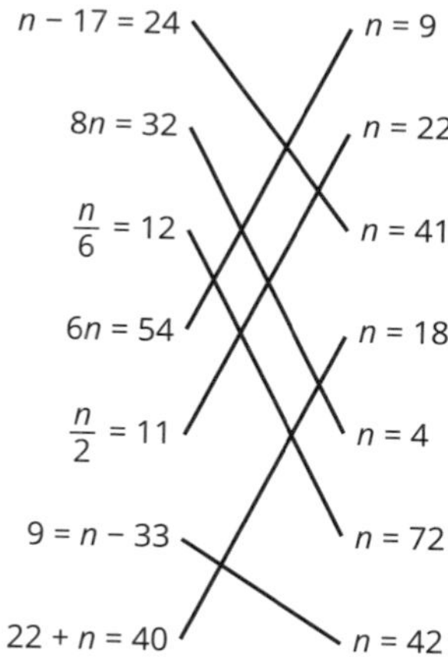

PAGE 146

$x = 4$	$x = 13$
$x = 18$	$x = 14$
$x = 7$	$x = 12$
$x = 19$	$x = 16$
$x = 9$	$x = 6$

MULTI-PLIERS!

Answer key

PAGE 147

$k = 8$ $c = 10$ $b = 6$

$x = 7$ $z = 9$ $w = 3$

$g = 2$ $a = 8$

PAGE 148

$\frac{p}{24} = 2$

$c + 12 = 36$

$2m = 800$

$s - 10 = 15$

$21.50h = 75.25$

PAGE 149

Equations may vary. Some possible equations are shown below.

$d + 8 = 21$
$13

$b - 15 = 25$
$40

$7p = 21$
3 points

$m + 1.25 = 2.75$
1.5 miles

$\frac{y}{4} = 1.5$
6 feet

PAGE 150

$n > 15$ $b \leq 33$

$5 < g$ $-28 \geq y$

$14.5 > c$ $2\frac{1}{2} \leq x$

$p + 7 < 19$ $4h \geq 36$

$a - 6 > 22$ $15 + w \leq 9$

PAGE 151

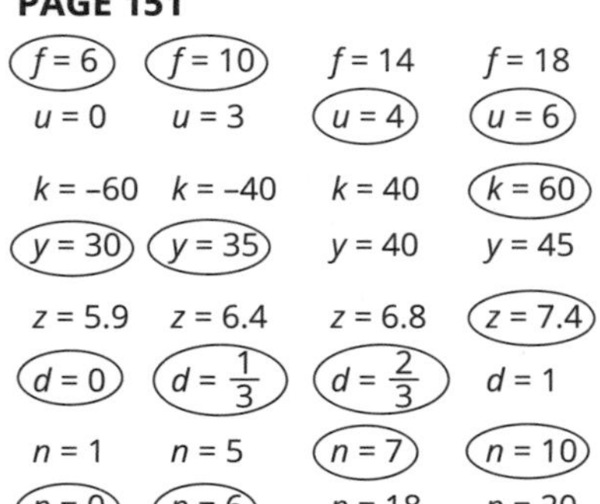

$f = 6$ (circled)	$f = 10$ (circled)	$f = 14$	$f = 18$
$u = 0$	$u = 3$	$u = 4$ (circled)	$u = 6$ (circled)
$k = -60$	$k = -40$	$k = 40$	$k = 60$ (circled)
$y = 30$ (circled)	$y = 35$ (circled)	$y = 40$	$y = 45$
$z = 5.9$	$z = 6.4$	$z = 6.8$	$z = 7.4$ (circled)
$d = 0$ (circled)	$d = \frac{1}{3}$ (circled)	$d = \frac{2}{3}$ (circled)	$d = 1$
$n = 1$	$n = 5$	$n = 7$ (circled)	$n = 10$ (circled)
$p = 0$ (circled)	$p = 6$ (circled)	$p = 18$	$p = 20$

PAGE 152

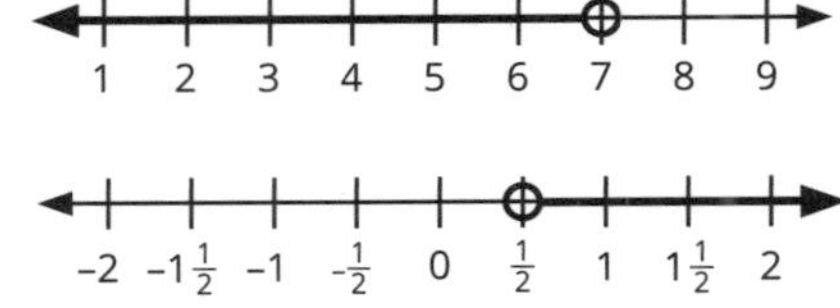

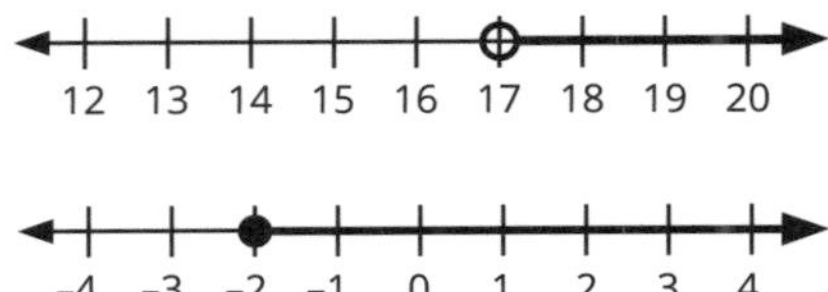

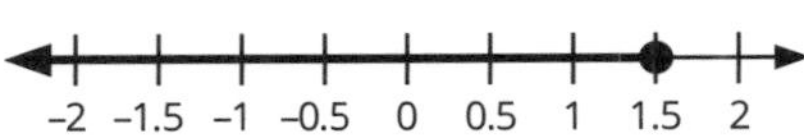

PAGE 153

$x > 3$ $x < 12$

$x \leq 7$ $x \geq 14$

$x \leq 5$ $x > -1$

$x \geq -2$ $x > \frac{3}{4}$

$x \leq -0.5$

PAGE 154

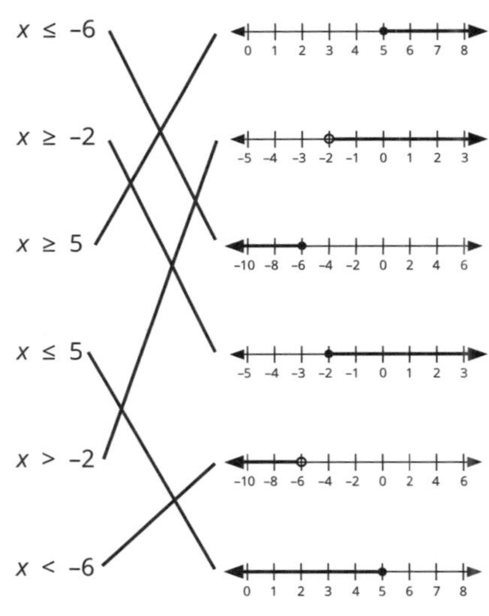

PAGE 155

$a \leq 10$

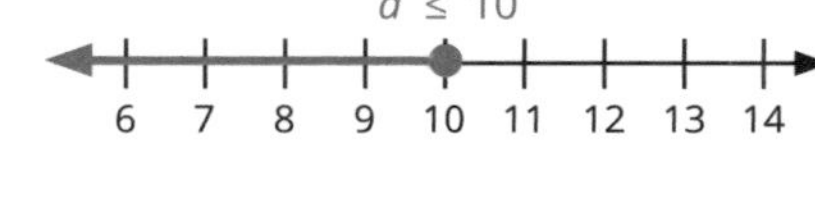

$y > 49$

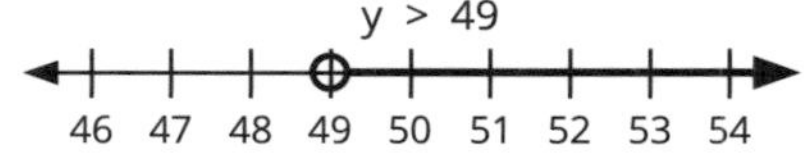

PAGE 155, *continued*

$p < 30$

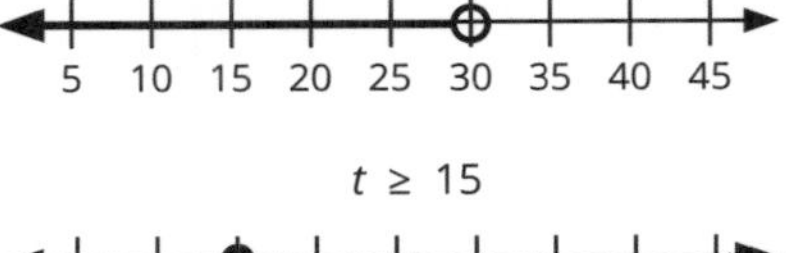

$t \geq 15$

5 10 15 20 25 30 35 40 45

$b \leq 5$

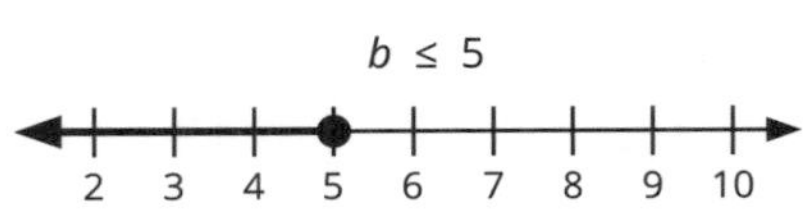

PAGE 156

No Yes

Yes Yes

No

PAGE 157

Independent variable: n
Dependent variable: t

Independent variable: p
Dependent variable: s

Independent variable: r
Dependent variable: a

Independent variable: d
Dependent variable: g

Independent variable: k
Dependent variable: u

PAGE 158

$y = 12$
$y = 16$
$y = 3$
$y = 4$
$y = 7$
$y = 25$

PAGE 159

x	y
1	5
2	10
3	15
4	20

x	y
1	3
3	5
5	7
7	9

PAGE 159, *continued*

x	y
3	1
6	2
9	3
12	4

x	y
10	2
11	3
12	4
13	5

x	y
3	0
4	3
5	6
6	9

PAGE 160

$y = x + 5$ $y = x - 4$

$y = 3x$ $y = \frac{x}{2}$

$y = x + 7$

PAGE 161

$y = x + 8$

x	y
1	9
2	10
3	11
4	12

$y = 6x$

x	y
1	6
2	12
3	18
4	24

$y = \frac{x}{4}$

x	y
4	1
8	2
12	3
16	4

$y = x - 2$

x	y
5	3
6	4
7	5
8	6

PAGE 162

x	y
1	5
2	6
3	7
4	8

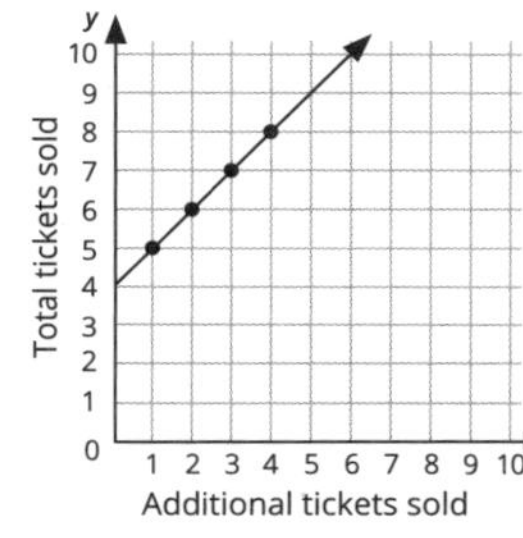

PAGE 162, *continued*

x	y
2	24
3	36
4	48
5	60

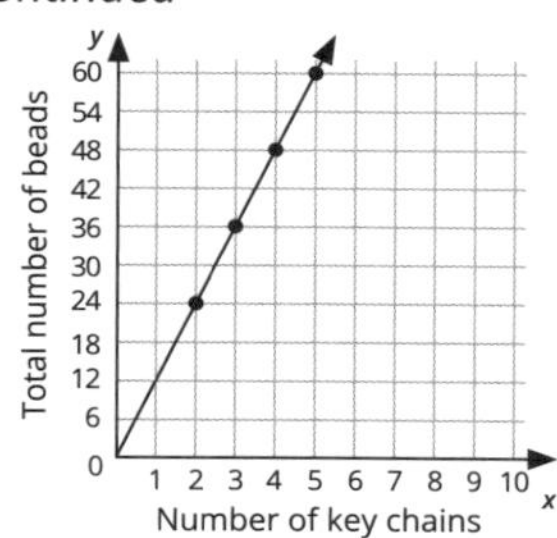

PAGE 163

x	y
10	90
20	80
30	70
40	60

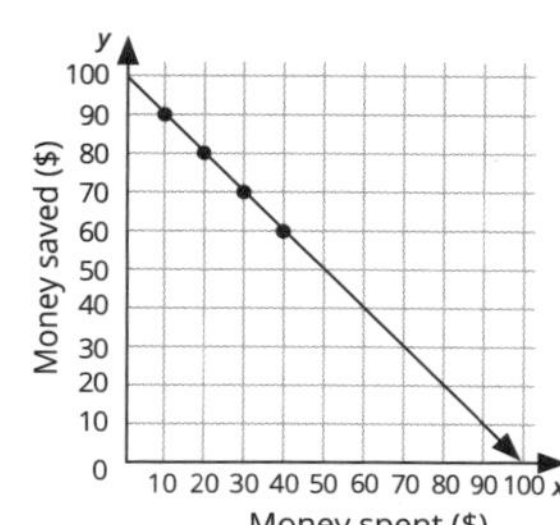

x	y
2	100
4	200
6	300
8	400

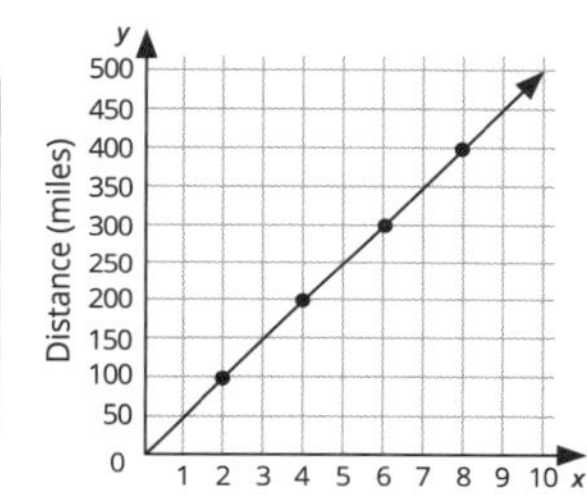

PAGE 164

No
Yes
No
No
Yes
Yes
No

PAGE 165

Mean = 3 Median = 3
Mode = 4 Range = 7

PAGE 166

Mean = 3 Median = 2
Mode = 1 Range = 11

Mean = 25 Median = 30
Mode = 30 Range = 15

Mean = 35 Median = 33
Mode = 46 Range = 33

Mean = 93 Median = 92.5
Mode = 90 Range = 7

PAGE 167

Mean = 7 Median = 7
Mode = 8 Range = 3

Mean = 18 Median = 18
Mode = 17 Range = 3

Mean = 77 Median = 80
Mode = 80 Range = 30

PAGE 168

MAD = 14 MAD = 2

PAGE 169

MAD = 3 MAD = 10.8
MAD = 13 MAD = 6
MAD = 15.25

PAGE 170

65
0
295
361
14
229

PAGE 171

173
183
increase

160
135
decrease

PAGE 172

Lower quartile = 5
Median = 8
Upper quartile = 11

Lower quartile = 17
Median = 21.5
Upper quartile = 24

Lower quartile = 40.5
Median = 47
Upper quartile = 49.5

Lower quartile = 25
Median = 28
Upper quartile = 31

Answer key

PAGE 173

IQR = 8

IQR = 17

IQR = 14

IQR = 3

IQR = 7.5

PAGE 174

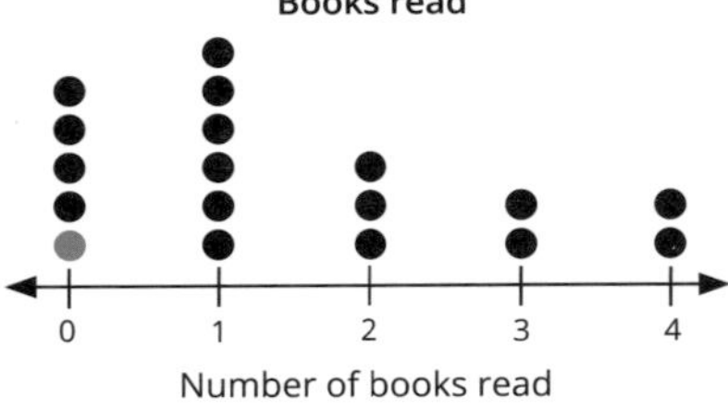

Height of players

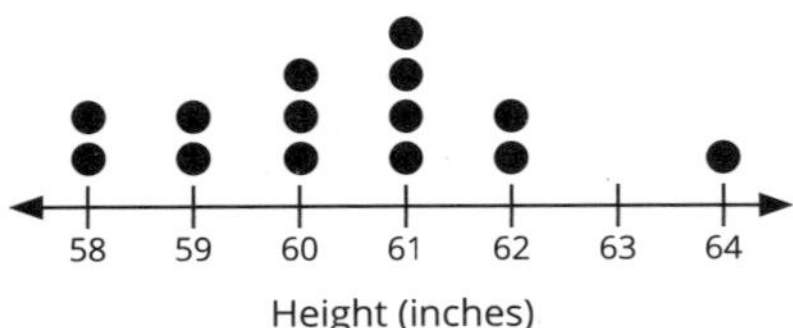

PAGE 175

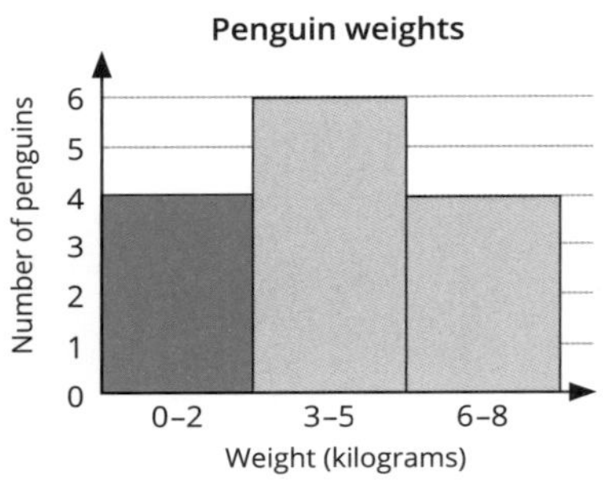

Time spent babysitting

Number of weekends

0 2 4 6 8 10

0–1 2–3 4–5 6–7

Number of hours

PAGE 176

Minimum = 9

Q_1 = 11

Median = 14

Q_3 = 16

Maximum = 18

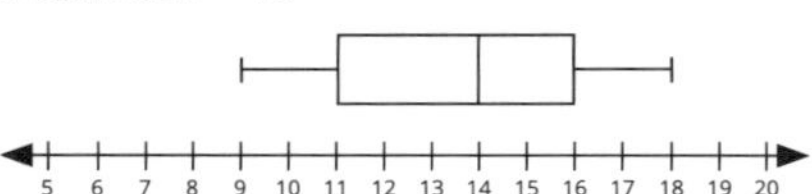

PAGE 177

Minimum = 28

Q_1 = 30

Median = 33

Q_3 = 34

Maximum = 36

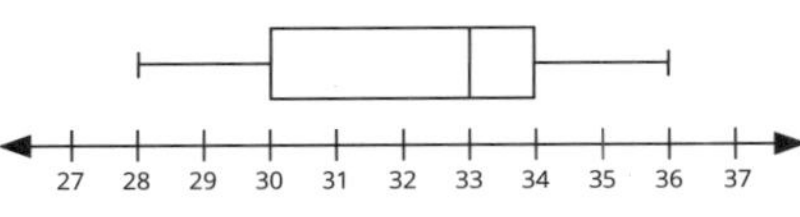

Minimum = 12

Q_1 = 14

Median = 18

Q_3 = 26

Maximum = 27

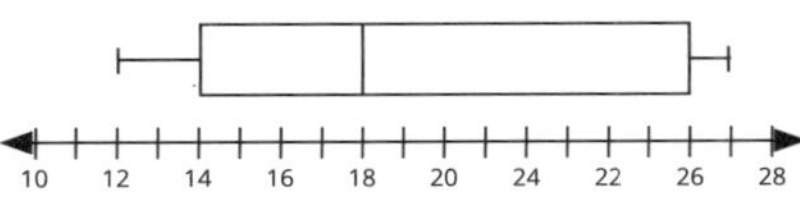

Minimum = 37

Q_1 = 38

Median = 41

Q_3 = 43

Maximum = 45

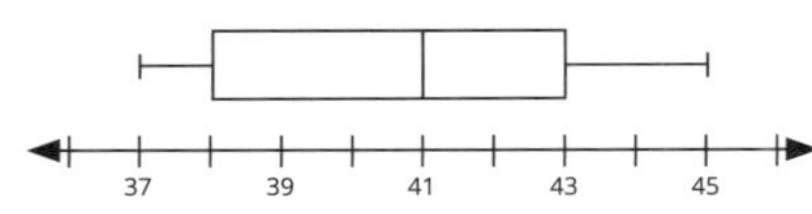

PAGE 178

Skewed
Median
IQR

Symmetric
Mean and Median
MAD and IQR

PAGE 179

Mean = 7
Mode = 9
Shape: Skewed left

Median = 8
Range = 9

Mean = 65
Mode = 65
Shape: Symmetric

Median = 65
Range = 6

Mean = 3
Mode = 3
Shape: Uniform or symmetric

Median = 3
Range = 6

PAGE 180

Shape: Skewed right
13 friends

Shape: Skewed left
0-14 minutes

Shape: Symmetric
20-29 students
10 clubs

PAGE 181

Median = 3
50%

IQR = 3

Median = 14
50%

Range = 11

Median = 3
25%

IQR = 4

PAGE 182

3 mm^2

60 in.^{2}

140 cm^2

14 ft.^{2}

2.5 ft.^{2}

30 in.^{2}

PAGE 183

9 in.

8 cm

8 ft.

7 cm

20 mm

PAGE 184

15 cm^2

$\frac{3}{8}$ m^2

120 ft.^{2}

48 in.^{2}

42 in.^{2}

PAGE 185

36 ft.^{2}

120 cm^2

40 in.^{2}

117 mm^2

$\frac{1}{4}$ m^2

PAGE 186

20 units   14 units

18 units   16 units

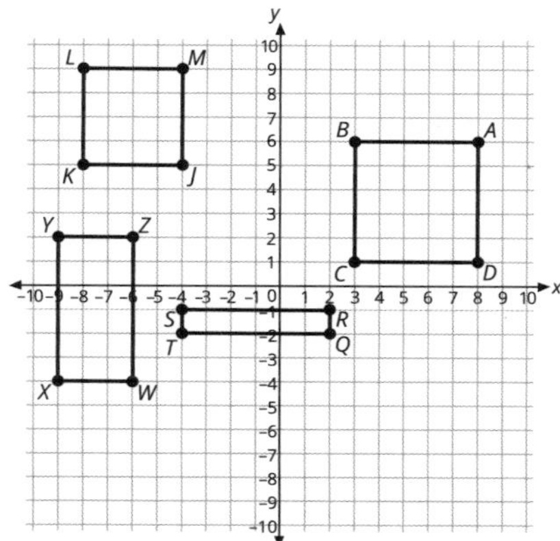

PAGE 187

10 square units   9 square units

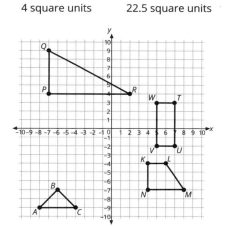

4 square units   22.5 square units

PAGE 188

Area of figure A = 14 cm^2

Area of figure D = 16 cm^2

Area of figure B = 16 cm^2

Area of figure E = 22.5 cm^2

Area of figure C = 9 cm^2

Area of figure F = 19 cm^2

PAGE 189

Figures will vary. Some possible figures are shown below.

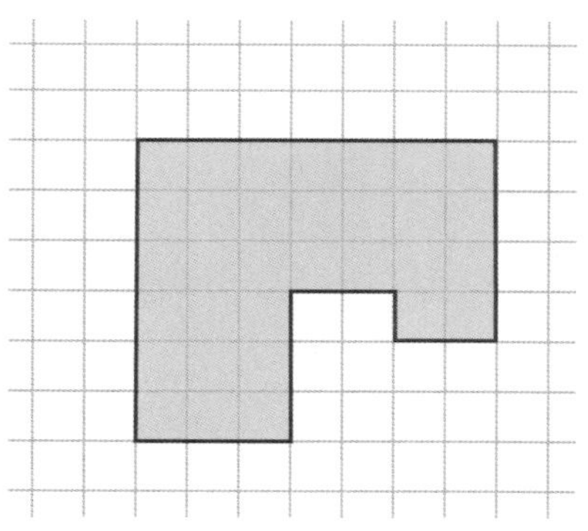

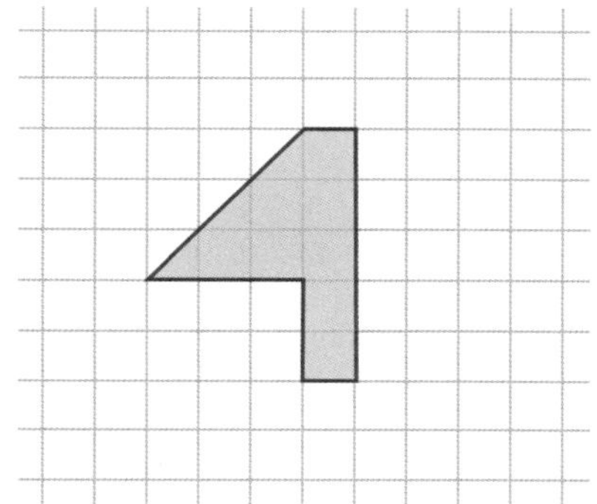

PAGE 190

100 in.^{2} 96 cm^2

80 ft.^{2} 192 mm^2

43 m^2

PAGE 191

53 ft.^{2} 284 cm^2

120 mm^2 130.5 in.^{2}

PAGE 192

rectangular prism

triangular pyramid

triangular prism

rectangular pyramid

PAGE 193

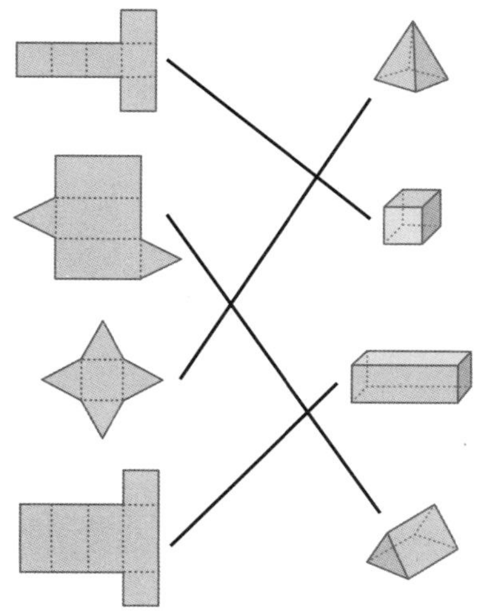

PAGE 194

96 cm^2

175.2 m^2

PAGE 195

202 in.^{2} 300 cm^2

486 ft.^{2} 408 yd.^{2}

432 mm^2

PAGE 196

400 in.^{2}

147.35 m^2

PAGE 197

132 cm^2 26.4 ft.^{2}

403.5 m^2 451 in.^{2}

576 mm^2

PAGE 198

184 square inches

95 square inches

216 square inches

547.5 square centimeters

Answer key

PAGE 199

11.25 m^3 — $2\frac{1}{4}$ cm^3

$\frac{1}{125}$ m^3 — $\frac{7}{64}$ $in.^3$

$\frac{8}{27}$ $ft.^3$

PAGE 200

$\frac{1}{2}$ ft. — $\frac{3}{4}$ in.

5 cm — $\frac{1}{3}$ ft.

0.5 cm — 4 in.

PAGE 201

$1\frac{7}{8}$ cubic feet

$91\frac{1}{8}$ cubic inches

$\frac{3}{100}$ cubic meters

$\frac{2}{5}$ cubic meters

$\frac{9}{16}$ cubic feet

PAGE 202

$16n$ — $2k + 4w$

$7a + 68$ — $3r + 33$

$\frac{1}{2}c + \frac{5}{12}$ — $12u + 2t$

$2m + 9$ — $3.9h + 2f$

$p = 8$ — $b = 5$ — $a = 16$

$v = 27$ — $t = 12$ — $z = \frac{9}{10}$

PAGE 203

Independent variable: h

Dependent variable: m

h	m
2	$50
4	$100
6	$150
8	$200
10	$250

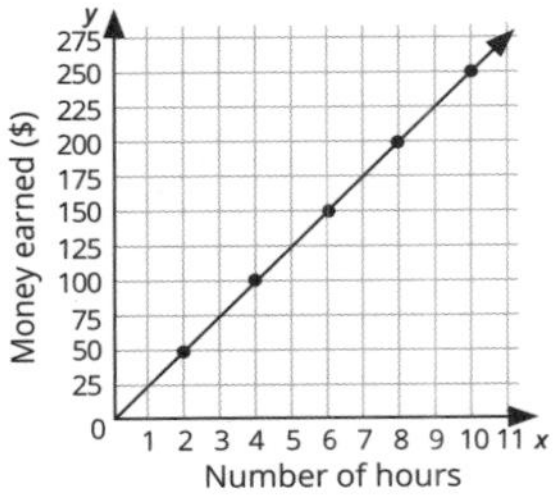

$m = 25h$

$375

17.5 hours

PAGE 204

$0.55 per pound

$0.60 per pound

Green Dot Flour

$0.35 per egg

$0.33 per egg

Carton of 12 eggs

PAGE 205

2 quarts

$\frac{1}{2}$-gallon

5 packages

$12.45

Item	Price
Flour	$2.75
Eggs	$3.96
Buttermilk	$3.84
Blueberries	$12.45
Cost (without tax)	$23.00

PAGE 206

$1\frac{3}{4}$ cups

$\frac{1}{4}$ of a cup

$\frac{1}{2}$ of a cup

2 times

PAGE 207

6 teaspoons

$6:\frac{1}{2}$

$2\frac{1}{2}$ cups

$\frac{1}{4}$ of a cup

5 cups

$2\frac{1}{2}$ pints